DOF
PLACE

DORSET
PLACE-NAMES

their origins and meanings

A. D. MILLS

COUNTRYSIDE BOOKS
NEWBURY, BERKSHIRE

Originally published by Roy Gasson Associates

This edition published 1998 by

Countryside Books
3 Catherine Road
Newbury, Berkshire

© A. D. Mills 1986 and 1998

ISBN 1 85306 544 7

Cover photograph of Abbotsbury
taken by Roger Holman

Printed by J. W. Arrowsmith Ltd., Bristol

CONTENTS

Acknowledgements **7**
Introduction **9**
Names as linguistic fossils
The importance of early spellings
The relative chronology of the names
and the different linguistic strata
Folk etymology, back-formation and euphemism
Place-names and the landscape
Place-names and human activity
Place-names and persons
Folklore and special allusions
Alphabetical List of Dorset Place-Names **23**
Glossary of the Elements found in Dorset Place-Names **167**

ACKNOWLEDGEMENTS

My best thanks are due to Professor Kenneth Cameron of Nottingham University, Director of the English Place-Name Survey, for permission to make use of copyright material, and to Miss Hilary Carpenter of Queen Mary College, London, for her kindness in typing the greater part of my manuscript.

INTRODUCTION

There is a perennial fascination about the origins and meanings of place-names, those familiar but often curious labels for places, not least in a county like Dorset which is blessed with such a rich variety of them. This book sets out to provide all those who know Dorset, whether fortunate enough to live in the county or only passing through, with information about the origins of its place-names, their history, their underlying meaning and their significance.

The alphabetical list of Dorset place-names includes most of the names to be found on the 1:50000 series of maps published by the Ordnance Survey, and also takes in the area of Bournemouth and Christchurch. Thus besides all names of towns, villages and hamlets, the list includes names of rivers and streams, hills, woods and archaeological sites, as well as many names of farms, mills, bridges, promontories and other features of the Dorset landscape.

The list provides the basic information about the history and origin of each name, as far as it is known:

(*a*) its modern form as it appears on map or signpost;

(*b*) some representative early spellings for the name, with dates, to show how the name has developed (where the name occurs in a particularly interesting early record, like the

Anglo-Saxon Chronicle, an Anglo-Saxon charter, or Domesday Book, this is mentioned);

(c) the probable original meaning of the name, deduced from those early spellings;

(d) the elements (i.e. words) or personal names from which the name is derived (the elements are also listed in the Glossary at the end of the book);

(e) other brief comments where appropriate on points of linguistic, geographical or historical significance.

NAMES AS LINGUISTIC FOSSILS

Most place-names today are, as it were, linguistic fossils. Although they began life as living units of speech – as descriptions, in a living language, of places in terms of their topography, appearance, situation, use, ownership, or other association – most have become, in the course of time, mere labels, no longer possessing a clear linguistic meaning. It is only by tracing each name back to its earliest spelling in the records that its original meaning can be discovered and its original significance appreciated.

Of course some place-names, even very old ones, have changed very little through the many centuries of their existence, and may still convey something of their original meaning when the words from which they are composed have survived in the ordinary language, and when the names themselves have, as it were, 'kept up to date' in spelling and pronunciation. Thus Dorset names like Okeford, Sandford and Thornford are still self-explanatory, even though they are several hundred years old and though the fords themselves from which the places took their names may long since have been replaced by bridges. Similarly, old names like Blackmoor, Marshwood and Woodbridge are shown by their early spellings to have had original meanings that still seem obvious today.

But even a casual glance at the alphabetical list of Dorset place-names will show that such instant etymologies are often a delusion. The modern form of a name can never be *assumed* to convey its original meaning without early spellings to confirm it. We find, for instance, that Wool has nothing to do with sheep, that Beer has no brewery, and that Kingcombe has no royal associations! Instead, these names, like many others, derive from words that survive only in a different form (like the word *well* as compared to Wool), or from old words that have disappeared from the general vocabulary altogether (like the *bǣr* or *bearu* found in Beer and the *cymed* in Kingcombe). An enormous number of such old words survive in a fossilized form in place-names, as is evident from the glossary of elements at the end of the book.

Many of the words found in Dorset place-names may live on in the Dorset dialect, even though they have not survived in Standard English, like the words *slait, botham* and *holm* evidenced in the names Sleight, Bothenwood and Sutton Holms. Even when the words used in Dorset place-names have not become obsolete or dialectal, it is apparent that they have often diverged a good deal in form, pronunciation, spelling or significance from their counterparts in the ordinary vocabulary. These divergences are not completely haphazard. For instance, in compound place-names, that is in names consisting of two elements the first of which usually qualifies the second, original long vowels have often been shortened, as in compound words in the ordinary vocabulary. Just as *holi-* and *bon-* in the words *holiday* and *bonfire* represent *holy* and *bone* with their historically long vowels, so in compound place-names the common Old English elements *brād* 'broad' and *stān* 'stone' occur with shortened vowels in Bradford and Stanton. Similarly, Stratton is from *strǣet* 'street' and *tūn* 'farm' (now the word *town*), and Waddon is from *wād* 'woad' and *dūn* 'down'.

This tendency for long vowels to be shortened in compound place-names, together with weakening of stress at the end of names, resulted in some originally distinct elements coinciding in form and pronunciation. Once shortened, the important and often early Old English habitative element *hām* 'homestead, village' (probably found in Gillingham and Wareham) came to sound like the quite separate topographical element *hamm* 'enclosure, river-meadow' (probable in Portisham and Tyneham). As a result, it is not possible to be sure whether a number of place-names, such as Edmondsham and Pulham, contain *hām* or *hamm*. The same combination of shortening of vowel and weakening of stress leads to the confusion of *-ton* from *tūn* 'farm', *-don* from *dūn* 'down', and *-den* from *denu* 'valley' in names like Farrington, Morden and Norden, and there are similar reasons for the replacement of *-mere* by *-more* in Ashmore and Enmore, *-cliff* by *-ley* in Catsley and Rockley, and *-hurst* by *-chester* in Bedchester and Hogchester.

THE IMPORTANCE OF EARLY SPELLINGS

The importance of early spellings in the elucidation of the original meanings of place-names has already been touched upon, but it is best illustrated by comparing pairs of apparently identical names that have quite different etymologies. Thus Hinton St Mary differs in origin from Hinton Martell, likewise Burton Bradstock from Long Burton. Of the two pairs of places called Orchard, one pair has the obvious meaning 'orchard', virtually unchanged through nine centuries, whereas the other pair has an even older Celtic name, now disguised, as it were, through changes in spelling. All three of the Dorset places called Holwell have quite different origins, as have the two places called Gummershay.

Dorset has its share of place-names, some of them very old, that are to be found in several other English counties. Names like Kingston, Knighton, Charlton, Buckland and Sherborne occur elsewhere in England, and their origins are usually straightforward. However here too the early spellings are crucial for correct interpretation. Dorset names that are apparently identical with names in other counties often turn out to be quite different in origin. The Dorset Acton could look as if it might be the common 'oak-tree farm', but early spellings show otherwise, that it is a unique name with a different derivation. Similarly, Dorchester and Gillingham both have different origins from their namesakes in Oxfordshire and Kent.

A good many Dorset place-names are unique to the county, often containing rare old words found in very few other English names and usually now obsolete. These include Blashenwell, Blandford, Gussage, Spettisbury, Tincleton, Worgret and many others. Here again, it is only through early spellings that probable etymologies can be arrived at. For many names, in fact, even early spellings do not always provide a clear unambiguous etymology, hence the large number of names for which alternative, or only tentative, explanations are suggested. Particularly common are names like Chelborough, Pamphill, Puncknowle and Shaftesbury, where the first element could be either a significant word or a personal name.

Not all the place-names can be satisfactorily explained, even in terms of alternative possibilities. A few names, like Caundle, Chickerell, Powerstock and Owermoigne, remain for the time being at least partly obscure, even though early spellings are available. On the other hand, there are a few names, such as Ballard Down, Durlston and Sugar Hill, for which a tentative etymology may be proposed, on the basis of analogy with similar names elsewhere, even though no early spellings are recorded.

THE RELATIVE CHRONOLOGY OF THE NAMES AND THE DIFFERENT LINGUISTIC STRATA

Most of the Dorset place-names so far mentioned (except for Dorchester and one of the pairs called Orchard) are of Old

English or Anglo-Saxon origin. This is the dominant stratum in the place-names of Dorset, as in other English counties apart from Cornwall, and is the legacy of the Germanic peoples, the Anglo-Saxons, who first came to Britain from about the fifth century AD, and who were settling in Dorset from the seventh century onwards. Thus the majority of Dorset towns and villages, and a good many hamlets, farms and landscape features, have names that were first coined in the language of the Anglo-Saxons, that is in Old English, between the seventh and eleventh centuries. Dorset of course was within the old kingdom of Wessex, that is within the area settled by the West Saxons, and many Dorset place-names, such as Chaldon, Marnhull, Shapwick and Wool, reflect the distinctive West Saxon dialect spoken in this region.

The names of Old English origin vary in age, but it is not always easy to tell which names belong to the earlier and which to the later part of the period. What is certain, however, is that names recorded in Domesday Book (compiled in 1086) or earlier, apart from the Celtic names mentioned in the next paragraph, will have had their origins in the Old English period. In fact many other names too, first on record in later medieval documents, may well have been coined in Old English times, since the date of the earliest occurrence of a name in a surviving manuscript is largely a matter of chance.

However, the oldest place-names in Dorset are those of British or Celtic origin. Such Celtic names as have survived are relatively few in number, but they are particularly interesting because they provide evidence of continuity and contact between the Celtic-speaking Britons and their English-speaking conquerors, the West Saxons. In fact the conquered Britons must have passed these names on during the Anglo-Saxon occupation of Dorset in the seventh century, so most of them are probably a good deal older than that (the original Celtic names for Dorchester and Badbury are recorded as early as the fourth century). Most of the surviving Celtic names are names of rivers or other natural features, although these have often been later transferred to settlements. They include river-names like Cerne, Char, Lim, Lydden, Tarrant, Trent and Wey, original stream-names like Fontmell, Winfrith and Wynford, hill-names like Creech, Crichel, Crook, Pen and Pentridge, and wood-names like Chideock, Lytchett and the Orchard already mentioned.

Only a few names in Dorset, as in most other English counties, are French in origin, in spite of the far-reaching effects of the Norman conquest on the English language in general. It is clear that by 1066, most settlements and landscape features already had established names, and the new Norman aristocracy only rarely gave French names to parts of their estates (Organ Ford may be an example of a name actually transferred from France). But the influence of this powerful French-speaking aristocracy is revealed in the way the names of the great feudal families were affixed to the names of the manors they possessed. These manorial additions result in a great many hybrid double-barrelled names which contribute considerable variety and richness to the map of Dorset. Most of these additions serve to distinguish one manor from another with an identical name, either in Dorset or some other county, like Langton Herring and Matravers, Fifehead Neville and St Quintin, Bradford Peverell, and Kingston Lacy. Some of the important Norman families are represented in more than one name, as in Okeford and Wootton Fitzpaine, Langton and Worth Matravers. Many of the manorial additions are now compounded with the original name itself, as in Hammoon, Owermoigne, and Stourpaine. The Norman-French influence also shows itself in rather different ways in a few other names like Corfe Mullen, Font le Roi, La Lee and Piddletrenthide. Beaulieu, however, although it now looks like a French name, is a refashioning of a purely English one.

Mention must also be made of the interesting presence of Latin among the place-names of Dorset. There are no names of purely Latin origin, but quite a number of names which have had a Latin affix added in medieval times. This reflects the widespread use of Latin by church and state – it was the language most often used by scribes in medieval documents relating to law and administration. Presumably so many of the Latin additions survive because they became fixed and accepted in writing, even though one suspects they may never have been used very much in popular speech. Many of them give an indication of ownership, as by the king (Bere Regis, Melcombe Regis), an abbey (Bradford Abbas, Compton Abbas) or other religious foundation (Whitchurch Canonicorum). Some allude to administrative arrangements (Ryme Intrinseca) or relative size (Kington Magna). Others are used to distinguish two manors with identical names, like Fontmell Magna and Parva or Toller Fratrum and Porcorum ('of the brethren' and 'of the pigs' – there is surely a medieval joke here, and one wonders who was being got at!).

Of course, not all the names on the modern map, even names of sizeable settlements, are as old as most of those so far mentioned. Many names for smaller settlements, farmsteads and topographical features probably originate in the Middle English period, that is from the twelfth to the fifteenth century inclusive. Names such as Bailey Ridge, Eastbury, Forston, Hermitage and Lenthay belong here. Others, like Burning Cliff and Decoy Heath, date only from the nineteenth century, as do transferred names like Botany and Waterloo. Relatively few names are of recent creation, but Northbourne, Southbourne, Springbourne and Westbourne for the modern districts of Bournemouth are examples.

FOLK ETYMOLOGY, BACK-FORMATION AND EUPHEMISM

Once the original meaning of an old place-name has been obscured or lost – because words have gone out of use, or because the person commemorated has been forgotten, or because of changes in pronunciation and spelling – there is often a tendency for a process of rationalization or reinterpretation to take place, a process sometimes known as folk etymology. Numerous Dorset place-names show the process at work. An early case is the name Dorchester, where part of the original Celtic name was rationalized and reinterpreted by the Anglo-Saxons by the middle of the ninth century. Other examples somewhat later in date include Devil's Brook, Goathorn, Hengistbury, Sixpenny Handley, Slaughtergate, Wadmill and Wolfridge. In all these names, familiar words, quite unhistorical but making a kind of sense, have been substituted for unfamiliar or obscure words.

Folk etymology sometimes results in a phenomenon known as back-formation. This is especially common in the creation of river-names in comparatively recent times. Thus Crane came to be the name of the river at Cranborne because the village name (historically 'crane stream, stream frequented by cranes') came to be understood as 'stream called Crane'. Other examples of back-formation include the river-names Allen, Asker, Mude and Simene.

Euphemism, the tendency to replace an offensive name by one that sounds less so, has also played its part in the history of some names. The names Arish Mell and Merritown may be instances. The medieval bluntness of Arish Mell contrasts with the relative coyness in recent times noted under Puddletown and Shitterton.

PLACE-NAMES AND THE LANDSCAPE

Obviously the place-names of Dorset relate very closely to the landscape they describe, a landscape seen through the eyes of the earlier inhabitants of the county. The importance of river valleys for early settlement – providing fertile soils and a water supply – is reflected in the number of Dorset places named from the rivers on which they are situated. The two rivers called Winterborne provide the names of over a dozen places, all distinguished one from another by additions. Similarly the River Tarrant gives its name to no less than eight different places, the River Piddle to six, the Rivers Frome and Wey to four each, and so on. Many other places are named from the quite small streams on which they stand, like Trent, Trill and Iwerne. The numerous places that take their names from fords, like Blandford and Canford, show the early importance of river crossings. Other topographical features – hills and valleys, moors and marshes, springs and pools, estuaries and promontories – are well represented among the names, as will be appreciated by a glance through the glossary of elements at the end of the book. The wide range and variety of this topographical vocabulary is to be noted. Many names indicate woodland, or clearings in woodland, like those containing *bearu, grāf, hyrst, lēah, holt, wudu,* and *sceaga;* these clearly reflect a period when wooded areas were much more extensive than they are today. Natural history is also well represented among the place-names of Dorset. Many different species of trees and plants, wild animals and birds, fish and even insects are evidenced, again as is apparent from the glossary of elements.

PLACE-NAMES AND HUMAN ACTIVITY

Obviously Dorset place-names also reflect the many and various aspects of human activity in the area during the different phases of its history – settlement, exploitation of the land, communications and trade, and industry. Many names refer to particular kinds of habitation, such as those containing *tūn, -ingtūn, hām, stoc, wīc, cot,* and *throp.* Words like *ceaster* and *burh,* as well as others like *beorg, hring* and *dīc,* usually have important archaeological implications. Names containing *cirice, hīwan, mynster,* and *prēost* have significant religious associations. Many names provide information about the agricultural economy of earlier times. Different words for

18

man-made enclosures include *worth, hamm* and *haeg*; and meadows, pastures and orchards are also well represented. Some names refer to the kind or quality of the soil, others to the livestock raised, others to the crops produced. Several names, besides those containing *ford* already mentioned, contain elements that suggest the importance of communication and trade in early times, among them *strǣt, weg, brycg, port* and *forum*. Other elements reflect local industries and occupations, like milling (*myln*), fishing (*wer*), salt-making (*salt-aern*), charcoal-burning (*col*), pot-making (*pott* and *crocc*), hunting (*hunta, heorot, coninger, warren*) and quarrying (*pytt, wince, whim, alum*).

PLACE-NAMES AND PERSONS

Many persons and families from many different periods of history are commemorated in the place-names of Dorset. Some of the Anglo-Saxon men and women who bore Old English names may have been among the settlers who colonized Dorset from the seventh century onwards, like the Gylla who gave name to Gillingham, but most of them probably occupied their estates at a somewhat later date. About many of them, like the Cana who gave name to Canford (and possibly to Canon Hill), nothing more is known, and even some of their personal names are hypothetical. Others, like the Here who gave name to Herston and the Beorn of Barnston are actually on record as known individuals. Quite a number of these early manorial landowners were women, like the Aelfrūn of Afflington and the Tola of Tolpuddle. However, it should be noted that some Old English personal names, like the Betti of Bettiscombe and the Ella of Elworth, are names of men even though they may resemble more recent women's names.

Besides such individuals, known and unknown, many families are likewise recalled in the place-names. As already mentioned, the great landowning families, often of Norman-

French descent, have left their mark on Dorset place-names in the manorial additions of names like Kingston Lacy, Fifehead Neville and Langton Matravers. Most of these families were influential and well documented. Others, like the families that gave name to places like Cruxton, Silkhay, Bluntshay and Moorcourt, were often rather less notable and only known in local records.

FOLKLORE AND SPECIAL ALLUSIONS

Some Dorset place-names, like Agglestone, Crab Farm, Elwell and Fortuneswell, are to be associated with popular beliefs and superstitions. Others refer to heathen gods (Grim's Ditch) or contain references to goblins (Puckstone, and possibly Pokedown) or to the devil (Old Harry). Motcombe refers to an old assembly place, and Pistle Down is an allusion to the ceremony of beating the bounds at Rogationtide. A few names are grim reminders of the violent punishments meted out to criminals in earlier times (Gallows Hill, Worgret, Yewstock). Some allude to sports and pastimes (Merry Field Hill, Miz Maze, Troy Town). In some the precise nature of the allusion is uncertain, since it may be figurative or ironical (Giddy Green, Gaulter Gap, Harp Stone, Stapehill, Three Legged Cross). A few names are transferred from other places outside England, and here too the exact significance is not always clear (Mount Ararat, Normandy, Waterloo). Others contain literary allusions (Branksome, Lilliput) or commemorate a historical event (Monmouth's Ash).

The introduction has only touched upon a few of the points of interest arising from a study of the place-names of Dorset. The alphabetical list of the names themselves, and the glossary of elements at the end of the book, will provide a lot more information which it is hoped will satisfy curiosity as well as stimulate further interest in the subject. Those seeking a more detailed coverage of the place-names (and field-names) of Dorset, together with a fuller discussion and analysis, should consult the series of county volumes published by the English Place-Name Society.

ALPHABETICAL LIST OF
DORSET PLACE-NAMES

Abbeycroft Down (in Tarrant Rushton) *Abbey Croft* 1542. From Old English *croft* 'enclosure'. It belonged to Tarrant Abbey.

Abbey House (in Witchampton) called *The Abbey Barn* in the 18th century, but by tradition once a chapel.

Abbotsbury *Abbedesburie* 946 (in a later copy of an Anglo-Saxon charter), *Abedesberie* 1086 (Domesday Book), *Abbodesberia* 1194, *Abbotesbir* 1227. 'Fortified house or manor belonging to the abbot', from Old English *abbod* and *burh*. The abbot in question was the abbot of Glastonbury who held lands here at an early date; the monastery at Abbotsbury itself was not founded until about 1026.

Abbot's Court Farm (in Winterborne Kingston) *Abescourte* 1553, *Abbots-Court* 1774. 'Court or manor house of the abbess', from Middle English *abbesse* and *court*. The allusion is to the abbess of Tarrant who held lands here from the 13th century. The modern form of the name, implying some connection with an *abbot*, is thus rather misleading.

Abbott Street (in Pamphill) *Abbodestrete* 1340, *Abbotestret* 1407. *Abbostrete* 1523. 'Abbot's hamlet', from Old English *abbod* and *strǣt*. The name refers to the possession of the manor by the Abbey of Sherborne.

Abbott's Wootton Farms (in Whitchurch Canonicorum)

Wudetune 1044 (Anglo-Saxon charter), *Widetone* 1086 (Domesday Book), *Wodeton Abbatis* 1268, *Wotton Abbatis* 1288. 'Farm in or by a wood', from Old English *wudu* and *tūn*. The Latin addition *abbatis* means 'of the abbot', with reference to the early possession of this manor by Abbotsbury Abbey.

Acton (in Langton Matravers) *Tacatone* 1086 (Domesday Book), *Tacton* 1283, *Taketon* 1305, *Acton* 1550. Probably 'farm where young sheep are reared', from Old English *tacca* and *tūn*. The original *T-* in this name was only dropped in the 16th century. Without the early spellings, a meaning 'oak-tree farm' from Old English *āc* and *tūn* (the usual origin of the common English place-name Acton), might have been wrongly assumed.

Adber (in Trent) *Eatan beares* 956 (in a later copy of an Anglo-Saxon charter), *Ateberie, Ettebere* 1086 (Domesday Book), *Adebere* 1429. 'Grove belonging to a man called Ēata', from Old English *bearu* and an Old English personal name.

Admiston, South (in Athelhampton) a more popular variant of the name Athelhampton itself.

Afflington Farm (in Corfe Castle) *Alvronetone, Alfrunetone* 1086 (Domesday Book), *Alfrington* 1244, *Aflington* 1586. 'Farm or estate belonging to a woman called Aelfrūn', from Old English *tūn* and an Old English personal name. The woman in question actually held the manor at the time of Domesday Book.

Affpuddle *Affapidele* 1086 (Domesday Book), *Affepidel* 1244, *Affepudele* 1289, *Afpudele* 1303. 'The estate on the River Piddle belonging to a man called Aeffa'. The Old English personal name *Aeffa* is probably a short form of *Aelffrith*. This is one of several places named from the River Piddle.

Agglestone (in Studland) *Adlingston* 1586, *Aglestone* 1773. 'Prince's stone', from Old English *aetheling* and *stān*. According to folklore, this massive block of sandstone was said to have been thrown by the Devil from the Isle of Wight with the intention of demolishing Corfe Castle!

Ailwood (in Corfe Castle) *Aleoude* 1086 (Domesday Book), *Ailewud* 1222, *Aylewood* 1409. 'Wood belonging to a woman called Aethelgifu', from Old English *wudu* and an Old English personal name.

Alcester (in Shaftesbury) *Alcestre* 1433, *Alyncestr* 1453, *Alcetor* 1577. This name was transferred from Alcester in Warwickshire, since Alcester Abbey possessed lands here from at least as early as the 13th century.

Alderholt *Alreholt* 1285, *Arleholte* 1318, *Halreholt* 1328, *Alderholt* 1509. 'Alder wood', from Old English *alor* and *holt*.

Alders Coppice (in Shillingstone) *Alres* 1330, *Alders* 1838. From Old English *alor* 'alder'.

Allen, River this river was originally called *Wimborne*, a name transferred to Wimborne Minster and Wimborne St Giles. Its present name is taken from the bridge at Wimborne Minster now called Canford Bridge but earlier *Aldewynebrigg* 1268, *Aldwynesbrigg* 1280, *Alwynsbrydge* 1500, *Aleynsbrydge* 1543, 'bridge belonging to a man called Ealdwine', from Old English *brycg* and an Old English personal name.

Aller (in Hilton) *Alre* 1332. From Old English *alor* 'an alder'.

All Hallows Farm (in Wimborne St Giles) *Opewinburne* 1086 (Domesday Book), *Vpwymbúrne All Saints* 1294, *Vpwymbourn Omnium Sanctorum* 1297, *Alhalowes Wimborn* 1575. For the meaning of *Vpwymburne*, see Wimborne St Giles. All Hallows (from Old English *hālga* 'saint') is from the dedication of the former church here. In medieval times this manor was sometimes called *Wymborn Karentham* (as in 1291) from a family of that name.

Allington *Adelingtone* 1086 (Domesday Book), *Alingetun* 1206, *Athelington* 1227, *Adelynton* 1268. 'Farm belonging to the princes', from Old English *aetheling* and *tūn*.

Allweston (in Folke) *Alfeston, Alveston* 1214, *Alfletheston* 1244, *Alueueston* 1268. 'Farm of a man called Aelf', from Old English *tūn* and personal name. Or 'stone of a woman called Aelfflǣd', from Old English *stān* and personal name.

27

Almer (in Sturminster Marshall) *Elmere* 943 (in a 15th century copy of an Anglo-Saxon charter), *Almere* 1212, *Aylmere* 1288, *Almer* 1431. 'Eel pool', from Old English *ǣl* and *mere*, with reference to the pool on the River Winterborne just south-east of the village.

Alton Pancras *Awultune* 1012, *Altone* 1086 (Domesday Book), *Aweltone Pancratii* 1226, *Alton Pancras* 1326. 'Farm at the source of a stream', from Old English *ǣwiell* and *tūn*; the River Piddle rises here. The addition Pancras (Latin *Pancratius*) is from the dedication of the church.

Alum Chine (in Bournemouth) first recorded in the 18th century, presumably an allusion to the earlier mining of alum here. Chine is from an Old English word *cinu* 'a deep valley, a ravine'.

Amen Corner (in Gussage All Saints) not recorded until the 19th century, but probably so named because according to tradition there was once a chapel here.

Ameysford (in Hampreston) first recorded in the 18th century, probably named from a local family called *Amey*. The ford was across the stream called Uddens Water.

Anderson *Wintreburne* 1086 (Domesday Book), *Wynterborn Fifasse* 1268, *Andreweston* 1331, *Wynturbourne Andreston alias Wynturbourne Vyueasshe* 1477. Originally named from the River Winterborne. The addition *Fifasse* means 'five ash-trees', from Old English *fīf* and *aesc*. The later *Andreweston* which forms the basis of the present name is probably from the dedication of the disused St Andrew's Church which lies a quarter of a mile from the manor house, with Old English *tūn* 'estate'.

Angers Farm (in Okeford Fitzpaine) *Aungiers* 1601. Named from a family called *Aunger*, here from the 14th century.

Ansty (in Hilton) *Anesty* 1219, *Ansty* 1244. 'Narrow track, or track linking other routes', from Old English *ānstīg*.

Arish Mell (in East Lulworth) *Arsmyll* 1454, *Arish Mill* 1634, *Arishmell* 1841. 'The mill near a topographical feature resembling a buttock', from Old English *ears* and *myln*. Our forefathers were not coy in using terms for parts of the body to describe their surroundings!

Armswell Farm (in Piddletrenthide) *Ermingewell* 1225, *Ermingyswelle* 1303, *Ermeneswell* 1366, *Armeswell* 1675. Probably 'spring or stream belonging to a man called Eormen', from Old English *wella* and an Old English personal name.

Arne *Arne* 1268, *Harne* 1285, *Arn* 1327, *Aren* 1575. Probably 'the house or building', from Old English *aern*, but alternatively a plural form of Old English *haer* 'rock, heap of stones, tumulus' is possible.

Ash (in Netherbury) *Esse* 1207, *Ashe* 1316, *Assh* 1377, *Aysshe* 1430. '(Place at) the ash-tree', from Old English *aesc*.

Ash (in Stourpaine) *Aisse* 1086 (Domesday Book), *Esse* 1244, *Assche* 1280, *Aysshe* 1372. Has the same origin as the previous name.

Ashcombe Farm (in Caundle Marsh) *Ascumbe* 1205, *Esscumbe* 1244, *Asshcomb* 1332. 'Valley where ash-trees grow', from Old English *aesc* and *cumb*.

Ashington (in Canford Magna) *Esseton* 1243, *Ashamton* 1327, *Asshton* 1463. Probably 'farm of the dwellers by the ash-tree', from Old English *aesc, hāeme* and *tūn*.

Ashley (in Long Bredy) *Asseleghe* 1246, *Ayhslegh* 1251, *Asshele* 1325. 'Wood where ash-trees grow', from Old English *aesc* and *lēah*.

Ashley (in St Leonards and St Ives) *Aisshele* 1280, *Asshele* 1317. Has the same origin as the previous name.

Ashley Barn (in Tolpuddle) *Asleg* 1268, *Aschlegh* 1327, *Asshleye* 1332. Has the same origin as the previous two names.

Ashley Wood (in Tarrant Keynston) *Ashelie Wood* 1624. Has the same origin as the previous names.

Ashmore *Aisemare* 1086 (Domesday Book), *Assemere* 1235, *Aysschemere* 1283, *Asshemore* 1316. 'Pool where ash-trees grow', from Old English *aesc* and *mere*, with reference to the pond at the centre of this hill-top village (situated at 700 feet above sea level). The second element has been confused with, and eventually replaced by, Old English *mōr* 'moor, marshy ground'.

Ashton Farm (in Hinton Parva) *Esseton* 1243, *Ashton* 1841. 'Farm by the ash-tree(s)', from Old English *aesc* and *tūn*.

Ashton Farm (in Winterborne St Martin) *Wintreburne* 1086 (Domesday Book), *Winterburn Asshe* 1275, *Aschtone* 1327, *Wynterbourne Aysshton* 1412. Originally named from the South Winterborne River on which it stands, but later with Old English *aesc* 'ash-tree' and *tūn* 'farm, estate'.

Asker, River a late back-formation from Askerswell.

Askerswell *Oscherwille* 1086 (Domesday Book), *Oskereswell* 1201, *Askereswell* 1208, *Askerswill* 1346. 'Spring or stream belonging to a man called Ōsgār', from Old English *wella* and an Old English personal name.

Athelhampton *Pidele* 1086 (Domesday Book), *Pidele Aleume* 1250, *(Pidele) Athelamston* 1285, *Athelhameston* 1303, *Adelmyston* 1547, *Admyston* 1560. Originally named from the River Piddle on which it stands, but later 'farm belonging to a man called Aethelhelm', from Old English *tūn* and an Old English personal name. The same name survives in a more popular form in South Admiston, a hamlet in this parish.

Atrim (in Netherbury) *Atrem, Atrum* 1086 (Domesday Book), *Atrom* 1200, *Attrum* 1210. Possibly the old name for the River Simene, but its origin is obscure.

Attisham (in Broadwindsor) *Hadesham* 1244, *Adesham* 1252, *Atesham* 1412, *Attysham* 1529. 'Enclosure belonging to a man called Aeddi', from Old English *hamm* and an Old English personal name.

Axe Farm (in Broadwindsor) *Axe* 1252. Named from the River Axe on which it stands. Axe is an old river-name of Celtic origin meaning originally 'water'; it also gives its name to Axminster and Axmouth in Devon.

Axnoller Farms (in Beaminster) *Axnolre* 1285, *Axnaldre* 1388, *Axinaller* 1431, *Axnollar* 1553. 'Alder-tree by the River

Axe', from Old English *alor*. For the origin of the river-name, see Axe Farm.

Badbury Rings (in Shapwick)   this Iron Age hill-fort was called *Vindocladia* in the 4th century, an old Celtic name meaning '(the town with) the white ditches', from *uindo-* and *clādo-*, clearly a reference to the chalk of which the hill-fort is constructed. The present name dates from Anglo-Saxon times, recorded as *Baddan byrig* in the 10th century (Anglo-Saxon Chronicle), *Baddebir* in 1244, *Badbury* in 1468. This probably means 'fortified place associated with a man called Badda', from Old English *burh* and an Old English personal name (perhaps that of a legendary hero).

Bagber (in Sturminster Newton)   *Bakeberge* 1201, *Bakebere* 1204, *Baggeber* 1244, *Bakkeber* 1428. Probably 'hill or grove belonging to a man called Bacca', from Old English *beorg* or *bearu* and an Old English personal name.

Bagman's Farm (in Woodlands)   *Bagerham* (probably an error for *Bagenham*) 1237, *Baggeham* 1305, *Bagenham* 1435, *Baggnam* 1551. The first element is probably Old English *bagga* 'bag', either as a topographical word for a hill or as the name of some animal, possibly the badger. The second element is probably Old English *hamm* 'enclosure'.

Bailey Ridge Farm (in Lillington)   *La Baillie* 1351, *Baillye* 1388, *Baylyrygge* 1496. From Middle English *baillie* 'a bailiff's jurisdiction or district', with the addition of *hrycg* 'ridge'.

Bailie Gate (in Sturminster Marshall)   *Baylye Yeate* 1516. 'The gate of a bailiwick or bailiff's district', from Middle English *baillie* and Old English *geat*. The bailiff may have had charge of a stretch of woodland or of the river-bank of the Stour.

Bainly Farm (in Gillingham)   *Binley* 1609. 'Clearing where beans are grown', from Old English *bēan* and *lēah*.

Ballard Down and Point (in Studland)   not on record until the 19th century, but probably 'smooth or rounded head or promontory', from Old English *balg* and *hēafod*.

Baltington (in Tyneham)   *Boltington* 1280, *Baltington* 1284,

Baltingeton 1287, *Baltyngton* 1300. Probably 'farm called after a man named Beald', from Old English -*ingtūn* and an Old English personal name.

Barcombe Farm (in Alton Pancras) *Berecombe* 1332. Probably 'valley where barley is grown', from Old English *bere* and *cumb*.

Bardolf Manor and Basan Hill (in Puddletown) *Pidelebardolveston* 1257, *Pidel Bardolf* 1264, *Bardelston* 1401, *Barson Hill* 1627. 'Estate on the River Piddle belonging to the *Bardolf* family', from Old English *tūn*. The *Bardolf* family held this manor in the 13th century. Basan is a much reduced form of *Bardolveston*.

Barford Farm (in Pamphill) *Bereford* 1244, *Berefford* 1427, *Barfford* 1444, *Barfforde* 1547. 'Ford by the woodland pasture or grove', from Old English *bǣr* or *bearu* and *ford*. The ford was on the River Stour.

Barnsfield Heath (near Hurn) *Barndefeld* early 12th century, *la Brendefeld* 1285, *Barnefeld* 1541. 'Tract of land cleared by burning', from Old English *berned* and *feld*.

Barnsley Farm (in Pamphill) *Bernardeslega* 1178, *Bernardesleye* 1285, *Barnardeslegh* 1479, *Barnesleye* 1535. 'Wood or clearing belonging to a man called Beornheard', from Old English *lēah* and an Old English personal name.

Barnston Farm (in Church Knowle) *Berneston* 1288, *Barneston* 1375. 'Farm belonging to a man called Beorn', from Old English *tūn* and an Old English personal name. The man in question is actually mentioned in Domesday Book as holding lands in Church Knowle.

Barton Hill (in Shaftesbury) named from the manor of *Berton* 1288, *La Bertone* 1293, *la Barton* 1471. From Old English *bere-tūn* 'a corn farm, an outlying grange'.

Basan Hill (in Puddletown) see Bardolf Manor.

Batcombe *Batecumbe* 1201, *Batecombe* 1268, *Batecoumb* 1314, *Badecombe* 1336. Probably 'valley belonging to a man called Bata', from Old English *cumb* and an Old English personal name.

Bay (in Gillingham)   first recorded 1791, probably from the word *bay* 'an embankment to form a dam'.

Beacon Hill (in Lytchett M.)   from *Lechiot becon* 1575.

Beaminster   *Bebingmynster* 862 (in a later copy of an Anglo-Saxon charter), *Beiminstre* 1086 (Domesday Book), *Begminister* 1091, *Bemenistre* 1228, *Beministre* 1284. 'Church associated with a woman called Bebbe', from Old English *mynster* and an Old English personal name.

Bearwood (in Canford M.)   from 1840, same origin as Beer(e).

Beaulieu Wood (in Buckland Newton)   *Beleye* 1288, *Belee* 1317, *Boelegh* 14th century, *Bewlywood* 1648. 'Wood or clearing frequented by bees', from Old English *bēo* and *lēah*. The modern spelling has been refashioned to resemble Beaulieu in Hampshire which is a place-name of French origin meaning 'beautiful place'.

Bedchester (in Fontmell Magna)   *Bedeshurste* early 12th century, *Bedeshurst* 1392, *Bedyshurst* 1395, *Bedcester* 1576. 'Copse or wooded hill belonging to a man called Bēdi or Bāede', from Old English *hyrst* and an Old English personal name. The second element had been modified to resemble a quite different element in the same way as in Hogchester.

Beere Farm (in Thorncombe)   *La Bere* 1281, *Bere* 13th century. Probably from Old English *bearu* 'a wood, a grove'.

Beer Hackett   *Bera* 1176, *Bere* 1244, *Berehaket* 1362, *Beere Haket* 1419. 'The woodland pasture' or 'the grove', from either Old English *bāer* or *bearu*. The manorial addition is from one *Haket de Bera* who held the manor from 1176.

Beerhall Farm (in Thorncombe)   *Berehalle* 1377. 'Hall or manor house by the grove', from Old English *bearu* and *heall*.

Belchalwell (in Okeford Fitzpaine)   *Chaldewelle* 1109, *Bell* 1207, *Belle and Chaldwell* 1286, *Belchalwell* 1575. Originally two distinct names. *Chaldwell* is 'cold spring or stream', from Old English *ceald* and *wella*; *Belle* is from Old English *belle* 'a bell-shaped hill', originally with reference to what is now Bell Hill (845 feet).

Belhuish Farm (in West Lulworth)   *Behylde Hywysche*

1303, *Belhywyssh* 1331, *Belehiwich* 1346, *Beelhewyssh* 1447. 'Measure of land belonging to a woman called Bēaghild', from Old English *hīwisc* 'measure of land sufficient to support a family' and an Old English personal name.

Bellows Cross (in Cranborne) *Bellyes Crosse* 1621, named from *Belleye* 1382, which probably means 'wood or clearing at the bell-shaped hill', from Old English *belle* and *lēah*.

Benville Manor (in Corscombe) *Benefeld* 1340. 'Arable land where beans are grown', from Old English *bēan* and *feld*.

Bere Farm (in Lytchett Minster) *Bearecourt* 1374, *Bere* 1420, *Bere Court* 1520, *Beere* 1534. Has the same origin as Bere Regis, with the addition of Middle English *court* 'a manor house' up to the 16th century.

Bere Marsh Farm and Mill (in Shillingstone) *molendinum* ('mill') *de la Bere* 1268, *Berre marshe* 1546. Probably from Old English *bāer* '(woodland) pasture', with *mersc* 'marsh'. The place is by the River Stour.

Bere Regis *Bere* 1086 (Domesday Book), *Beere* 1242, *Kyngesbyre* 1264, *Bire Regis* 1495. 'Woodland pasture', or 'wood, grove', from Old English *bāer* or *bearu*. The manor was anciently royal demesne, hence the Latin addition *Regis* 'of the king'. In fact there was also once a royal forest here.

Berne Farm (in Whitchurch Canonicorum) *La Berne* 1281, *Le Bernes* 1431, *Berne* 1462, *Barne* 1488. 'The barn or barns', from Old English *bere-aern*.

Berry Hill (in Bournemouth) possibly to be associated with a place called *la Bury* recorded at the end of the 13th century, from Old English *burh* 'a fortified place'.

Berwick (in Swyre) *Berewich* 1194, *Berewyk* 1250, *Berewik* 1265, *Berwyke* 1431. From Old English *bere-wīc*, literally 'barley-farm' but often denoting 'the outlying part of an estate'.

Bestwall (in Wareham) *Beastewelle* 1086 (Domesday Book), *Biestewalle* 1293, *Byestwall* 1412, *Bestwall* 1547. '(Place) to the east of the wall', from Old English *bī* 'by, near', *ēastan* and *weall*.

Bettiscombe *Bethescomme* 1129, *Betescumbe* 1244, *Bettescumbe* 1288, *Bettyscombe* 1436. 'Valley belonging to a man called Betti', from Old English *cumb* and an Old English personal name.

Bexington (in Puncknowle) *Bessintone* 1086 (Domesday Book), *Buxinton* 1212, *Bexinton* 1243, *Bexingtun* 1285. 'Farm where box-trees grow', from Old English *byxen* and *tūn*. East and West Bexington are separately recorded as early as the 13th century.

Bhompston (in Stinsford) *Frome* 1086 (Domesday Book), *Frome Bonevileston* 1285, *Boneleston* 1478, *Bolmeston* 1492. 'Manor on the River Frome belonging to the Boneville family', from Old English *tūn*. This family was here from the 13th century.

Bibbern Farm (in Stalbridge) *Bydeburnan* 933 (in a later copy of an Anglo-Saxon charter), *Biddeburn* 1244. 'Stream in a hollow', from Old English *byden* and *burna*. The stream is now called Bibbern Brook.

Bidcombe Mill (in Gussage All Saints) probably named from *Bitcombe* 1327, *Bitecomb* 1332, which may mean 'valley belonging to a man called Bitta', from Old English *cumb* and an Old English personal name.

Biddlesgate Farm (in Cranborne) *bi talayate* 946 (in a 14th century copy of an Anglo-Saxon charter), *Butelesheite* 1236, *Butlesgate* 1283, *Byddelgates* 1570. Probably 'gate belonging to a man called Butel', from Old English *geat* and an Old English personal name. It is on the county boundary where a road from Damerham in Hampshire enters Dorset.

Bidlake Farm (in Netherbury) *Bitelak* 1225, *Bitelake* 1356, *Bydelake* 1431. 'Stream belonging to a man called Bitta', from Old English *lacu* and an Old English personal name.

Bilshay Farm (in Allington) *Bilesheye* 1244, *Billeshage* 1285, *Bilshegh* 1340, *Billeshey* 1397. 'Enclosure belonging to a man called Bil', from Old English *haeg* and an Old English personal name.

Bincombe *Beuncumbe* 987 (in a 13th century copy of an

Anglo-Saxon charter), *Beincome* 1086 (Domesday Book), *Bincumbe* 1244, *Benecumbe* 1288. Probably 'valley where beans are grown', from Old English *bēan* and *cumb*.

Bindon Hill, Little Bindon (in West Lulworth) *Binedon, Old Bynedon* 1279, *Byndoun* 1399, *Litle Bindon* 1535. '(The place) within the hill', from Old English *binnan* and *dūn*. This was the site of the original foundation of Bindon Abbey before it was transferred to Wool in 1172. It was called *Little* or *Old* to distinguish it from Bindon Abbey itself.

Bingham's Farm (in Netherbury)   originally called *Woth* in 1207, *Bynghams Wothe* in 1448. *Woth* is the earlier name of the River Brit, see Wooth Grange also in this parish. An estate on this river was held by the *Bingham* family from the 13th century.

Bingham's Melcombe (in Melcombe Horsey) *Melcome, Melecome* 1086 (Domesday Book), *Bynghammes Melcombe* 1412, *Melcombe Byngham* 1431. See Melcombe Horsey. The manorial addition is from the *Bingham* family, here from the 13th century. In medieval times this manor was sometimes called *Nethermelcombe*, from Old English *neotherra* 'lower', to distinguish it from Melcombe Horsey.

Binnegar (in East Stoke) *Beningere* 1299, *Benegar* 1318. Possibly 'slope where beans grow', Old English *bēan, hangra*.

Birdsmoor Gate (in Broadwindsor) *Birds moore* 1663.

Bishop's Down (in Folke) *Doune* 1332, *Downe* 1460, *Bysshopysdoune* 1468. 'The hill or down belonging to the bishop', from Old English *dūn*, the later addition of 'Bishop's' referring to the Bishop of Salisbury.

Bittles Green (in Motcombe) *Biddles Greene* 1609. From the family of John *le Budel* 1327.

Blackdown Hill (in Broadwindsor) *Blakedon* 1275. 'Dark-coloured down', from Old English *blaec* and *dūn*. Blagdon Hill in the same parish is identical in origin.

Blackmanston Farm (in Steeple) *Blachemanestone* 1086 (Domesday Book), *Blakmanton* 1288, *Blakemestone* 1376, *Blakmanston* 1458. 'Farm belonging to a man called Blaec-mann', from Old English *tūn* and an Old English personal name.

Blackmoor Forest and Vale *Blakemor* 1212, *Blakemore* 1217, *Blakamor* 1239. 'Dark-coloured moor', from Old English *blaec* and *mōr*.

Blackney Farm (in Stoke Abbott) *Blakenhey* 1327, *Blakenheye* 1332. 'Dark-coloured enclosure', from Old English *blaec* and *haeg*.

Blackrow Common (in Lydlynch) *Blakerewe* 1421, *Blackrewe* 16th century. 'Dark-coloured row (of trees or houses)', from Old English *blaec* and *rǣw*.

Blackven Common (in Fontmell Magna) *Blakkefennys-mersche* 1395, *Blakevenne* 1450, *Blackfenne* 1505. '(Marsh at) the dark-coloured fen', from Old English *blaec* and *fenn* with *mersc*.

Black Venn (in East Stour) *la Blakeuenne* 13th century, *Blakefenne* 1247, *Blacke Fenn* 1609. 'The dark-coloured fen', from Old English *blaec* and *fenn*.

Blackwater (near Hurn) so called from the 18th century, perhaps originally an earlier name for the Moors River, with *black* in the sense 'dark-coloured'.

Blagdon Farm and Hill (in Cranborne) *Blakedone* 1237, *Blakedun* 1251, *Blakedoun* 1399, *Blagdon* 1535. 'Dark-coloured hill', from Old English *blaec* and *dūn*. The hill reaches 529 feet and lies on the county boundary. There was a large medieval deer-park here.

Blagdon Hill (in Broadwindsor) *Blakedon* 1324. Identical in origin with Blackdown Hill in the same parish.

Blandford Forum *Blaneford* 1086 (Domesday Book), *Blaneford Forum* 1297, *Blanford Forum* 1340, *Blandford Forum* 1506. Possibly 'ford where blay or gudgeon are found', from Old English *blǣge* and *ford*. Blay and gudgeon are small freshwater fish. The Latin addition *forum* means 'market', alluding to the early importance of Blandford as a market town. In medieval times an alternative name for Blandford was

Cheping Blaneford (as in 1288), from Old English *cēping* also meaning 'market'.

Blandford St Mary   *Bleneford, Blaneforde* 1086 (Domesday Book), *Blaneford St Mary* 1254, *Seyntmaryblandford* 1450. For the origin of Blandford, see Blandford Forum. The addition *St Mary* is either from the dedication of the church or because the manor once belonged to the nunnery of St Mary at Clerkenwell in London. In medieval times Blandford St Mary was sometimes called *Parva Blaneford* (from Latin *parva* 'small'), or *Blaneford Martel* (from a family called *Martel* which possessed the manor in the 12th century).

Blashenwell Farm (in Corfe Castle) *Blechenenwelle, Blachenwelle* 956 (in a later copy of an Anglo-Saxon charter), *Blachenewell* 1285, *Blachyngwell* 1316. 'Spring or stream where cloth is bleached', from Old English *blǣcen* 'bleaching' and *wella*, referring either to the calcareous spring near the farm or to the stream here.

Bleet Farm (in Gillingham)   first recorded in the 18th century, but perhaps from Old English *blēat* 'wretched, miserable'.

Bloxworth   *Blacewyrthe* 987 (in a 13th century copy of an Anglo-Saxon charter), *Blocheshorde* 1086 (Domesday Book), *Blokeswurthe* 1201, *Blokkesworth* 1244. 'Enclosure belonging to a man called Blocc', from Old English *worth* and an Old English personal name.

Bluntshay (in Whitchurch Canonicorum)   *Blondelesheye* 1312, *Blundleshay* 1329, *Bloundeleshey* 1399, *Blontyshay* 1431. 'Enclosure belonging to a family called Blundel', from Old English *haeg*.

Bluntsmoor Farm (in Mosterton)   this place, called *Blountescourte* in 1486, is named from the *Blunt* or *Blount* family, here from the 13th century.

Blynfield Farm (in Cann)   *Blinchesfelde* 932 (in a later copy of an Anglo-Saxon charter), *Blinchefeld* 1244, *Blyntesfeild* 1283, *Blynfelde* 1550. Probably 'tract of open land by the shining stream', from Old English *blinc* and *feld*.

Bockhampton (in Stinsford)   *Bochehamtone* 1086 (Domesday Book), *Bocameton* 1212, *Bukhamton, Bokhampton* 1244. Probably 'farm of the dwellers by the beech-tree', from Old English *bōc, hǣme* and *tūn*.

Bockhampton, Middle, North and South (in Christchurch)   *Bachamton* 1199, *Bachampton* 1236, *Bochamton* 1295. Possibly 'homestead by the beech-tree', from Old English *bōc* and *hām-tūn*, but the first element may be Old English *baec* 'a ridge'.

Bokerly Ditch (in Pentridge)   *Bockedic* 1280, *Bucke Ditche* 1618. 'Ditch where bucks are to be found', from Old English *bucc* and *dīc*, an allusion to the hunting of bucks in Cranborne Chase. The ditch itself, which crosses four miles of downland, is of Romano–British origin, dating from the end of the 4th century.

Bonscombe (in Shipton Gorge)   *Bonescumb* 13th century, *Bondscombe* 1618. From Old English *cumb* 'valley'. The first element is probably a surname; there is record of a William *Boun* here in 1332.

Bonsley Common (in Shillingstone)   *Bowslye Common* 1583, *Bonslate* 1774, *Bonsley* 1811. The first element may be the Old English personal name *Buna*, the second element is probably Old English *slaeget* or *slege* 'a sheep pasture'.

Bookham (in Buckland Newton)   *Bobbecombe* 14th century, *Bubbecome* 1317, *Bowcombe* 1616. 'Valley belonging to a man called Bubba', from Old English *cumb* and an Old English personal name.

Boscombe (in Bournemouth)   *Boscumbe* 1273, *Bascombe* 1593. Possibly 'valley overgrown with spiky plants', from Old English *bors* and *cumb*.

Botany Farm (in East Lulworth)   first so called in the 19th century. This is a transferred name from Botany Bay in Australia, usually denoting a remote spot.

Bothenhampton   *Bothehamton* 1268, *Bothenamtone* 1285, *Bothenhampton* 1322, *Baunton* 1497. 'Home farm in the valley bottom', from Old English *bothm* and *hām-tūn*.

Bothenwood (in Holt) *Bothenewode* 1323, *Bothenwode* 1462. The first element is probably an Old English plant-name *bothen* 'rosemary, darnel, or thyme', with *wudu* 'wood'. The word survives in Dorset dialect as *botham* or *bothen* in the sense 'corn marigold'.

Bourne Farm (in Piddlehinton) *la Bourne* 1270. 'The stream', from Old English *burna*.

Bournemouth *la Bournemowthe* 1407, *Burnemouthe* 1575, *Bournemouthe* 1585. 'The mouth of the stream', from Old English *burna* and *mūtha*. The stream is still called the Bourne.

Bourton *Bureton* 1212, *Burton* 1244, *Borton* 1268, *Buryton* 1288. 'Fortified farmstead', or 'farmstead near a fortified place', from Old English *burh-tūn*.

Boveridge (in Cranborne) *Bovehric* 1086 (Domesday Book), *Bogerugg* 12th century, *Boverig* 1256, *Bouerigg* 1268. '(Place) above the ridge', from Old English *bufan* and *hrycg*, or 'bow-shaped, i.e. curved, ridge', from Old English *boga* and *hrycg*.

Bovington (in Wool) *Bovintone* 1086 (Domesday Book), *Bovynton* 1280, *Bovyngton* 1288. 'Farm called after a man named Bōfa', from Old English *-ingtūn* and an Old English personal name.

Bowden (in Kington Magna) *Bouedon* 1332. '(Place) above the hill, i.e. on top of the hill', from Old English *bufan* and *dūn*.

Bowerswain Farm (in Gussage All Saints) *Boresfen* 1288, *Boreswain* 1546. 'Fen or marshland belonging to a man called Bār', from Old English *fenn* and an Old English personal name. In the 12th century the same place, or somewhere nearby, was known as *Baresfeld*, 'Bār's open country', the second element here being Old English *feld*.

Bowldish Pond (in Wimborne St Giles) not mentioned in early records, but possibly 'bull pasture', from Old English *bula* and *edisc*. The name may have been altered by folk etymology because the round pond here was thought to resemble a bowl or a dish.

Bowleaze Cove (near Preston)   *Bolheys* 1461, *Bolhaise* 1531, *Bolehaies* 1586, *Bow Leaze* 1838. 'Enclosures where bulls were kept', from Old English *bula* and *haeg*.

Bowood, North and South (in Netherbury)   *Bovewode* 1086 (Domesday Book), *Buwod* 1207, *Bowode* 1244, *Bouewode* 1288. '(Place) above the wood', from Old English *bufan* and *wudu*.

Bowridge Hill (in Gillingham)   *Poghrigge* 1292, *Pogherygge* 1306, *Porridge Hill* 1609. Probably 'pouch-shaped ridge', from Old English *pohha* and *hrycg*.

Boys Hill (in Holnest)   *Boies hill* 1582. Named from the family of William *de Boys* who was here in the early 14th century.

Boywood Farm (in Mappowder)   *Boywode* 1494. Possibly 'wood belonging to a man called Boia', from Old English *wudu* and an Old English personal name.

Bradford Abbas   *Bradan forda* 933 (in a later copy of an Anglo-Saxon charter), *Bradeford* 1086 (Domesday Book), *Braddeford Abbatis* 1386, *Bradfford* 1462. '(Place at) the broad ford', from Old English *brād* and *ford*, referring to a crossing of the River Yeo. The addition is Latin *abbas* 'an abbot', alluding to the early possession of this manor by Sherborne Abbey.

Bradford Farm (in Pamphill)   *Bradeford* 1212, *Braddeford* 1553. Identical in origin with the previous name. The ford was no doubt on the tributary of the River Allen flowing to the north of the farm. From the late 13th century on, this place was often called *Bradeford Brian*, from the *Brian de Insula* who also gave his name to Bryanston.

Bradford Peverell   *Bradeford* 1086 (Domesday Book), *Bradeford Peuerel* 1244, *Bradford Peverell* 1352. Identical in origin with the previous two names. The ford was across the River Frome. The addition is from the family of *Peverel*, here in the 13th and 14th centuries.

Bradle Farm (in Church Knowle)   *Bradelege* 1086 (Domesday Book), *Bradele* 1170, *Bradeleghe* 1243, *Bradeley* 1285.

'Broad wood or clearing', from Old English *brād* and *lēah*.

Bradpole *Bratepolle* 1086 (Domesday Book), *Bradepol* 1212, *Bradepole* 1219, *Bradpole* 1457. 'Broad pool', from Old English *brād* and *pōl*.

Branksome (in Poole) a recent name, taken from a house called *Branksome Tower* in the 19th century which in turn was probably named from the setting of Sir Walter Scott's *Lay of the Last Minstrel* published in 1805; Scott's *Branksome Tower* is near Hawick in Roxburghshire, Scotland. *Chine* in Branksome Chine is from an Old English word *cinu* 'a fissure, a ravine'.

Breach Farm (in Marnhull) *la Breche* 1482. From Old English *brǣc* 'land broken up for cultivation'.

Breach Woods (in Hilton) *la Brache* 1399, *la Breche* 1400. Identical in origin with the previous name.

Bredy Farm (in Burton Bradstock) *Bridie* 1086 (Domesday Book), *Bridye* 1303, *Bonevylesbryde* 1431, *Bonvyles-Bridy* 1486. Named from the River Bride on which it stands, see next name. The manorial addition in the 15th century forms is from the family of Stephen *de Bonevil*, here from the 13th century.

Bredy, Little and Long *Bridian* 987 (in a later copy of an Anglo-Saxon charter), *Litelbride, Langebride* 1086 (Domesday Book), *Litlebridie* 1204, *Langebridie* 1244. Both these places take their names from the river (now called Bride) on which they are situated. The river-name is Celtic and means 'gushing or surging stream'. *Long* refers to the elongated shape of Long Bredy parish, *Little* to the relatively smaller size of Little Bredy, from Old English *lang* and *lȳtel* respectively.

Brenscombe Farm (in Corfe Castle) *Brunescume* 1086 (Domesday Book), *Brynnescombe* 1376, *Brunscombe* 1449, *Brenscomb* 1509. 'Valley belonging to a man called Brȳni', from Old English *cumb* and an Old English personal name.

Briantspuddle (in Affpuddle) *Pidele* 1086 (Domesday Book), *Brianis Pedille* 1465, *Pudell Bryan* 1504, *Brientes Piddell*

1588. Named from the River Piddle, like Affpuddle itself. The addition *Briants* is from *Brian de Turbervill* who held the manor in the early 14th century (the *t* is quite unhistorical). In fact from the 13th century the place was often known as *Pudele Turberville* or *Turberville Pudele* because it was held by other members of this same family.

Briar's Wood (in Stockwood) *Priureswode* 1274, *Prioreswode* 1403, *Bryars Wood* 1685. 'Wood belonging to a prior (of a religious house)', from Old English *prior* and *wudu*. The alteration of *P-* to *B-* first appears in the 17th century.

Bride, River see Bredy.

Bridge Lane (in Abbotsbury) *Brugelane* 1492. Self-explanatory, from Old English *brycg* and *lane*.

Bridport *Brideport* 1086 (Domesday Book), *Bridiport* 1157, *Brudiport* 1207, *Bredeport* 1266. 'Harbour or market town belonging to Bredy', from Old English *port* which could have the sense 'port' or 'market'. The place referred to is Long Bredy, which was at the time a relatively important 'borough'. The present name of the river which flows through the town, the Brit, is taken from the name Bridport; its earlier name the *Woth*, is still found in Wooth Grange in Netherbury.

Brimbley Farm (in Stoke Abbott) *Bromlegam* 12th century, *Bromleye* 1295, *Bromeleye* 1298, *Bremeleygh* 1412. 'Clearing where broom grows', from Old English *brōm* and *lēah*. Brimbley Coombe Farm nearby is called simply *Cumb* in 1221, *Cume* in 1236, from Old English *cumb* 'valley'.

Brinsham Farm (in Netherbury) *Brinsham* 1288, *Brynsham* 1340, *Brynshaump* 1412, *Brynysham* 1430. 'Enclosure belonging to a man called Brȳni', from Old English *hamm* and an Old English personal name.

Brit, River see Bridport.

Broadenham Farm (in Netherbury) *Brodeham* 1268, *Bradenham* 1327. 'Broad enclosure', from Old English *brād* and *hamm*.

Broadley Wood (in Bryanston) *Bradele* 1334, *Bradelegh*

43

1344, *Bradeley* 1431, *Broadly* 1650. 'Broad wood or clearing', from Old English *brād* and *lēah*.

Broadmayne *Maine* 1086 (Domesday Book), *Brademaene* 1202, *Brodemaynne* 1288, *Brodemaygne* 1392. From Celtic *main* 'a rock, a stone', no doubt with reference to the many large sarsens scattered to the north-east of the village. These are apparently a natural phenomenon, in spite of their resemblance to a man-made stone circle. 'Broad' (Old English *brād*) to distinguish this manor from Little Mayne in the adjacent parish of West Knighton. Broadmayne was often known as *Mayne Martel* in medieval times, from the *Martel* family.

Broad Oak (in Symondsbury) *Brode Woke* 1493. 'Large oak-tree', from Old English *brād* and *āc*.

Broadstone (in Poole) first recorded 1765.

Broadwey *Wai(a)* 1086 (Domesday Book), *Waie* 1166, *Brode Way* 1243, *Bradeweye* 1249. One of several places named from the River Wey, others being Causeway, Upwey and Weymouth. *Broad-* is from Old English *brād*, referring to the width of the river here or to the size of the manor. Wey is an old Celtic river-name identical with the River Wey in Surrey and the River Wye in Herefordshire.

Broadwindsor *Windesore* 1086 (Domesday Book), *Windlesor* 1202, *Magna Wyndesor* 1249, *Brodewyndesore* 1324. 'River-bank with a windlass', from Old English *windels* and *ōra*. This place is thus identical in origin with Windsor in Berkshire. *Broad-* from Old English *brād*, alternated with Latin *magna* 'great' to distinguish this manor from Littlewindsor.

Brockham (in Turnworth) *Brocam* early 13th century, *le Brokham* 16th century, *Brokeham* 1546. Possibly 'enclosure or meadow by a brook', from Old English *brōc* and *hamm*, although there is no brook here now. Alternatively the first element could be Old English *brocc* 'badger'.

Brockhampton Green (in Buckland Newton) *Brokhampton* 1288, *Brochampton* 1332, *Brokehampton* 1478. 'Homestead by the brook', from Old English *brōc* and *hām-tūn*, or identical in origin with Brockington Farm.

Brockhill (in Turners Puddle) *Brockholes* 1664, *Brockhall* 1811, *Brockhill* 1838. 'Badger holes', from Old English *brocc-hol*.

Brockington Farm (in Gussage All Saints) *Brochemtune* 1086 (Domesday Book), *Brochamton* 1204, *Brochampton* 1225, *Brokinton* 1575. Probably 'farm of the dwellers by the brook', from Old English *brōc, hǣme* and *tūn*. The farm lies beside the River Allen.

Bronkham Hill (in Winterborne St Martin) *Bromcomb* 1445, *Brancombe* 1473. 'Valley where broom grows', from Old English *brōm* and *cumb*.

Broom Hill (in Holt) first recorded as *Bromehill* in 1591. Identical in origin with the next name.

Broomhill Bridge (in Moreton) *Brumel Bridge* 1791, named from Broomhill in Winfrith Newburgh which is *Bromhill* 1244, *Bromhull* 1280, *Bromehill* 1464, 'broom-covered hill' from Old English *brōm* and *hyll*.

Brownsea Island *Brunkeseye* 1241, *Bronkesye* 1319, *Brounkeseye* 1381, *Brownesey* 17th century. Probably 'island belonging to a man called Brūnoc', from Old English *ēg* and an Old English personal name.

Bryanston *Blaneford Brian, Brianeston* 1268, *Bryanston* 1280, *Bryenston* 1297. 'Brian's estate', from Old English *tūn*. The man in question was *Brian de Insula* who held this manor (originally called *Blaneford* = Blandford) in the early 13th century. Bryanston may be one of the manors called *Blaneford* in Domesday Book (1086).

Buckham (in Beaminster) *Bochenham* 1086 (Domesday Book), *Bukeham* 1244, *Bukkeham* 1285, *Bukham* 1288. Probably 'enclosure where he-goats are kept', from Old English *bucca* and *hamm*, but alternatively 'enclosure belonging to a man called Bucca', from an Old English personal name.

Buckhorn Weston *Westone* 1086 (Domesday Book), *Boukeresweston* 1275, *Bokerne Weston* 1346, *Weston Bukkehorne* 1535. 'West farm', from Old English *west* and *tūn*, perhaps referring to its situation in relation to Gillingham. The addition is probably manorial, from the surname *Bouker* of some medieval owner. The possessive *-es* in *Boukeres-* seems to have been interpreted as a plural ending and to have been replaced by the old *-en* plural (as in the word *oxen*) often found in Dorset dialect. The change to Buckhorn from the 16th century is due to folk etymology.

Buckland Newton *Boclonde* 941 (in a later copy of an Anglo-Saxon charter), *Bochelande* 1086 (Domesday Book), *Bokeland* 1212, *Newton Buckland* 1576. From Old English *bōc-land* 'charter land', i.e. 'land in which certain rights and privileges were granted by charter'. The relatively recent addition Newton is from Sturminster Newton, because at one time the Hundreds of Sturminster Newton and Buckland were combined.

Buckland Ripers (near Radipole) *Bocheland* 1086 (Domesday Book), *Bokeland* 1268, *Boklond Ripers* 1359, *Buklond Rivers* 1425. Identical in origin with the previous name. *Ripers* is a manorial addition from the family of *de Riuers* or *de Ripariis* (from Rivière in Normandy) here in the 13th century.

Bucknowle House (in Church Knowle) *Bubecnolle* 1285, *Bubbeknolle* 1306, *Bouknolle* 1412, *Bucknoll* 1584. 'Hill-top belonging to a man called Bubba', from Old English *cnoll* and an Old English personal name.

Buckshaw House (in Holwell) *Buggechage* 1194, *Bugeshagh* 1342, *Bukshawe* 1420. Probably 'small wood belonging to a woman called Bucge', from Old English *sceaga* and an Old English personal name, but alternatively the first element could be Middle English *bugge* 'a boggart, a hobgoblin'.

Bugley (in Gillingham) *Bogeley* 1275, *Boggeley* 1280, *Bugeley* 1300. From Old English *lēah* 'wood, clearing', with a first element as in the previous name.

Bulbarrow Hill (in Stoke Wake) *Buleberwe* 1270, *Bulbaro* 1555. From Old English *beorg* 'barrow, tumulus'. The second element may be Old English *bula* 'bull' or an Old English personal name *Bula*.

Bulbury Camp (in Lytchett Minster) *Burlebury, Bulrebury* 1306, *Bulberye* 1567, *Bullbury* 1774. The final element is clearly Old English *burh* 'earthwork', with reference to the hill-fort here. The first part of the name is probably 'wood or clearing by the earthwork' from the same word *burh* and Old English *lēah*.

Bullhill (in Alderholt) first recorded in the 17th century, and self-explanatory, from Old English *bula* and *hyll*.

Burcombe Farm (in North Poorton) *Burcumbe* 1244, *Burcome* 1346, *Burcombe* 1386, *Borcombe* 1431. 'Valley by or belonging to a fortified place', from Old English *burh* and *cumb*.

Burleston *Bordelestone* 934 (in a later copy of an Anglo-Saxon charter), *Burdeleston* 1212, *Burdleston* 1383, *Burleston* 1535. 'Farm belonging to a man called Burdel', from Old English *tūn* and an Old French personal name.

Burngate Farm (in West Lulworth) *Brumzete* 1233, *Brunnegate* 1262, *Bronyate* 1436, *Burneyate* 1462. Probably 'brown gate', from Old English *brūn* and *geat*.

Burning Cliff (in Owermoigne) so called from the spontaneous ignition of the bituminous shale here in 1826, giving rise to a fire that lasted for four years.

Burstock *Burewinestoch* 1086 (Domesday Book), *Burgestok* 1200, *Burghestok* 1244, *Burstok* 1291. 'Farm belonging to a woman called Burgwynn or a man called Burgwine', from Old English *stoc* and an Old English personal name.

Burton (in Charminster) *Burton* 1204, *Bourton* 1289, *Borton* 1300. 'Farm near the fortification', from Old English *burh-tūn*. The *burh* referred to is Poundbury Camp in Dorchester.

Burton (in Christchurch) *Buretone* 1100, *Buriton* 1236, *Burton* 1248, *Bourton* 1316. Identical in origin with the previous name, although the meaning here might be 'fortified farmstead' rather than 'farm near a fortification'.

Burton (in Marnhull) *Burtun* 1244, *Borton* 1268, *Burtone* early 14th century. Identical in origin with the previous two names. In medieval times it was often called *Ashburton* or

Nashburton because of its proximity to Nash Court. The name survives now only as a street name.

Burton Bradstock *Bridetone* 1086 (Domesday Book), *Briditona* 1244, *Brytton* 1327, *Berton* 1381. 'Farm on the River Bride', from Old English *tūn*. The river-name is Celtic in origin, see under Bredy. The relatively late addition *Bradstock* is from the Wiltshire abbey of Bradenstoke, to which this manor belonged from the 13th century.

Burton, East and West (in Winfrith Newburgh) *Bureton* 1212, *Burton* 1244, *Borton* 1271, *Estburton, Westburton* 1280. 'Fortified farm' or 'farm near a fortification', from Old English *burh-tūn*. There is no archaeological evidence for a fortification here.

Burton, Long *Burton* 1244, *Buryton* 1285, *Bourton* 1316, *Langebourton* 1460. Identical in origin with the previous name. 'Long' because of the length of the village, from Old English *lang*.

Burwood (in Cranborne) *Borwode* 1285, *Borewode* 1292, *Burwod* 1369. Probably 'wood at or near the fortified place', from Old English *burh* and *wudu*.

Bushey (in Corfe Castle) *Burshawe* 1299, *Bursewe* 1550, *Bershew* 1623, *Bushy* 1740. Probably 'small wood or copse with a cottage', from Old English *būr* and *sceaga*.

Bussey Stool Farm (in Tarrant Gunville) *Burcyes* 1432, *Burces* 1558, *Burses Stolle* 1590, *Burcistoole* 17th century. Named from a family called *Burcy*, here in the 14th century. *Stool* is from Old English *stōl* 'stool, seat', perhaps used here of 'a flat-topped hill'.

Butterwick Wood (in Folke) *Buterwik, Buterwyk* 1288, *Boterwyk* 1332, *Butterwyke* 1553. 'Farm where butter is made', from Old English *butere* and *wīc*.

Buzbury Rings (in Tarrant Keynston) the name of this Iron Age enclosure is not recorded before the 19th century, but the second element is no doubt Old English *burh* 'fortified place, earthwork', the first may be an Old English personal name *Beorhtsige*.

Cale, River   an old Celtic river-name of uncertain origin, first recorded in the 10th century as *Cawel*.

Cam, River   a tributary of Caundle Brook not mentioned in early records, but it may be an old Celtic river-name with a meaning 'crooked, winding'.

Camesworth (in Netherbury)   *Kaymmswoth* 1288, *Kaymesworth* 1332, *Caymeswouth* 1340, *Caymyswothe* 1518. An estate on the River *Woth* (now called the River Brit) held by a family called *Kaym* or *Caym*, see Wooth Grange also in this parish.

Canford, Little (in Hampreston)   *Parva Caneford* 1263, *Lytel Canefford* 1381, *Litelcaneford* 1386. From Old English *lӯtel*, alternating with Latin *parva*, to distinguish it from Canford Magna on the opposite bank of the River Stour.

Canford Magna   *Cheneford* 1086 (Domesday Book), *Kaneford* 1195, *Greate Canford* 1612, *Canford Magna* 1774. 'Ford belonging to a man called Cana', from Old English *ford* and an Old English personal name. The ford was across the River Stour. The additions *Great* and *Magna* (Latin 'great') distinguish it from Little Canford across the river.

Cann   *Canna* early 12th century, *Canne* 1202, *Kanne* 1288, *Can* 1575. From Old English *canne* 'a can, a cup', used topographically for 'a hollow, a deep valley' with reference to the situation of this place in a steeply sided valley.

Canon Hill (in Colehill)   this name perhaps preserves the name of the old Hundred of *Canendone*, first recorded in Domesday Book, meaning 'Cana's down or hill', from Old English *dūn* and the Old English personal name found in Canford.

Cards Mill Farm (in Whitchurch Canonicorum)   *Cassymulle* 1399, *Casemyll* 1462. Probably 'mill where cress grows', from Old English *caerse* and *myln*.

Carey (in Wareham)   *Kerre, Keire* 1220, *Carry* 1318, *Carye* 1611. Perhaps an old Celtic river-name for the lower course of the River Piddle or Trent.

Castle Hill (in Cranborne)   *Castlehill* 1553. Self-explanatory, with reference to the undated motte and bailey here, first recorded as *Castell* in 1324.

Castleton *Castleton* 1332, *le Castellton* 1429, *la Casteltoune* 1448, *Casteltown* 1535. 'Farm or estate by the castle', from Old English *tūn* with *castel*, here referring to Sherborne Castle.

Caswell Farm (in Ryme Intrinseca) *Carsewell* 1413, *Carswell* 1476, *Cassewell* 1621. 'Spring or stream where cress grows', from Old English *caerse* and *wella*.

Catherston Leweston *Chartreston* 1268, *Chartereiston* 13th century, *Cardeston et Lesterton* 1316, *Katherston Lewson* 1576. The names were originally those of adjacent estates, Catherston meaning 'estate of a family called Charteray' and Leweston 'estate of a family called Lester', both from Old English *tūn*.

Catsley Farm (in Corscombe) *Catesclive* 1086 (Domesday Book), *Katesclive* 1200, *Cattescliue* 1244, *Catscliffe* 1632. 'Cliff or steep slope frequented by wild-cats', from Old English *catt* and *clif*. A similar late development of -*cliff* to -*ley* occurs in Rockley.

Cattistock *Cattesstoke* 934 (in a later copy of an Anglo-Saxon charter), *Stoche* 1086 (Domesday Book), *Kattestok, Cattestok* 1288. 'Secondary settlement belonging to a man called Catt', from Old English *stoc* and a personal nickname from Old English *catt* 'a cat'.

Caundle, Bishop's and Purse *Candel* 1086 (Domesday Book), *Purscaundel* 1241, *Caundel Bishops* 1294. The meaning of the name Caundle, found in these two names as well as in Caundle Marsh, Caundle Wake and Stourton Caundle, has not yet been satisfactorily explained. It may originally have been a name for the chain of hills in the vicinity, but its exact origin remains obscure. The addition *Bishop's* is from the possession of this manor by the Bishop of Salisbury. *Purse* is probably also a manorial addition, the family name of an early owner. Caundle Brook is named from the places.

Caundle Marsh *Candelemers* 1245, *Caundelmarys* 1288,

Caundelmersh 1333, *la Mersshe* 1361. See Bishop's Caundle. *Marsh* is self-explanatory, from Old English *mersc* 'marsh'.

Caundle Wake (in Bishop's Caundle) *Caundelwak* 1288, *Caundel Wake* 1360. See Bishop's Caundle. *Wake* is a manorial addition from the family which gave name to Stoke Wake and which was here in the late 13th century.

Causeway Farm (near Radipole) *Caucesweie* 1371, *Causweye* 1381, *Cawesway* 1570. 'The manor on the River Wey held by the Kauz family', see Broadwey. A certain John *de Kauz* or *le Kauz* held land here in 1299.

Cerne, River an old Celtic river-name, identical in origin with the River Char, from Celtic *carn* 'a cairn, a heap of stones'. It gives its name to Cerne Abbas, Nether Cerne and Up Cerne, as well as to Charminster (parish).

Cerne Abbas *Cernel* 1086 (Domesday Book), *Cerne* 1175, *Cerne Abbatis* 1288, *Serne Abbas* 1447. Like Nether Cerne and Up Cerne, taking its name from the River Cerne. The addition is Latin *abbas* 'an abbot', with reference to the abbey here.

Cerne, Nether *Nudernecerna* 1206, *Nudercerne* 1244, *Nethercerne* 1288, *Nithercerne* 1291. *Nether* means 'lower down' from Old English *neotherra*, with reference to its situation on the River Cerne.

Cerne, Up *Obcerne* 1086 (Domesday Book), *Upcerne* 1202, *Uppecerne* 1218. *Up* means 'higher up' from Old English *upp*, with reference to its situation on the River Cerne.

Chaffeymoor House (in Bourton) *Chauye* 1327, *Chavie* 1609, *Chaffey* 1839. Probably from Old English *ceaf* 'chaff' (perhaps in the sense 'rubbish, fallen twigs') and *īeg* 'land partly surrounded by water, with the later addition of *mōr* 'marshy ground'.

Chalbury (parish) *cheoles burge* 946 (in a 14th century copy of an Anglo-Saxon charter), *Chelesbyr* 1244, *Chalesbury* 1361, *Challebury* 1504. 'Fortified place associated with a man called Cēol', from Old English *burh* and an Old English personal name, with reference to the hill-fort here.

Chalbury (near Preston)   *Charlebury* 1452, *Cherlebury* 1461, *Chalbury* 1838. 'The encampment of the peasants', from Old English *ceorl* and *burh*. Chalbury is an Iron Age hill-fort.

Chaldon Herring   *Celvedune, Calvedone* 1086 (Domesday Book), *Chalvedon* 1224, *Chaluedon Hareng* 1243, *Chaldon Hearynge* 1574. 'Hill where calves are pastured', from Old English *cealf* and *dūn*. The manorial addition is from the family of *Harang*, here from the 12th century; the same family gave its name to Herrison, Langton Herring and Winterborne Herringston.

Chaldon, West, or Chaldon Boys (in Chaldon Herring) *West Chalvedon* 1269, *Chalvedon Boys* 1280. 'West' in relation to Chaldon Herring; *Boys* from the family of *de Bosco* or *Boys*, here from the 13th century.

Challow Farm (in Corfe Castle)   *Challway* 1716. Probably 'chalk way', from Old English *cealc* and *weg*.

Chalmington (in Cattistock)   *Chelmyntone* 934 (in a later copy of an Anglo-Saxon charter), *Chelminton* 1212, *Chalmington* 1268, *Chalmynton* 1280. 'Farm called after a man named Cēolhelm or Cēolmund', from Old English *-ingtūn* and an Old English personal name.

Chamberlayne's Farm (in Bere Regis)   *Chaumberleynesmylle* 1411, *Chamberlain Mill* 1546, *Chamberlynes* 1682. Named from the family called *Chamberlayn*, on record in the area from the 13th century. The mill would have been on the River Piddle or Trent.

Champernhayes Farm (in Wootton Fitzpaine)   *Chapronheys* 1440, *Champrenheghe* 1482. 'Enclosure belonging to the Champernon family', from Old English *haeg*. Names ending in *-hay* from this Old English word are particularly common in West Dorset, just as they are in East Devon.

Chantmarle (in Cattistock)   *Chauntemerle* 1288, *Chammerle* 1310, *Chantemerle* 1345. Named from the *Chauntemerle* family, recorded as having lands in this area from the 13th century.

Chapel Court (in Mosterton)   named from the chapel here, referred to as *Chapell* in 1486.

Chapel Marsh (in Beaminster)   *Chappell Marsh* 1615. Self-explanatory; a chapel here was recorded in the 13th century.

Chapman's Pool (in Worth Matravers)   *schort mannes pol* 948 (in a later copy of an Anglo-Saxon charter), *Shortmanpole* 1489, *Shipmans poole* 1575, *Chapmans Pool* 1811. Either 'small pool used in common', from Old English *sceort, mǣnnes* and *pōl*, or alternatively 'pool belonging to a man called Sceort-mann' if the first part of the name is an Old English personal name. It will be noted that the modern form of the name dates only from the early 19th century.

Char, River   an old Celtic river-name, identical in origin with the River Cerne. It gives its name to Charmouth.

Charborough House (in Morden)   *Cereberie* 1086 (Domesday Book), *Chereberge* 1212, *Chernebrug* 1219, *Charbergh* 1340). The second element is Old English *beorg* 'a hill, a barrow'. The first is uncertain. It may be either an old Celtic name for the River Winterborne (on which Charborough is situated) identical with the River Cerne, or Old English *cearr* 'a turn, a bend' (with reference to the gentle curve in the river here).

Charing Cross (in Alderholt)   at a cross roads. The name is not on early record, but is no doubt humorously transferred from the well-known London place (OE *cerring* 'a bend').

Charlestown (in Chickerell)   first recorded 1893.

Charlton Dairy Farm (in Woodlands)   *Cherleton* 1266, *Charleton* 1432. 'Farm belonging to the peasants', from Old English *ceorl* and *tūn*.

Charlton Higher Down (in Charminster)   *Cherlton* 1226, *Cherleton* 1242, *Charleton* 1303, *Charlton* 1412. Identical in origin with the previous name.

Charlton Marshall   *Cerletone* 1086 (Domesday Book), *Cheorleton* 1187, *Cherleton Marescal* 1288, *Charleton Marshall* 1571. Identical in origin with the previous two names. The addition *Marshall* is from the same family which gave name to

Sturminster Marshall; members of the family had lands here from the 13th century.

Charminster (parish) *Cerminstre* 1086 (Domesday Book), *Cerneministr* 1223, *Chermynstr* 1289, *Charminstr* 1376. 'Church on the River Cerne', from Old English *mynster*. See under Cerne for the meaning of the river-name.

Charminster (in Bournemouth) a recent name for a modern district of the town, presumably transferred from the previous place.

Charmouth *Cernemude* 1086 (Domesday Book), *Cernemue* 1189, *Cernemuth* 13th century, *Charnemothe* 1394, *Chermouth* 1432. 'Mouth of the River Char', from Old English *mūtha*.

Chartknolle (in Stoke Abbott) *Charteray* 1240, *Charterey* 1431. Probably a manorial name from a family so called, see Catherston Leweston. The modern place-name seems to have had Old English *cnoll* 'a hillock' added.

Chebbard Farm (in Dewlish) *Ceatwanberge* 870 (in a later copy of an Anglo-Saxon charter), *Scaborthe* 1335, *Chebbord* 1765. Rather obscure, but possibly 'the hill and border of a man called Ceatwa', from Old English *beorg* and *bord* with an Old English personal name.

Chedington *Chedinton* 1194, *Cedindun* 1226, *Chedington* 1230, *Cetindon* 1244. 'Farm called after a man named Cedd or Cedda', from Old English *-ingtūn* and an Old English personal name. The final element shows alternation with Old English *dūn* 'hill or down'.

Chelborough, East and West *Celberge* 1086 (Domesday Book), *Cheleberg* 1204, *Estchelberewe* 1343, *Westchelbergh* 1346. Probably 'hill belonging to a man called Cēola', from Old English *beorg* and an Old English personal name, but the first element could alternatively be Old English *ceole* 'a throat, a channel, a gorge'.

Chescombe Farm (in Winterborne Whitechurch) *Churchecombe* 1539, *Chescombe Farm* 1771. 'Church valley', from Old English *cirice* and *cumb*, with reference to St Mary's Church in Winterborne Whitechurch.

Cheselbourne *Chiselburne* 869 (in a later copy of an Anglo-Saxon charter), *Ceseburne* 1086 (Domesday Book), *Cheselburne* 1212, *Cheselborn* 1285. 'Gravel stream', from Old English *cisel* and *burna*.

Chesil Beach *the Chisil, Chisille bank* 1535–43. From Old English *cisel* 'shingle'. This ridge of pebbles extends along the coast for some 16 miles, and gives its name to the village of Chesil (recorded as *Chesill* 1608) on the Isle of Portland.

Chetnole *Chetenoll* 1242, *Chattecnolle* 1268, *Chetecnolle* 1288, *Chetnoll* 1535. 'The hill-top or hillock of a man called Ceatta', from Old English *cnoll* and an Old English personal name.

Chetterwood (in Moor Crichel) *Chetred* 1215, *Cetred* 1242, *Chetreth* 1243, *Chyttheryd* 1331. Probably a very old name, the first element of which is Celtic *cēd* 'a wood'. The second element may be Celtic *rid* 'a ford' or Old English *rīth* 'a stream'; there is now no ford or stream, but there is a marked valley. The 'rationalization' of *-ed* to *-wood* dates only from the 19th century.

Chettle *Ceotel* 1086 (Domesday Book), *Chetel* 12th century, *Chettel* 1233, *Chetil* 1288. Probably from Old English *ceotol* 'a kettle', here in the topographical sense of 'a deep valley surrounded by hills', with reference to the situation of the village.

Chettle Head Copse (in Pentridge) *cheotoles heafde* 955 (in a 14th century copy of an Anglo-Saxon charter), *Chetelesheved, Chytelheved* 1281, *Chettlehed* 1618. From Old English *ceotol* 'a kettle', used in a topographical sense as in the previous name, with Old English *hēafod* 'head', either in the sense 'hill, ridge' or 'upper end of a valley'.

Chewton Bunny (in Christchurch) *Chiventon* 12th century, *Cheveton, Chyveton* 1280. Probably 'farm belonging to a man called Cifa', from Old English *tūn* and an Old English personal name. Bunny is recorded as *la Bonye* in the early 14th century and may have originally meant 'island or marshy land overgrown with reeds', from Old English *bune* and *ēg*, though now it refers to the chine here.

Chickerell *Cicherelle* 1086 (Domesday Book), *Chikerel* 1227, *Chykerel* 1280, *Chekerell* 1375. This unique name remains obscure. It is one of the few Dorset names that have not yet been satisfactorily explained.

Chideock *Cidihoc* 1086 (Domesday Book), *Cidioc* 1240, *Chidihoc* 1248, *Chidioc* 1268. An old name of Celtic origin, meaning 'wooded', from a derivative of *cēd* 'wood'. The River Chid is a back-formation from this name.

Chilbridge Farm (in Pamphill) *Chelebruga* 12th century, *Chilbrigg* 1307, *Chelbrigg* 1326, *Chylbrygge* 1412. The second element is Old English *brycg* 'bridge', probably used here in the sense 'causeway through marshy ground'. The first element may be Old English *ceole* 'channel, gorge' or the Old English personal name *Cēola*.

Chilcombe *Ciltecombe* 1086 (Domesday Book), *Childecumb* 1198, *Chiltecumb* 1268, *Chylcombe* 1558. Probably 'valley at a steep hill or hill-slope called *Cilte*', from an Old English or pre-English hill-name and Old English *cumb*. Chilcombe lies at the foot of a steep slope.

Childhay (in Broadwindsor) *Childheya* 1234, *Childehey* 1244, *Childheye* 1250, *Childehaye* 1256. 'Enclosure belonging to the young noblemen', from Old English *cild* and *haeg*.

Child Okeford   see under Okeford.

Chilfrome *Frome* 1086 (Domesday Book), *Childefrome* 1206, *Childesfrome* 1268, *Chillfroome* 1653. 'Estate on the River Frome belonging to the noble-born sons', from Old English *cild*. In Domesday Book the manor is stated to have formerly belonged jointly to three thegns or noblemen.

Chilmore (in Hilton) *Childemore* 1399. 'Moor or marshy ground of the younger sons', from Old English *cild* and *mōr*.

Christchurch *Tweoxneam* 10th century (Anglo-Saxon Chronicle), *Twynham* 934 (in a later copy of Anglo-Saxon charter), *Thuinam* 1086 (Domesday Book), *Ecclesia Christi de Twinham* 12th century, *Cristeschirche of Twynham* 1318, *Crischurch* 1354. The old name means '(place) betwixt or between the streams', from Old English *betweoxn* or *betwēonan* and *ēa* (in the dative plural form *ēam*), referring to its situation between the Rivers Stour and Avon. The newer name is self-explanatory.

Christmas Close (in Wareham) first recorded in 1707 and named from the family of one Robert *Crissmasse* mentioned in 1532.

Church Knowle *Cnolle, Chenolle* 1086 (Domesday Book), *Cnoll* 1202, *Churchecnolle* 1346. Originally 'the hill-top', from Old English *cnoll*, later with the addition of Old English *cirice* 'church'. There is mention of a priest here at the time of Domesday book.

Clandon (Hill) (in Winterborne St Martin) *Clandon* 1594. 'Clean (i.e. cleared) hill', from Old English *clǣne* and *dūn*.

Clapgate (in Colehill) first recorded 1811. 'Gate that shuts to on its own', probably a gate to Holt forest.

Clatcombe Farm (near Sherborne) *Klatcombe* 1569. 'Valley where burdock grows', from Old English *clāte* and *cumb*.

Claylake (in Verwood) not recorded before the 19th century, but the meaning is 'clay stream', from Old English *clǣg* and *lacu*.

Claywell (in Studland) *Cleywoll* 1332, *Claywell* 1667. 'Clay spring or stream', from Old English *clǣg* and *wella*.

Cliff, The (in Shillingstone) *La Clive* 1270. From Old English *clif* 'cliff, bank'; it is beside the River Stour.

Clifton Maybank *Cliftune* 1012, *Clistone* 1086 (Domesday Book), *Clifton Mabank* 1319, *Clifton Maubank* 1404. 'Farm on the hill slope' or 'farm on the river bank', from Old English *clif* and *tūn*. The manorial addition is the name of the family which held the manor in medieval times, the first of them, William *Malbeenc*, having held the manor at the time of Domesday Book.

Clinger Farm (in Buckland Newton) *Clehangr'* 1206, *Cleyhangere* 1288, *Cleyangre* 1317. 'Clayey wooded slope', from Old English *clǣg* and *hangra*.

Clyffe Farm and House (in Tincleton) *Clyue* 934 (in a later copy of an Anglo-Saxon charter), *Clive* 1086 (Domesday Book), *Clyff* 1535, *Cliffe* 1664. '(Place) at the cliff', from Old English *clif*, with reference to the steep slope on the side of a 300 foot ridge.

Cobb (in Lyme Regis)   *la Cobbe* 1295, *le Cobbe* 1328, *Cobbe* 1380. Originally referring to the famous semi-circular pier, from an Old English word *cobb* 'a rounded mass'.

Cobley Farm (in Pentridge)   *Cobley, Cobly* 17th century. From Old English *lēah* 'wood, clearing', possibly with Old English *cobb* 'rounded mass' (perhaps here 'hill') or an Old English personal name *Cobba*.

Cockhill Farm (in Stourton Caundle) *Cokhull* 1332, *Cockill* 1709. 'Hill frequented by woodcocks or other wild birds', from Old English *cocc* and *hyll*, though alternatively the first element may be a different word *cocc* meaning 'heap, hillock'.

Cocknowle (in Church Knowle)   *Kokenulle, Kokenhule* 14th century. Possibly 'hill, or hollow, frequented by woodcocks', from Old English *cocc* and *hyll* or *hylu*. The modern name has been adjusted to resemble the name of the parish.

Coker's Frome (in Stinsford)   recorded as such only from the 18th century; called *East Froome* in the 17th century. 'Manor on the River Frome belonging to the Coker family', this family being noted here from 1433.

Cold Harbour (in Wareham)   first recorded at the end of the 18th century. 'Shelter from the cold', or 'cold shelter', from Old English *ceald* and *here-beorg*. Cold Harbour is a common English name, and like most other examples, this one is to be found by an important old road.

Colehill *Colhulle* 1431, *Colhill* 1518, *Collehill* 1547, *Colehill* 1578. The first element may be Old English *col* 'charcoal' or *coll* 'hill', with *hyll* 'hill'.

Cole Hill Wood (in Winterborne Came)   *Coldehull, Coldhull* 1406. 'Cold hill', from Old English *ceald* and *hyll*.

Cole Street Farm (in East Stour)   *Colstrete* 1504, *Colestrete*

1557. Probably 'street along which charcoal was carried', from Old English *col* and *strǣt*.

Cole Wood (in Wool) *Colewode* 1452. Probably 'wood where charcoal was burnt', from Old English *col* and *wudu*.

Colmer Farm (in Marshwood) *Colemer* 1332, *Colemere* 1399. 'Cool pool', from Old English *cōl* and *mere*.

Coltleigh Farm (in Mapperton) *Cottelegh* 1244, *Cotele* 1246, *Cotteleye* 1285, *Coltley* 1608. 'Wood or clearing belonging to a man called Cotta', from Old English *lēah* and an Old English personal name. The change of the first element to *Colt-* seems only to date from the 17th century.

Colway (in Lyme Regis) *Coleweye* 1243, *Colweheye* 1268, *Caluweye* 1288, *Calwehegh* 1346. Possibly 'bare enclosure', from Old English *calu* and *haeg*.

Combe Almer (in Sturminster Marshall) *Cumbe* 1228, *Combe* 1268, *Coumbe* 1280, *Combe Almere* 1327. 'The valley (near Almer)', from Old English *cumb*.

Combs Ditch (near Winterborne Whitechurch) *cunucces dich* 942 (in a 15th century copy of an Anglo-Saxon charter), *Cunekesdich* 1207, *Coombes Ditch* 1664. The first element is a Celtic word *conōg* of doubtful meaning, with Old English *dīc* 'ditch'. This earthwork is a boundary bank and ditch of Iron Age origin, but it also gave its name to a Hundred from the 11th century.

Compton Abbas *Cumtune* 956 (in a later copy of an Anglo-Saxon charter), *Cuntone* 1086 (Domesday Book), *Cumpton Abbatisse* 1293, *Compton Abbas* 1676. 'Farm or estate in a valley', from Old English *cumb* and *tūn*, one of five Dorset parishes with this name. This manor belonged to Shaftesbury Abbey from 956, hence the addition *Abbas*, a reduced form of Latin *abbatissa* 'abbess'.

Compton, Over and Nether *Cumtun* 951 (in a later copy of an Anglo-Saxon charter), *Contone* 1086 (Domesday Book), *Ouerecumton* 1268, *Nethercumpton* 1288. Identical in origin with the previous name. The additions *Over* and *Nether* mean 'higher' and 'lower' respectively. In medieval times Over

Compton was sometimes called *Compton Hawey*, from the *Hawey* family here in the 13th century.

Compton Valence *Contone* 1086 (Domesday Book), *Cumton* 1212, *Cumpton* 1252, *Compton Valance* 1280. Identical in origin with the previous names. The manorial addition is from William *de Valencia*, Earl of Pembroke, who was granted the manor in 1252. In medieval times it was sometimes called *Compton Pondelarge* from the family of William *Pont del Arch* which held the manor in the early 13th century.

Compton, West, or Compton Abbas West *Comptone* 934 (in a later copy of an Anglo-Saxon charter), *Contone* 1086 (Domesday Book), *Cumpton Abbatis* 1291, *West Compton* 1811. Identical in origin with the previous names. The addition is Latin *abbas* 'abbot' because this manor belonged to Milton Abbey. It is now usually called West Compton to distinguish it from the other Compton Abbas near Shaftesbury.

Conegar Hill (in Broadwindsor)   named from *Le Conyngere* 1496, from Middle English *coninger* 'a rabbit warren'.

Conygar Hill (in Winterborne Herringston)   first recorded in the 19th century, identical in origin with the previous name.

Coombe, Coombe Down Hill (in Beaminster)   *Combe* 1517, *Coombe, Coomdowne* 1625. From Old English *cumb* 'valley' with *dūn* 'hill or down'.

Coombe (in Bradford Abbas)   *Comb* 1332. 'The valley', from Old English *cumb*.

Coombe Bottom (in Corfe Castle)   *cumb* 948 (in a later copy of an Anglo-Saxon charter), *la Combe* 14th century. 'The valley', from Old English *cumb*, with *bottom* in the sense 'valley bottom'.

Coombe Farm (in Castleton)   *Combe* 1316. 'The valley', from Old English *cumb*.

Coombe, Higher and Lower (in Litton Cheney)   *Cumbe* 1220, *Combe* 1392. From Old English cumb *'valley'*.

Coombe Keynes *Cume* 1086 (Domesday Book), *Cumbe Willelmi de Cahaignes* 1199, *Combe Kaynes* 1299, *Coumbe Caynes* 1302. '(Place in) the valley', from Old English *cumb*. *Keynes* is a manorial addition from the family of William *de Cahaignes*, who held the manor in 1199.

Coppleridge (in Motcombe) *Copidockridge* 1609, *Copulridge* 1811. 'Ridge at the pollarded oak-tree', from Old English *coppod, āc* and *hrycg*.

Corfe Castle *Corf* 955 (in a later copy of an Anglo-Saxon charter), *Corffe* 1217, *Corffe Castell* 1302, *Corfecastle* 1545. 'A cutting, a pass', from Old English *corf*, aptly describing the gap in the central ridge of the Purbeck Hills at this place. In the annals of the Anglo-Saxon Chronicle during the 11th and 12th centuries it was sometimes called *Corfesgeate*, meaning 'gap (Old English *geat*) called *Corf*'. The castle here is mentioned in Domesday Book, but *Castle* is not attached to the name of the village until the 14th century.

Corfe Hill (near Radipole) *Corfhull* 1303, *Corfhill* 1457, *Corffehill* 1705. 'Hill at a gap', from Old English *corf* and *hyll*.

Corfe Mullen *Corf* 1086 (Domesday Book), *Corf le Mulin* 1176, *Corf Molyn* 1268, *Corff Moleyn* 1448. From Old English *corf* 'a cutting or pass', with reference to its situation between two hills. The addition *Mullen* is from Old French *molin* 'a mill', referring to the valuable mill here in early times which rendered 20 shillings (a high value) at the time of Domesday Book. In the 14th to 16th centuries it was sometimes called *Corf Hubert* from a medieval landowner of that name.

Corner, The (in Motcombe)   the home of John *atte Cornere* 1381, that is John 'at the corner or nook', from Middle English *corner*.

Corscombe *Corigescumb* 1014 (in a later copy of an Anglo-Saxon charter), *Coriescumbe, Corscumbe* 1086 (Domesday Book), *Corescumb* 1244. Possibly 'valley of the road in a pass', from Old English *corf, weg* and *cumb*. Alternatively, the first element may be an old name of the stream here, identical with that found in the Somerset place name Curry.

Corton (in Portesham)   *Corfetone* 1086 (Domesday Book), *Corfton* 1204, *Corftun* 1285, *Corton* 1327. 'Farm by a cutting or gap', from Old English *corf* and *tūn*, see also Coryates which is named from the same feature.

Coryates (in Portesham)   *Corf getes* 1024 (Anglo-Saxon charter), *le Corueyatis* 1473, *Corryatts* 1698. 'Gate at the cutting or gap', from Old English *corf* and *geat*. The final -*s* in this name is not a plural but an old possessive case, as is clear from the context of the earliest spelling: *Corf getes westran cotan*, 'the west cottages of *Corf gete*'.

Cothayes Dairy (in Hilton)   *Cotehay* 1412. 'Enclosure by a cottage', from Old English *cot* and *haeg*.

Cowdon Hill (in Charminster)   *Cowdon* 14th century, *Cowden* 1546. 'Cow down or hill', from Old English *cū* and *dūn*.

Cowgrove (in Pamphill)   *Cugrave* 1288, *Cougrave* 1317, *Cougrove* 1358, *Cowegrove* 1453. 'Cow grove or copse', from Old English *cū* and *grāf*.

Cowherd Shute Farm (in Motcombe)   *Cowards Shoot* 1811. From a surname *Coward*; Shute may be from Old English *scēot* or *scyte* both of which mean 'steep slope'.

Crab Farm (in Shapwick)   not on early record, but presumably an allusion to the legend of the 'Shapwick monster' (in local proverb a term for any unusual object, since an ordinary crab was considered a monster by the wise man of Shapwick).

Crab Orchard (in Verwood)   first recorded in the 19th century, from Old English *crabbe* 'crab-apple'.

Cranborne   *Creneburne* 1086 (Domesday Book), *Craneburna* 1163, *Craneborne* 1207, *Cranbourn* 1252. 'Stream frequented by cranes or herons', from Old English *cran* and *burna*, originally with reference to the stream here now called the River Crane (a back-formation from the place-name).

Cranborne Chase   first recorded in 1236, from Middle English *chace* 'tract of land for hunting wild animals'.

Crate Wood (in Woolland)   *Croftewood* 1384, *Crafte Woode*

1545. 'Wood by the small enclosure', from Old English *croft* and *wudu*.

Crawford Bridge (in Spettisbury) 'the bridge of *Crauford*' 1242, *Craufordesbrigge* 1337, *Craffordbrigge* 1468. 'Ford frequented by crows', from Old English *crāwe* and *ford*, with *brycg* 'bridge'. The ford gave its name to the former manor of *Great Crawford* in Spettisbury (this is *Craveford* in 1086 Domesday Book, *Crawford* 1244, later *Magna Crauford* 1308, *Great Crauford* 1386) as well as to Tarrant Crawford on the other side of the River Stour.

Creech Barrow (in Church Knowle) giving its name to East Creech in this parish and to Creech Grange and West Creech in the neighbouring parish of Steeple. The name appears as *Cric, Criz* and *Crist* in 1086 (Domesday Book), later as *Crich* 1224, *Weste Crych* 1324, *Estcriche* 1337. This is the oldest name in the Isle of Purbeck, being from a Celtic word *crūg* 'mound, hill or barrow', no doubt originally with reference to Creech Barrow itself, a conspicuous conical hill which must have been an important landmark in early times.

Creech Hill Farm (in Wimborne St Giles) not on record before the 19th century, but perhaps identical in origin with Crichel; the hill is 300 feet high and stands where the boundaries of three parishes meet.

Crendell (in Alderholt) *Crendall* 1620, *Crundall* 1622, *Crundole* 17th century. From Old English *crundel* 'a pit, a quarry' (with reference to a clay or chalk pit).

Crichel, Long *Circel* 1086 (Domesday Book), *Langecrechel* 1208, *Langecrichel* 1268, *Longe Curchel* 1280. A very old name, from Celtic *crūg* 'mound, hill or barrow' to which an explanatory Old English *hyll* 'hill' was added at an early date. The hill referred to is now called Crichel Down (from Old English *dūn* 'hill, down'). *Long* (from Old English *lang*) distinguishes this place from the neighbouring parish of Moor Crichel. In medieval times the eastern and western parts of Long Crichel were sometimes known as *Crichel Lucy* and *Crichel Govis* respectively, from families so named.

Crichel, Moor   *Mor Kerchel* 1212, *Morkerchil* 1288, *Mour Curchil* 1328, *Moore Crechill* 1541. For the origin of Crichel, see previous name. *Moor* is from Old English *mōr* 'marshy ground'.

Cripplestyle (in Alderholt)   not recorded before the 19th century, but probably 'stile that could be crept through (by sheep)', from Old English *crypel* and *stigel*.

Cripton (in Winterborne Came)   *Cribbeton* 1457, *Cribton* 1460, *Krybton* 1461, *Cripton* 1543. 'Farm with a crib, cattle farm', from Old English *cribb* and *tūn*.

Crocker's Knap (in Leigh)   probably to be associated with *Crockeresrewe* 13th century, from Old English *croccere* 'a potter', *rāew* 'row of houses or trees', *cnaepp* 'hill-top, hillock'.

Crockerton Hill (in Cranborne)   probably to be associated with *Crokkerneweye* 1325, *Crockherne yate* 17th century, which may mean 'way to the pottery' and 'gate at the pottery' respectively, from Old English *crocc* 'crock, pot' and *aern* 'building', with *weg* and *geat*.

Crook Hill (in Corscombe)   *Cruc* 1035 (in a later copy of an Anglo-Saxon charter), *Crokehulle* 1407, *Crockhill* 1684. An ancient name, from Celtic *crüg* 'hill' to which an explanatory Old English *hyll* 'hill' has later been added.

Cruxton (in Maiden Newton)   *Frome* 1086 (Domesday Book), *Fromma Johannis Croc* 1178, *Crocston* 1195, *Crokeston* 1204. At first 'estate on the River Frome (belonging to John Croc)' later 'Croc's farm', from Old English *tūn*. The *Croc* family was obviously here in the 12th century.

Cudnell (in Kinson)   *Codnell* 1520, *Cuddnell* 1544. Possibly 'hill or nook belonging to a man called Cuda', from Old English *hyll* or *healh* and an Old English personal name.

Culeaze House (in Bere Regis)   *Culyes* 1617, *Culeaze* 1664. 'Cow pasture', from Old English *cū* and *lāes*.

Cut Mill (in Hinton St Mary)   *Cuttemylle, Cutmyll* 16th century. 'Mill with a water-channel', from Middle English *cut* and *myln*.

Daggons (in Alderholt)   *Daggans* 1553, *Dagens* 1574, *Dagons* 1618, *Daggens* 1621. Named from the family of Richard *Dagon*, here in the 14th century.

Dancing Ledge (in Langton Matravers)   first on record in 1811, perhaps so called from the action of the waves breaking over the flat rock ledges.

Darknoll Farm (in Okeford Fitzpaine)   *Derkenhull* 1286, *Darkenell* 1640, *Darknell* 1811. 'The dark hill', from Old English *deorc* and *hyll*. It gives name to Darknoll Brook.

Deadmoor Common (in Fifehead Neville)   only on record from the 18th century, from Old English *dēad* 'dead', probably in the sense 'disused', and *mōr* 'moor, marshy ground'.

Dean (in Sixpenny Handley)   *la Dene* 1280, *Dene* 1332, *Deane* 1500. 'The valley', from Old English *denu*.

Dean Farm, Deans Leaze Farm (in Witchampton)   *La Dene* 1243, *Dene* 1412, *Deane* 1591, *Deane's Leaze* 1633. 'The valley', from Old English *denu*, with the later addition of *lǣs* 'pasture'.

Dean Hill (in Studland)   *Dene* 1449, *le Deane* 1546. 'The valley', from Old English *denu*.

Deanland (in Sixpenny Handley)   *Daine Lane* 1664. 'Lane in a valley', from Old English *denu* and *lane*.

Decoy Heath (in Wareham)   first recorded in 1811, from *decoy* 'pool with netted approaches for the capture of wildfowl'.

Densham Farm (in Folke)   *Denesham* 1332, *Densham* 1516. Possibly 'enclosure or river-meadow of a man called Dene', from Old English *hamm* and an Old English personal name.

Deverel Farm (in Milborne St Andrew)   *Muleborn* 1261, *Muleburn Deverell* 1316, *Milbourne Deverel* 1332. Originally a manor on the same 'mill stream' as Milborne St Andrew itself, held by the family of *Deverell* (from Deverill in Wiltshire) from the middle of the 13th century.

Devil's Brook   see Dewlish.

Dewlands Common (in Verwood)   not on early record,

but from Old English *dēaw* 'dew' in the sense 'moist, damp'.

Dewlish   *Devenis* 1086 (Domesday Book), *Deueliz* 1194, *Douelis* 1212, *Dewelisshe* 1481. Originally the name of the stream, now called Devil's Brook, which runs through the village. This old stream name is Celtic and means 'black stream'. The modern name of the stream is an interesting example of folk etymology: the name must at one time have been associated with the word 'devilish'.

Dibberford   (in Broadwindsor) *Dibberwurthe* 1001–12 (Anglo-Saxon writ), *Diberwurth* 1244, *Diberwrth* 1252, *Dibreworth* 1268. 'Enclosure belonging to a man called Dycgbeorht', from Old English *worth* and an Old English personal name. The substitution of *ford* for the final element is only relatively recent.

Didlington Farm (in Chalbury)   *Didelingtune* 946 (in a 14th century copy of an Anglo-Saxon charter), *Dedilintone* 1086 (Domesday Book), *Dudelinton* 1244, *Dydelington* 1288. 'Farm called after a man named Dydel', from Old English *-ingtūn* and an Old English personal name.

Divelish, River   an old Celtic river-name, with the same origin as Dewlish.

Dodding's Farm (in Bere Regis)   *Bere* 1086 (Domesday Book), *la Doddingg* 1268, *Dodingesbere* 1288, *Dodyngs Beare* 1546. 'Part of Bere at or called Dodding', the name *Dodding* meaning either 'place characterized by a rounded hilltop', from *-ing* and the word *dodde*, or 'place belonging to a man called Dodda' if the first element is an Old English personal name.

Dogbury (in Minterne Magna)   *Doggeneberwe* 941 (in a later copy of an Anglo-Saxon charter), *Doggebery* 1270, *Dogbury* 1527. 'Hill frequented by dogs', from Old English *dogga* and *beorg*.

Donedge Lodge Farm (in Motcombe)   *Donnedge-lodge* 1627. Probably 'edge or end of the down', from Old English *dūn* and *ecg*.

Dorchester   *Durnovaria* 4th century (Antonine Itinerary),

Dornwaraceaster 864 (in a later copy of an Anglo-Saxon charter), *Dorecestre* 1086 (Domesday Book), *Dorsestre* 1244. The original name of this Roman city, *Durnovaria*, is Celtic; *durno-* means 'fist' (probably in the sense 'fist-sized pebble'), but *varia* is obscure. The Anglo-Saxons added Old English *ceaster* 'city' to this name, perhaps at the same time associating *-varia* with Old English *ware* 'dwellers'.

Dorset   *Dorset* 891 (in a 14th century copy of an Anglo-Saxon charter), *Dornsaetum* late 9th century (Anglo-Saxon Chronicle), *Dorsete* 1086 (Domesday Book). Originally a tribal name, 'the people of the region about Dorchester', from *Dorn-* (a shortened form of *Dornwaraceaster* = Dorchester) and Old English *sǣte*.

Dowerfield Farm   (in Long Bredy) *Dowerland* 1431, *Dowersfields* 1650. 'Land or fields given as a dowry', from Middle English *dowere*.

Downshay Farm   (in Worth Matravers) *Dunshay* 1586, *Duncehay* 1646. Probably 'Dun's enclosure', from the surname *Dun(n)* and Old English *haeg*.

Drimpton   (in Broadwindsor) *Dremeton* 1244, *Dremintun* 1250, *Dremyton* 1268, *Drempton* 1288. 'Farm belonging to a man called Drēama', from Old English *tūn* and an Old English personal name.

Droop   (in Hazelbury Bryan) *Thorpe* 1580, *Throop, Thrupp* 1607, *Droop* 1799. From Old English *throp* 'an outlying farm, a secondary settlement'.

Druce Farm   (in Puddletown) *Drewes* 1431, *Druwes* 1447, *Druse, Druce* 1641. 'Estate belonging to Drew', the man in question being the 13th century *Drew Bardolf* whose family gave name to the nearby Bardolf Manor.

Duddle Farm and Heath   (in Puddletown) *Doddle* 1270, *Duddell* 1459, *Duddle* 1580. Perhaps 'the small rounded hilltop', from a derivative of the word *dodde* that is possibly present in Dodding's Farm in Bere Regis.

Dudmoor Farm   (in Christchurch) *Duddemore* 1269, *Dudmore* 17th century. 'Marshy land belonging to a man called Dudda', from Old English *mōr* and an Old English personal name.

Dudsbury, Duds Bury Camp (in West Parley) *Dodesberie* 1086 (Domesday Book), *Dudesbir* 1236, *Dodesbery* 1280, *Duddesbury* 1312. 'Fortified place associated with a man called Dudd', from Old English *burh* and an Old English personal name, with reference to the Iron Age hill-fort here.

Dullar Farm (in Lytchett Matravers) *Dulre* 1268, *Dolere* 1288, *Dullere* 1296, *Duller* 1468. A difficult name, but possibly 'house in a valley', from Old English *dulu* and *aern*.

Dunbury (in Winterborne Houghton) *Dunbaro* 1603, *Dunberry* 1838. 'Barrow on the down', from Old English *dūn* and *beorg*.

Duncliffe Hill (in Stour Provost) *Dunclive* 1247, *Donclyfe* 1364, *Duncliffe* 1568. 'Dark escarpment', from Old English *dunn* and *clif*.

Dungrove Hill (in Tarrant Gunville) *Dongroue* 1408, *Doune Grove* 1541, *Dungroue* 1618. 'Copse on the down or hill', from Old English *dūn* and *grāf*.

Dunster Farm, Little (in Marshwood) *Donstrowe* 1376, *Dunstrowe* 1396. Probably 'hollow or valley belonging to a man called Dunn', from Old English *trog* and an Old English personal name.

Duntish (in Buckland Newton) *dounen tit* 941, *Donetys* 1268, *Dunetys* 1280, *Donetisshe* 1289. 'Pasture on a hill', from Old English *dūn* and *etisc*.

Durdle Door (in West Lulworth) *Dirdale Door* 1811. Perhaps 'hill with a hole in it', from a derivative of Old English *thyrel* 'hole' and *hyll* 'hill'.

Durlston Bay and Head (in Swanage) not recorded before the 18th century, but probably an old name meaning 'rock with a hole in it', from Old English *thyrel* and *stān*, referring perhaps to some coastal feature that has now disappeared.

Durweston *Derwinestone* 1086 (Domesday Book), *Durwinestona* 1166, *Derewineston* 1204, *Durweston* 1412. 'Farm belonging to a man called Dēorwine', from Old English *tūn* and an Old English personal name.

Earl's Hill (in Tarrant Gunville) *Earles hill* 1618. The manor of Tarrant Gunville was held in turn by the earls of Gloucester and Hertford, of March, and of Cambridge.

East Brook (in Wimborne Minster) *Byestebrouk* 1286, *Biestebrok* 1348, *Byyestebroke* 1426, *Estbroke* 1444. '(Place) to the east of the brook', from Old English *bī, ēastan* and *brōc*, with reference to its situation by the River Allen.

Eastbury House (in Tarrant Gunville) *Estbury* 1391, *Gunvil-Eastbury* 1511, *Gounvyle Estbury* 1547, *Eastbury* 1619. From Middle English *bury* in the sense 'manor house, centre of an estate', with *ēast* 'east' to contrast with Westbury Farm in the same parish.

Easthay Farm (in Thorncombe) *Estehegh* 1356. 'East enclosure', from Old English *ēast* and *haeg*.

Eastcombe Wood (in Shillingstone) not recorded before the 19th century, from Old English *cumb* 'valley'.

Eastington Farm (in Worth Matravers) *Estinton* 1209, *Estington* 1259, *Estyngton* 1285. '(Land) east in the village', from Old English *ēast, in* and *tūn*.

East Moors Farm (in St Leonards and St Ives) *Great or East Moors* 1591, named in relation to West Moors.

Easton (on Isle of Portland) *Eston* 1323, *Easton* 1608. 'East farm or village', from Old English *ēast* and *tūn*, in contrast to Weston.

Ebblake (in Verwood) *Abbelake, Abbeslake* 1280, *Albelake* 1618. Probably 'stream belonging to a man called Abba', from Old English *lacu* and an Old English personal name, originally with reference to Ebblake Stream. The modern form of the name has probably been influenced by the word *ebb*.

Eccliffe (in Gillingham) *Eggcliue* 1292, *Ecclyue* 1300, *Egglive* 1364, *Ecliffe* 1609. Probably 'bank belonging to a man called Ecga', from Old English *clif* and an Old English personal name. The place is on the River Stour.

Edmondsham *Amedesham* 1086 (Domesday Book), *Edmundesham* 1195, *Edmodesham* 1196, *Edmondesham* 1332. 'Homestead or enclosure belonging to a man called Ēadmōd or Ēadmund', from Old English *hām* or *hamm* and an Old English personal name.

Eggardon Farms and Hill (in Askerswell) *Giochresdone* 1086, *Jekeresdon* 1204, *Ekerdon* 1244, *Egerdone* 1316. 'Hill or down belonging to a man called Eohhere', from Old English *dūn* and an Old English personal name.

Egliston (in Tyneham) *Egelineston* 1202, *Eggleneston* 1285, *Eglyneston* 1288, *Egliston* 1325. 'Farm belonging to a man called Eggelin', from Old English *tūn* and a Continental Germanic personal name.

Ellston Hill (in Sydling St Nicholas) *Helistun* 1227, *Eliston* 1293, *Elyston* 1303, *Eylyston* 1482. Possibly 'farm belonging to a man called Eli', from Old English *tūn* and a personal name.

Elwell (in Upwey) *Helewill* 1212, *Hellewell* 1249, *Elwell* 1460, *Helwell* 1492. 'The sound, healthy spring', or 'the spring which heals or gives good health', or 'the spring of good fortune', from either Old English *hǣle* 'healthy', *hǣlu* 'health', or *hǣl* 'good fortune', with *wella*. The reference may well be to the spring called Wishing Well where the River Wey rises about half a mile from here.

Elwell Farms and Lodge (in Netherbury) *Ellewell* 1332, *Elle-Wille* 1372, *Elwill* 1417. Possibly 'spring or stream belonging to a man called Ella', from Old English *wella* and an Old English personal name, but the first element could alternatively be Old English *ellen* 'an elder-tree'.

Elworth (in Abbotsbury) *Aleurde* 1086 (Domesday Book), *Elleworthe* 1221, *Ellewurth* 1285, *Elworthe* 1361. 'Enclosure belonging to a man called Ella', from Old English *worth* and an Old English personal name.

Empool Bottom and Heath (in West Knighton) only on record from the end of the 18th century, but possibly 'even or smooth pool' from Old English *emn* and *pōl*, with *botm* in the sense 'valley bottom'.

Encombe (in Corfe Castle) *Hennecumbe* 1244, *Henycumbe* 1280, *Enecumbe* 1285, *Encombe* 1489. 'Valley of the hens (i.e. water-hens or other wild birds)', from Old English *henn* and *cumb*.

Enmore Green (in Shaftesbury) *Hendemer* 1258, *Enedemere* 1275, *Enmer* 1475, *Enmore greene* 1527. 'Duck pool', from Old English *ened* and *mere*, with the later addition of *grēne* 'a green'. The second element has been confused with *mōr* 'moor' as in Ashmore.

Ensbury (in Kinson) *Eynesburgh* 1463, *Emysborowe* 1544. Probably 'fortified place associated with a man called Aegen', from Old English *burh* and an Old English personal name.

Evershot *Teversict* 1202, *Theuershet* 1268, *Evershet* 1286, *Evershute* 1432. Probably 'corner or nook of land frequented by wild boars', from Old English *eofor* and *scēat* or *scīete*. However if the initial *T-* or *Th-* in the early spellings is original, and not from the preposition *at* or the definite article, the first element could be Old English *tēafor* 'red lead', perhaps in allusion to red soil.

Eye Mead (in Pamphill) *Eye* 1253, *Ey, Ymede* 1468, *Ey mede* 1547, *Eye Meade* 1591. From Old English *īeg* 'an island', with *mǣd* 'meadow'. It is encircled by the River Stour and its tributaries.

Eype (in Symondsbury) *Estyep* 1300, *Estrhep* 1329, *Yepe* 1365, *Yep* 1406. From Old English *gēap* 'a steep place', with *ēast* 'east' or *ēasterra* 'more easterly' in the earliest forms.

Farnham *Fernham, Ferneham* 1086 (Domesday Book), *Farnham* 1199, *Farnam* 1263. 'Homestead or enclosure where ferns grow', from Old English *fearn* and *hām* or *hamm*.

Farrington (in Iwerne Courtney) *Ferendone* 1285, *Farendon* 1315, *Farindon* 1377, *Farrington* 1664. 'Fern-covered hill', from Old English *fearn* and *dūn*. The spelling in *-ton* is relatively recent, dating only from the 17th century.

Feltham Farm (in Silton) *Fyletham* 1327, *Filtham* 1332,

Fyltam 1541. 'Hay enclosure', from Old English *filethe* and *hamm*.

Fernbrook Farm (in Motcombe) *Fernbroc, Farnbroc* 1251, *Ferenbroken* 1275. Self-explanatory, from Old English *fearn* and *brōc*, with reference to the stream still called Fern Brook, a tributary of the River Lodden.

Ferndown (in Hampreston) originally *Fyrne* 1321, *Ferne* 1358, from either Old English *fergen* 'wooded hill' or *fierne* 'ferny place', with the later addition of *dūn* 'down, hill'.

Fiddleford (in Okeford Fitzpaine) *Fitelford* 1244, *Fitilford* 1340, *Fytelford* 1342. 'Ford belonging to a man called Fitela', from Old English *ford* and an Old English personal name.

Field Grove (in Durweston) *Fylgrove* 1564, *Great Feyldegrove Woodd* 1567, *Filgroes* 1583, *Filgraves* 1590. 'Grove in open country', from Old English *feld* and *grāf*.

Fifehead Magdalen *Fifhide* 1086 (Domesday Book), *Fifyde Maudaleyne* 1388, *Vifyde Maudeleyne* 1393, *Fifehead Magdelen* 1664. '(Estate of) five hides', from Old English *fíf* and *hīd*. The manor was assessed at five hides in Domesday Book, a hide having originally been the amount of land that would support one free family and its dependants. The addition *Magdalen* is from the dedication of the church.

Fifehead Neville *Fifhide* 1086 (Domesday Book), *Fyfhud Neuyle* 1287, *Fifhide Neuile* 1288, *Vyfhyde Nevyle* 1303. Identical in origin with the previous name. The addition is manorial, from the family of William *de Nevill* who was here in the mid 13th century; the family came from Néville or Neuville in France.

Fifehead St Quintin (in Fifehead Neville) *Fifhide* 1086 (Domesday Book), *Fifhide Quintyn* 1268, *Fifhide Seint Quyntyn* 1323, *Fyffyde Seynt Quyntyn* 1412. Identical in origin with Fifehead Neville. The manorial addition is from the family of *de Sancto Quintino*, here in the 13th century. The same family, from one of the places called St Quentin in France, gave its name to Frome St Quintin.

Filcombe Farm (in Chideock) *Vilcumbe* 13th century,

Filcombe 1430, *Fylcombe* 1477, *Fillecomb* 1491. 'Valley where hay is made', from Old English *filethe* and *cumb*.

Filford (in Netherbury) *Filleforde* 1327, *Fulleford* 1332, *Feleford* 1382, *Filleford* 1405. Probably 'ford by the clearing where hay is made', from Old English *filethe, lēah* and *ford*.

Fitzworth Farm (in Corfe Castle) *Fitoure* 1545, *Fitworth* 1561, *Fitzworth* 1571, *Fitzoure* 1661. Probably 'shore subject to dispute', from Old English *fitt* and *ōra*, though the second element has been replaced by Old English *worth* 'enclosure'.

Fleet *Flete, Flote* 1086 (Domesday Book), *Fleota* 1213, *Flete* 1244. From Old English *flēot* 'estuary, inlet', with reference to the long channel still called East and West Fleet between Chesil Beach and the mainland.

Flower's Barrow (in East Lulworth) *Flouresberi* 1381, *Flouresbury* 1462, *Flowrysburye, Flowerborrow hill* 1586. The second element is Old English *burh* 'pre-English earthwork' with reference to the hill-fort here. The first element could be Old English *flōr* 'a floor' or the surname of some medieval owner.

Folke *Folk* 1244, *Folke* 1337, *Foolke* 1453, *Fowlke* 1563. 'The folk or people', from Old English *folc*, no doubt indicating 'land held (in common) by the people'.

Font le Roi (in Folke) *Fontleroy Mershe* 1582. Named from the *Fauntleroy* family, here from the 13th century, with Old English *mersc* 'marsh'.

Fontmell Magna *Funtemel* 877 (in a later copy of an Anglo-Saxon charter), *Fontemale* 1086 (Domesday Book), *Magnam Funtemell* 1391, *Great Funtmill* 1704. Originally a Celtic stream-name, the name of Fontmell Brook, meaning 'stream or spring by the bare hill' from Celtic *funtōn* and *mailo-*. The addition is Latin *magna* 'great', distinguishing it from Fontmell Parva.

Fontmell Parva (in Child Okeford) *Parva Funtemel* 1360, *Lytel Fountemel* 1431. Named from Fontmell Brook. The addition is Latin *parva* 'little', distinguishing it from Fontmell Magna.

Ford Farms (in Netherbury) *la Forde* 1288, *Forde* 1510. From Old English *ford* 'a ford'.

Forde Abbey (in Thorncombe) *Ford* 1189, *Forda* 1204, *Ford* 1227, *Forde* 1291. 'The ford' (over the River Axe), from Old English *ford*. The Cistercian abbey was founded in 1141.

Fordington (in Dorchester) *Fortitone* 1086 (Domesday Book), *Fordinton, Fordington* 1155, *Fordynton* 1280, *Fordyngton* 1288. Probably 'farm at the ford place', from Old English *ford, -ing* and *tūn*. The ford was no doubt across the River Frome.

Forest Farm and Forest Side (in Gillingham) named from the royal forest of Gillingham which is mentioned as early as the 13th century.

Forston (in Charminster) *Fosardeston* 1236, *Forsardeston* 1285, *Forston* 1431, *Forreston* 1553. 'Manor or estate of the Forsard family', from Old English *tūn*. This family was here from the early 13th century. Forston is probably one of the several manors called *Cerne* or *Cernel* in Domesday Book (from its situation on the River Cerne).

Fortuneswell (on Isle of Portland) first recorded in 1608. The meaning is 'lucky well or spring', or 'well or spring in which fortunes could be told'.

Fossil, East and West (in Winfrith Newburgh and Chaldon Herring respectively) *Foresteshull* 1227, *Forshulle* 1244, *West-foreshull* 1319, *Estforshull* 1398. The second element is Old English *hyll* 'hill'. The first element is probably an Old English word *forst* 'a ridge', but an Old English personal name *Forst* is a possible alternative.

Frampton *Frantone* 1086 (Domesday Book), *Fromton* 1188, *Frompton* 1253, *Frampton* 1264. 'Farm or estate on the River Frome', from Old English *tūn*.

France Farm (in Stourpaine) *Franc'* 1368, *France or Fraunce* 1774, earlier called *Nodford* 1086 (Domesday Book), *Notford-locky* 1265, *Nutford Locky* 1288, *Nutford Lockey alias France* 1587. The earlier name is the same as Nutford Farm in Pimperne to which this farm lies adjacent, with the manorial addition *Locky* from a family here in the 13th century. The later name France may be an allusion to land held here by the French abbey of Fontevrault from about the same time.

Frankham Farm (in Ryme Intrinseca) *Frankeham* 1244, *Francham* 1327, *Frankham* 1383. 'Enclosure belonging to a man called Franca', from Old English *hamm* and an Old English personal name.

French's Farm (in Wimborne St Giles) *Frensshes, le Frenche* 1394, *Freinsshes* 1422. A manorial name, from a family here in the 13th and 14th centuries.

Friar Waddon see Waddon.

Frith House (in Stalbridge) *la Frithe* 1244. From Old English *fyrhth* 'wood, wooded countryside'.

Frogmore Dairy House (in Toller Porcorum) *Froggemore* 1268, *Frogmore* 1340. 'Moor or marshy ground frequented by frogs', from Old English *frogga* and *mōr*.

Frogmore Hill (in Chideock) *Frogghemore* 1324, *Froge mor* 1498, *Frogmore* 1504. Identical in origin with the previous name.

Frome, River an old Celtic river-name, first recorded in the 9th century and probably meaning 'fair' or 'fine'. Rivers with the same name occur in Somerset, Gloucestershire and Herefordshire. The Dorset river gives its name to four parishes on its banks, namely Chilfrome, Frampton, Frome St Quintin and Frome Vauchurch.

Frome Hill (in West Stafford) named from the former manor of Frome Billet (*Frome* 1086 Domesday Book, *Frome Belet* 1268) which in turn takes its name from the River Frome and the Norman family of *Belet*.

Frome Mead (in Puddletown) *Fromemede* 1325, *Fromede* 1440, *Frome Mede* 1571. 'Meadow on the River Frome', from Old English *mǣd*.

Frome St Quintin *Litelfrome* 1086 (Domesday Book), *Litlefrome* 1202, *Fromequintin* 1288, *Fromeseyntquynteyn* 1452. At first, 'little estate on the River Frome' from Old English *lȳtel*, later with a manorial addition from the family of *St Quintin*, here in the 13th century.

Frome Vauchurch *Frome* 1086 (Domesday Book), *Frome Fowechirch* 1288, *Frome Voghechurche* 1297, *Frome Vouchurche* 1352. 'Estate on the River Frome with a coloured church', from Old English *fāh* and *cirice*.

Frome Whitfield (in Stinsford) *Frome* 1086 (Domesday Book), *Froma Witefeld* 1243, *Frome Wytefeld* 1268, *Frome Whitfeld* 1288. 'Manor on the River Frome belonging to the *de Witefeld* family'. This family was here in the early 13th century.

Fryer Mayne (in West Knighton) *Frarenemayne* 1337, *Freremayn* 1449, earlier called *Mayne Hospitalis* 1244, *Meyne Hospitalis* 1280. For the meaning of Mayne, see under Broadmayne. The additions *Frarene-*, *Frere-* ('of the brothers', from Middle English *frere*) and *Hospitalis* ('of the hospital', from the Latin) refer to the Knights Hospitallers who had a preceptory and lands here from the 13th century.

Furleigh Cross (in Netherbury) *Ferlegh* 1288, *Farleghe* 1427, *Firley* 1489. Probably 'clearing where ferns grow', from Old English *fearn* and *lēah*.

Furzehill (in Colehill) *la furshulle* 14th century. Self-explanatory, from Old English *fyrs* and *hyll*.

Furzey Island (in Poole Harbour) *Fursey* 1545. 'Furze island', from Old English *fyrs* and *ēg*, with the later explanatory addition of *Island*.

Gallows Hill (in Bere Regis) *Gallis Hill* 1682. A name that speaks for itself, from Old English *galga* and *hyll*.

Galton (in Owermoigne) *Gaveltone, Galtone* 1086 (Domesday Book), *Gaulton* 1244, *Gawlton* 1392. 'Farm subject to tax or rent', from Old English *gafol* and *tūn*.

Garston Down (in Sixpenny Handley) *La Garston* 15th century, *Gaston* 1575. 'The grass enclosure or paddock', from Old English *gaers-tūn*.

Gatemerston (in East Lulworth) *Gatemareston* 1236, *Gatemorestone* 1260, *Gatemerston* 1280. Probably 'the farm (Old

English *tūn*) belonging to a family called *Gatemore*'; one Richard *de Gatemore* is mentioned in a British Museum charter of the 13th century. The surname is from a place-name meaning 'moor where goats are kept', from Old English *gāt* and *mōr*.

Gaulter Gap (in Kimmeridge)   *Goldehorde* 1451, *Goulthred* 1614, *Goulthard* 1842. 'Gold-hoard, treasure of gold', from Old English *gold-hord*, perhaps an allusion to the discovery of a hidden treasure here long ago, although the name could be ironical. The 'gap' refers to a low part of the shore.

Gaunt's Common and House (in Hinton Martell)   probably named from the famous John of Gaunt, Duke of Lancaster 1372–99, who possessed the large manor of Kingston Lacy; lands here were called *the great Gawntz* in 1535, and *Gantts farme* is mentioned in 1646.

Giddy Green (in Wool)   not in the early records but possibly a derogatory name, from Old English *gydig* 'mad, foolish' and *grēne* 'a green'.

Gillingham   *Gillinga ham* 11th century (Anglo-Saxon Chronicle), *Gelingeham* 1086 (Domesday Book), *Gillingeham* 1156, *Gillingham* 1198. Probably 'homestead or village of Gylla's people', from Old English *-inga* and *hām*, with an Old English masculine personal name.

Glanvilles Wootton   *Widetone* 1086 (Domesday Book), *Wotton* 1268, *Wotton Glaunuill* 1288, *Wotton Glanvyll* 1361. 'Farm in or by a wood', from Old English *wudu* and *tūn*. The manorial addition is from the *Glanville* family, here from the 13th century. In medieval times the place was sometimes called *Wolfrenewotton*, where the addition is probably the feminine Old English personal name *Wulfrūn*.

Goathill   *Gatelme* 1086 (Domesday Book), *Gathulla* 1176, *Gothull* 1256, *Gotehill* 1495. 'Hill where goats are pastured', from Old English *gāt* and *hyll*.

Goathorn Plantation and Point (in Studland)   *Gotowre* 1286, *Gotoure* 15th century, *Gotehorn Point* 1575. Probably 'bank or shore where goats are kept', from Old English *gāt*

77

and *ōra*. The second element was replaced by *horn*, probably because the promontory resembles the horn of a goat.

Godlingston Hill and Manor (in Swanage) *Godlington* 1299, *Godelyngston* 1345, *Godelyngton* 1381, *Godlingston* 1458. 'Farm or estate belonging to a man called Godelin or Godling', from Old English *tūn* and a personal name.

Godmanstone *Godemanestone* 1166, *Godmaneston* 1201, *Godmanneston* 1251, *Godmanston* 1268. 'Farm belonging to a man called Godmann', from Old English *tūn* and an Old English personal name.

God's Blessing Green (in Holt) first recorded as *God-blessing* in 1694, no doubt a name for productive or pleasant land.

Gore Farm (in Ashmore) probably to be associated with *Gore Close* and *Gores Coppices* 1590, from Old English *gāra* 'triangular plot of ground, point of land'; the farm is situated in the pointed north-west corner of the parish.

Gore Farm (in Margaret Marsh) *Gora* 1282, *la Gore* 1358, *Gore* 1431. 'The triangular plot of ground', from Old English *gāra*, still an accurate description of this northern part of the parish.

Gore Heath (in Wareham) *Gore heathe* 1597. From Old English *gāra* 'gore of land', originally describing a large triangular area of ground.

Gorwell Farm (in Long Bredy) *Gorewull* 1285, *Gorwell* 1290, *Gorewell* 1360, *Gorwyll* 1471. 'Dirty spring or stream', from Old English *gor* and *wella*.

Gotham (in Edmondsham) *Goathams* 1838. Although not in the early records, probably 'goat enclosure(s)', from Old English *gāt* and *hamm*.

Grange (in Holt) *Graunge* 1327, *Grange* 1654. From Middle English *grange* 'a grange, an outlying farm where crops were stored'.

Grange Farm (in Pulham) so called because there was once a *grange* here, first mentioned in the 13th century, belonging to Bindon Abbey.

Graston (in Burton Bradstock) *Gravstan* 1086 (Domesday Book), *Grauestañe* 1210, *Grauston* 1269, *Graveston* 1280. Probably 'stone by a grove or copse', from Old English *grāf* and *stān*.

Great Coll Wood (in Sturminster Marshall) *Colwod* 1284, *Colwode* 1460, *Colewoode* 1549, *Coll Wood* 1587. Possibly 'wood where charcoal was burnt', from Old English *col* 'coal, charcoal' and *wudu*, but alternatively the first element may be Old English *coll* 'hill' with reference to the hill spur here.

Great Coombe (in Whitchurch Canonicorum) *Comb* 1332, *Combe* 1399. From Old English *cumb* 'valley'.

Great Ebb (in Symondsbury) *Hebbe* 1329. From Old English *ebba* 'ebb', in the sense 'shore visible at low tide'.

Green Island (in Poole Harbour) only known by this name from the 18th century, earlier (from the 14th century) called *St Helen's Island* (e.g. *Insula Sancte Elene* 1310, from Latin *insula* 'island' and *sancta* 'saint').

Grim's Ditch (in Pentridge) *Grymesdiche, Grimesdych* 1280, *Grymes Ditche* 1618. 'Ditch associated with Grīm', from Old English *dīc*. This is a common name for ancient earthworks such as this one, which crosses the county boundary into Wiltshire. *Grīm* is probably a nickname for the heathen Germanic god Woden, to whose activities these earthworks were ascribed (Wansdyke, another earthwork in Wiltshire, is in fact 'Woden's ditch').

Grimstone (in Stratton) *Grimeston* 1212, *Grimston* 1268, *Grymeston* 1278, *Grymmeston* 1288. 'Farm belonging to a man called Grīm', from Old English *tūn* and an Anglo-Danish personal name first introduced into England by the Vikings.

Grove (on Isle of Portland) *le Groue* 1323, *Grove* 1608. 'The grove or copse', from Old English *grāf*.

Gulliver's Farm (in West Moors) named from Isaac *Gulliver* 1745–1822.

Gummershay Farm (in Stalbridge) *Gumersheye* 1268, *Gommeresheye* 1315, *Gummeresheye* 1327. 'Enclosure of a man called Gūthmǣr', from Old English *haeg* and an Old English personal name.

Gummershay Farm (in Whitchurch Canonicorum) *Gomboldesheye* 1332, *Gombeldesheye* 1340. 'Enclosure belonging to a man called Gumbeald', from Old English *haeg* and an Old English personal name.

Guppy (in Wootton Fitzpaine) *Guppehegh* 1254, *Gopeheye* 1332, *Gowpey* 1577. 'Enclosure belonging to a man called Guppa', from Old English *haeg* and an Old English personal name.

Gussage All Saints *Gyssic* 10th century, *Gessic* 1086 (Domesday Book), *Gersich Omnium Sanctorum* 1155, *Gussich All Saints* 1245. Probably 'gushing stream', from Old English *gyse* and *sīc*, originally with reference to the stream rising at Gussage St Andrew which flows through this parish to join the River Allen. *All Saints* (Latin *Omnium Sanctorum*) is from the dedication of the church.

Gussage St Andrew (in Sixpenny Handley) *Gissic* 877 (in a later copy of an Anglo-Saxon charter), *Gyssyh* early 12th century, *Gissik St Andrews* 1258. See Gussage All Saints. The addition is from the dedication of the church, earlier a chapel.

Gussage St Michael *Gessic* 1086 (Domesday Book), *Gersich* 1168, *Gyssiche Sancti Michaelis* 1280, *Gussich St Michael* 1297. See Gussage All Saints. The addition is from the dedication of the church. In medieval times this place was sometimes called *Gussiche Dynaunt* or *Gussiche Bohun*, from families which held the manor in the 12th and 13th centuries.

Gutch Pool Farm (in Gillingham) *Gowge Pole* 1568, *Gutch Poole House* 1650. Perhaps from the word *gouge* 'to hollow out', with *pōl* 'pool'.

Guy's Marsh (in Cann) *Gyesmersch* 1401, *Gyes Marshe* 1564. 'Marshy ground belonging to a man called Guy', from Old English *mersc*.

Half Hide Down (in Farnham) named from *Halueyde* 1288, *Halfhide* 1618, 'the half hide of land', from Old English *healf* and *hīd*. This is no doubt one of the two manors in

Farnham assessed at half a hide in Domesday Book.

Halstock *Halganstoke* 998 (in a 12th century copy of an Anglo-Saxon charter), *Halgestoch* 1212, *Haleghestok* 1244. 'Holy outlying farmstead', from Old English *hālig* and *stoc*, so called because in early times it belonged to the monastery at Sherborne.

Halstock Leigh (in Halstock) *Legh* 1268, *Lye, Leigh* 1684. From Old English *lēah* 'a wood, a clearing in a wood'.

Ham Common (in Gillingham) *Hamme* 12th century, *la Hamme* 1270, *Hampe* 1461, *Ham common* 1627. From Old English *hamm* 'enclosure, river-meadow'.

Hambledon Hill (in Child Okeford) *Hameledun* 1270, *Hamildon hill* 1773. 'The scarred or mutilated hill', from Old English *hamel* and *dūn*, no doubt with reference to the earthworks of the Neolithic causewayed enclosure and Iron Age hill-fort here.

Hambury House and Tout (in West Lulworth) *Hamborough* 1589, *Hanbury* 1597, *Hambury-taut, or toote* 1790. Possibly 'high hill or barrow', from Old English *hēah* and *beorg*, with the addition of Old English *tōte* 'a look out'.

Hamlet (in Yetminster) first on record in the 19th century, from the word *hamlet* 'small village'.

Hammond Street Farm (in Mappowder) *Hamondes Streete* 1602, cf. *Hamondes londes* 1536. From the *Hamund* family, here from the 14th century, with Old English *strǣt* and *land*.

Hammoon *Hame* 1086 (Domesday Book), *Ham Galfridi de Moiun* 1194, *Hamme Moun* 1280, *Hammemowne* 1408. 'The enclosure or river-meadow belonging to the *Moion* family', from Old English *hamm*. This family, deriving its name from Moyon in Normandy, already held the manor at the time of Domesday Book.

Hampreston *Hame* 1086 (Domesday Book), *Hamme* 1204, *Hamme Preston* 1244, *Hamepreston* 1299. Originally 'the enclosure or river-meadow', from Old English *hamm* (it is on the River Stour). The later addition *Preston* is 'priest farm or estate', from Old English *prēost* and *tūn*, probably an allusion

81

to lands here belonging to the College of Wimborne Minster.

Hamworthy (in Poole)   *Hamme* 1236, *Hamworthy* 1463, *Southamme* 1465, *Hamwurthy* 1535. From Old English *hamm* 'enclosure', here possibly used in the sense 'peninsula'. The later addition *-worthy* is from Old English *worthig* which also meant 'enclosure'. It was sometimes called *South-* in relation to Hampreston.

Handfast Point (in Studland)   *Hanfast* 16th century, *Handefaste Pointe* 1583. Probably 'rock stronghold', from Old English *hān* and *faesten*, perhaps with reference to Studland Castle which was situated on this promontory. Handfast Point is alternatively known as The Foreland, from the word *foreland* 'cape, headland'.

Handley   see Sixpenny Handley.

Hanford   *Hanford* 1086 (Domesday Book), *Hamford* 1197, *Haunford* 1228, *Hampford* 1241. Probably 'ford at the stone', from Old English *hān* and *ford*. The original ford was on the River Stour.

Harbin's Park (in Tarrant Gunville)   originally referred to as simply *parcus de Tarente Gundeuile* 1280, *la Park de Goundevile* 1423, from Middle English *park* (this is the best preserved of Dorset's medieval deer parks). The present name of the park is from the *Harbin* family which possessed the manor of Tarrant Gunville in the 18th century.

Hargrove Farm (in Stalbridge)   *Haregroue, Haregraue* 1268, *Haregrave* 1285, *Hargrove* 1538. Possibly 'grove frequented by hares', from Old English *hara* and *grāf*, but alternatively the first element may be Old English *hār* 'grey'.

Harley Down (in Gussage All Saints)   *Hardelyedun, Hardeleydune* 1281, *Harendeledone* 1294. 'Hill or down at the hard clearing', from Old English *heard, lēah* and *dūn*.

Harman's Cross (in Worth Matravers)   not recorded before the 19th century, from the surname *Harman* and *cross* in the sense 'crossroads'.

Harpitts Farm (in Kington Magna)   *Harpete* 1206. 'Grey pit', from Old English *hār* and *pytt*.

Harp Stone, Hurpston (in Steeple)   the 'Harp Stone' is situated near Hurpston and both names go back to *Herpere* 1086 (Domesday Book), *Herperston* 1340, *Harpeston* 1376. Originally 'the harper', from Old English *hearpere*, referring figuratively either to the stone or to the stream here, later with *stān* 'stone' added.

Hartgrove (in East Orchard)   *Haregrave* early 12th century, *Hardgrove* 1395, *Haregrove* 1450, *Hartgrove* 1698. 'Grove frequented by hares', or 'grey grove', from Old English *hara* or *hār* and *grāf*. The *-t-* (earlier *-d-*) in the modern spelling is quite unhistorical.

Hartland Moor (in Arne)   earlier called *Harttesknolle* 1545, *Hartnole* 1632, 'hart's hill-top or hillock', from Old English *heorot* and *cnoll*.

Hartley Farm (in Minterne Magna)   *Herleg* 1212, *Hertlegh* 1223, *Herteleye* 1268, *Hartleygh* 1431. 'Wood or clearing frequented by harts', from Old English *heorot* and *lēah*.

Hatherly Farm (in Hilton)   *Hetherle* 1227, *Hederlegh* 1400. 'Clearing where hawthorn or (less probably) heather grows', from Old English *haeg-thorn* (or *hǣddre*) and *lēah*.

Hatts Barn (in Ashmore)   first recorded in the 19th century, but in 1618 a coppice here was called *Winsons Hatts*, probably from Old English *haet* 'a hat-shaped hill' with reference to the prominent hill rising to 800 feet west of Hatts Barn. *Winson* is a surname.

Haydon (parish)   *Heydone* 1163, *Heidon* 1202, *Haydon* 1268, *Haydoun* 1385. 'Hill or down where hay was made', from Old English *hēg* and *dūn*.

Haydon (in Lydlinch)   *Haydon, Haydun* 13th century. Identical in origin with the previous name.

Haydon Hill (in Charminster)   *Haydon, Haydowne* 1617. Identical in origin with the previous names.

Hayes Farm (in Marnhull)   *Heis* 16th century. From Old English *hǣs* 'brushwood'.

Haythorn (in Horton)   *Heythorne* 1551. From Old English *haeg-thorn* 'hawthorn'.

Hayward Bridge (in Child Okeford) *bridge of Hayford* 1268, *Haifordesbrigge* 1337, *Hayford Bridge* 1618. 'Hay ford', i.e. 'ford used at haymaking time', from Old English *hēg* and *ford*. There is a crossing of the River Stour here.

Hazelbury Bryan *Hasebere* 1201, *Haselber* 1237, *Heselbere* 1380, *Hasilbere Bryan* 1547. 'Hazel wood', from Old English *haesel* and *bearu*. The manorial addition is from the *Bryene* family, here in the 14th century; the surname is from Brienne in France.

Heath Farm (in Hampreston) named from *Heath* 1541, *le Hethe* 1583. Self-explanatory, from Old English *hǣeth*.

Hemsworth (in Witchampton) *Hemedesworde* 1086 (Domesday Book), *Hemeleswurth* 1224, *Hemedeswurth* 1243, *Hemmesworth* 1428. 'Enclosure belonging to a man called Hemede', from Old English *worth* and an Old English personal name.

Henbury (in Sturminster Marshall) *Hennbyr* 1244, *Hymbur* 1249, *Hymbury* 1327, *Henbury* 1546. Probably 'the high or chief fortified place', from Old English *hēah* and *burh*, though alternatively the first element could be Old English *henn* 'water-hen or other wild bird'.

Hengistbury Head (in Bournemouth) *Hedenesburia* 12th century, *Hedenesbury* 14th century, *Hensbury* 1540, *Hengestbury heade* 1610 (Speed's map). 'Fortified place associated with a man called Heddīn', from Old English *burh* and an Old English personal name. The later form of the name is due to folk etymology, presumably through an antiquarian association of the place with the 5th century Germanic chieftain called *Hengest* mentioned in the Anglo-Saxon Chronicle.

Heniford Farm (in Melbury Bubb) *Humerford* 1328. 'Ford across the River Humber', from Old English *ford* and an old river-name which must at one time have been applied to what is now called the Wriggle River.

Henley (in Buckland Newton) *Henneleghe*, *Henelee* 13th century, *Henlegh* 1311. 'Wood or clearing frequented by hens (of wild birds)', from Old English *henn* and *lēah*.

Hermitage *the hermitage of Blakemor* 1309, *Ermytage* 1389, *le Hermitage* 1469, *Harmitage* 1650. Named from the priory or hermitage founded here in Blackmoor Forest in the 13th century.

Herrison (in Charminster) *Harengestun* 1224, *Haringeston* 1227, *Heryngeston* 1303, *Herriston* 1837. 'Manor or estate of the *Harang* family', from Old English *tūn*. This family was here from the early 13th century, and also gave name to Chaldon Herring, Langton Herring and Winterborne Herringston. Herrison is probably one of the several manors called *Cerne* or *Cernel* in Domesday Book (from its situation on the River Cerne).

Herston (in Swanage) *Herstune* 1086 (Domesday Book), *Hereston, Herston* 1288, *Hearston* 1656. 'Farm or estate belonging to a man called Here', from Old English *tūn* and an Old English personal name. The man in question actually held part of this manor at the time of Domesday Book.

Hethfelton (in East Stoke) *Elfatune, Hafeltone* 1086 (Domesday Book), *Hethfelton* 1280, *Hethefeldton* 1535. 'Farm by the open land overgrown with heather', from Old English *hǣth, feld* and *tūn*.

Hewish Farm (in Milton Abbas) *Hywysch* 1385. From Old English *hīwisc* 'measure of land that would support a family'.

Highcliffe (in Christchurch) self-explanatory. The cliff here is called *High Clift* in 1759, but is *Black Cliffe* on Speed's map of 1610.

High Hall (in Pamphill) *High Hall farm* 1663. Self-explanatory, with Old English *heall* in the sense 'large residence, manor house'.

High Lea Farm (in Hinton Martell) named from land called *High Ley* in 1838, from Old English *lēah* 'wood or clearing', also 'meadow'.

High Stoy (in Minterne Magna) *Staweyesfote* 1270, *Stoweye* 1550, *the Stoye* 1618. 'Stony way', from Old English *stān* and *weg*. The earliest spelling contains Old English *fōt* 'foot (of a hill)'.

Highwood (in East Stoke) *Highwood(s)* 17th century. Self-explanatory.

Hilfield *Hylfelde* 934 (in a later copy of an Anglo-Saxon charter), *Hulfeld* 1212, *Hullefeld* 1412, *Hilfeild* 1613. 'Tract of open country on a hill', from Old English *hyll* and *feld*.

Hillamsland (in Hampreston) *Hillamlands* 1553, *Hullam-lande* 1562, *Hullomslonde* 1620, originally simply called *Hull* 1330, from Old English *hyll* 'hill', with the later addition of *hamm* 'enclosure' and *land* 'estate'.

Hillbutts (in Pamphill) not recorded before the 19th century, possibly from Old English *butt* 'an archery butt', but alternatively from *butte* 'a short strip ploughed at right angles to others'.

Hillcombe Coppice (in Shillingstone) *Elcombe* 1330, *Elcomb Wood* 1811. From Old English *cumb* 'valley'. The first element is clearly not Old English *hyll* 'hill'; it may be the Old English masculine personal name *Ella*.

Hill Farm (in Iwerne Minster) *Hille* 1086 (Domesday Book), *Hulle* 1270, *Hull* 1291, *Hill* 1346. '(Place at) the hill', from Old English *hyll*. The farm is situated at 619 feet, the highest part of the parish.

Hilton *Eltone* 1086 (Domesday Book), *Halcton* 1210, *Helton* 1212, *Hilton* 1280. From Old English *tūn* 'farm, estate', but the first element is uncertain, possibly Old English *hielde* 'slope', *helde* 'tansy' or *healh* 'nook'.

Hincknoll Hill (in Netherbury) *Hennecnolle* 1288, *Henknoll* 1441. Probably 'knoll or hillock frequented by wild birds', from Old English *henn* and *cnoll*.

Hinton Martell *Hinetone* 1086 (Domesday Book), *Hinetun* 1212, *Hineton Martel* 1226, *Henton Martell* 1412. 'Farm or estate belonging to a religious community' (probably the former monastery of Wimborne Minster), from Old English *hīwan* and *tūn*. *Martell* is a manorial addition from a family of this name which held the manor in the 13th century.

Hinton Parva *Parva Hyneton* 1285, *Hynton Parva, Lytle-hyneton* 1288, *Lytell Hynton* 1459. The Latin addition *parva* 'little' (alternating since the 13th century with Old English *lȳtel*), distinguishes this place from Hinton Martell.

Hinton St Mary *Hamtune* 944 (in a later copy of an Anglo-Saxon charter), *Haintone* 1086 (Domesday Book), *Henton* 1244, *Hinton Marye* 1627. 'High farm, farm situated on high land', from Old English *hēah* and *tūn*. Although Hinton is a common place-name, the other Dorset Hintons have a different origin, see Hinton Martell and Parva. This village occupies a 300 foot hill overlooking the River Stour. The addition is from the possession of the manor by the abbey of St Mary, Shaftesbury.

Hoburne (in Christchurch) *Hoburne* 1086 (Domesday Book), *Huburne* 1313, *Houburne* 1333. 'Stream by the heel of land', from Old English *hōh* and *burna*.

Hod Hill (in Stourpaine) originally *Hod* 1270, from Old English *hōd* which could mean either 'hood' (perhaps an allusion to the shape of the hill) or 'shelter' (with reference to the Iron Age hill-fort crowning it). *Hill* is not added until the 18th century. The fort here may be *Dunium*, see Maiden Castle.

Hogchester (in Wootton Fitzpaine) *Hoggeshurst* 1236, *Hoggehurste* 1425, *Hoggescestre* 1427, *Hoggecestre* 1436. Probably 'copse or wooded hill where hogs (or wild boars) are found', from Old English *hogg* and *hyrst*, but alternatively the first element could be an Old English personal name *Hogg*. The change from *-hurst* to *-chester* occurs also in Bedchester.

Hogleaze Farm (in Frampton) *Hoglease, Hogslease* 1670. 'Pasture for hogs', from Old English *hogg* and *lǣs*.

Hogstock (in Tarrant Rushton) *Hogstocke, Hogstoke* 1609. Probably from Old English *stoc* 'an outlying farmstead, a secondary settlement' with either *hogg* 'a hog' or an Old English personal name *Hogg*.

Holcombe Farm (in Alton Pancras) *Holcombe* 1480. 'Deep or hollow valley', from Old English *hol* and *cumb*.

Holdenhurst (in Bournemouth) *Holehest* 1086 (Domesday Book), *Holeherst* 1172, *Holnhurst* 1397, *Holnest* 1540. Identical in origin with Holnest.

Holditch Court (in Thorncombe) *Holedich* 1219, *Holdyche* 1364, *Holdich* 1397. 'Hollow ditch', from Old English *hol* and *dīc*.

Holebrook Green (in Lydlinch) *Holambrok* 968 (in a later copy of an Anglo-Saxon charter), *Holebrouk* 1332, *Holebrok* 1412. 'Hollow brook', i.e. 'brook running in a deep hollow', from Old English *hol* and *brōc*.

Holm and Ivy Farm (in Cann) *la Holmene Theuele* 1341, *la Holmunthevel* 1394, *Holemandivile* 1548. 'The holly bush or thicket', from an adjectival derivative of Old English *holegn* (which gives Dorset dialect *holm*) and *thȳfel*. Obviously the original meaning of this compound was forgotten by the 16th century, and the modern form, with its conventional association of holly and ivy, is due to folk etymology.

Holmebridge (in East Stoke) *Holmebrygge* 1530. 'The bridge near Holme', from Old English *brycg*. The reference is to East and West Holme.

Holme, East *Holne* 1086 (Domesday Book), *Holm* 1218, *Estholn, Estholm* 1288. '(Place at) the holly tree', from Old English *holegn*, 'east' in relation to West Holme.

Holme, West (in East Stoke) *Westholn, Westholm* 1288. See under East Holme.

Holmwood (in Hampreston) not on early record, but no doubt from Dorset dialect *holm* 'holly' (Old English *holegn*).

Holnest *Holeherst* 1185, *Holenhurst* 1268, *Holnest* 1316, *Holnhurst* 1375. 'Copse or wooded hill where holly grows', from Old English *holegn* and *hyrst*. Holdenhurst is identical in origin.

Holt *Winburneholt* 1185, *Wynburneholt* 1221, *Holte* 1372, *le Holte* 1427. 'The wood near Wimborne (Minster)', from Old English *holt*. This was a royal chase and forest, first recorded as *foresta de Winburne* in 1086 (Domesday Book).

Holt Farms (in Melbury Osmond) *la Holte* 14th century. From Old English *holt* 'wood, thicket'.

Holton (in Wareham) *Holtone* 1086 (Domesday Book), *Holton* 1211. 'Farm in or near a hollow', from Old English *hol* and *tūn*. Alternatively the first element could be Old English *holt* 'a wood'.

Holway Farm (in Cattistock) *Holeweia* 1206, *Holeweye* 1291, *Holloway* 1577. 'Hollow way, way in a hollow', from Old English *hol* and *weg*.

Holwell (parish) *Holewala* 1188, *Holewal* 1194, *Holewale* 1201, *Holewell* 1206. 'Ridge or bank in a hollow', from Old English *hol* and *walu*.

Holwell (near Broadwey) *Halegewelle* 1086 (Domesday Book), *Halghewell* 1244, *Halewell* 1346, *Holywell* 1530. 'Holy well, spring or stream', from Old English *hālig* and *wella*.

Holwell Farm (in Cranborne) *Holewella* 1194, *Holewelle* 1328, *Holwelle* 1378, *Holewyll* 1393. 'Hollow stream, stream in a deep valley', from Old English *hol* and *wella*.

Holworth (in Owermoigne) *Holewertthe, Holewourthe* 934 (in later copies of Anglo-Saxon charters), *Holverde* 1086 (Domesday Book), *Holewrth* 1204. 'Enclosure in a hollow', from Old English *hol* and *worth*. There is the site of a deserted medieval village here.

Honeybrook Farm (in Holt) *Honybrock* 1300, *Honybrok* 1327, *Honybrouk* 1332. 'Brook by which honey is found', from Old English *hunig* and *brōc*; the place is by a small tributary of the River Allen.

Honeycomb Wood (in Castleton) *Honycombe Wode* 1538. 'Valley where honey is produced', from Old English *hunig* and *cumb*, with *wudu*.

Hooke *Lahoc* 1086 (Domesday Book), *Hok* 1209, *La Hoke* 1244, *Houc* 1268. 'The hook or angle, the land in a river-bend', from Old English *hōc*. The River Hooke takes its present name from this place, its earlier name being *Toller*, see Tollerford.

Hookswood Farm (in Farnham) *Hookes-Wood* 1774, probably named from *Hoke* 1621 which is Old English *hōc* 'a hook, an angle or bend' (perhaps originally with reference to the valley in which the farm lies).

Horn Hill and Park (in Broadwindsor) *Horhulle* 13th

century, *Horne hill, Horne Park* 1621. From Old English *horn* 'horn-shaped hill, projecting piece of land'.

Horton   *Hortun* 1033 (in a 12th century copy of an Anglo-Saxon charter), *Hortune* 1086 (Domesday Book), *Horton* 1212. 'Dirty or muddy farm', from Old English *horu* and *tūn*.

Hound Hill (in Pamphill)   *Houne Hill* 1591. Probably 'hill where hounds were kept', from Old English *hund* and *hyll* (there are still kennels nearby), but the first element could alternatively be the plant-name *hūne* 'hoarhound'.

Huish (in Winterborne Zelstone)   *Hiwysh* 1327, *Ywyssch* 1332, *Haiwyssh* 1419, *Huwyssh* 1423. From Old English *hīwisc* 'a household, a measure of land that would support a household'.

Huish Farm (in Sydling St Nicholas)   *Hywyssh* 1280, *Hiwische* 1321. Identical in origin with the previous name.

Hummer (in Trent)   *Humbre* 1106, *Homere* 1311, *Homer* 1504. Originally the name of the small stream here, a tributary of the River Yeo; Humber is an ancient pre-English river-name of uncertain origin.

Huntingford (in Gillingham)   *Hunteneford* 1258, *Huntingford* 1300, *Huntyngford* 1333, *Huntenford* 1338. 'The hunters' ford, the ford used by people going hunting', from Old English *hunta* and *ford*. This was on the boundary of the royal forest of Gillingham, so the association with hunting is clear.

Hurn   *Herne* 1086 (Domesday Book), *Hurne* 1242, *Hyrne* 1256, *la Hurne* 1367. 'The angle or corner of land', from Old English *hyrne*, perhaps originally with reference to the piece of land between Moors River and the River Stour.

Hurpston (in Steeple)   see Harp Stone.

Hursey (in Burstock)   *Herstanesheia* 1201, *Herstanseg* 1244, *Herstenesheye* 1268, *Hestoneshegh* 1336. 'Enclosure belonging to a man called Heorstān', from Old English *haeg* and an Old English personal name.

Hurst (in Moreton)   *Herste* 1251, *Urste, Hurste* 1300, *Hurst* 1318. 'Copse or wooded hill', from Old English *hyrst*.

Hyde (in Bothenhampton)   *la Hyde* 1244, *atte Hide* 1327, *le*

Hyde 1482, *Hyde* 1497. 'The hide of land', from Old English *hīd*; *atte* means 'at the'. Originally a hide was an amount of land sufficient to support one free family and its dependants.

Hyde Farm (in Tarrant Hinton) *Hydam* 1227, *Hida* 1242, *la Hyde* 1288, *la Hide* 1358. Identical in origin with the previous name. From the 15th century the place was sometimes called *Stokehyde*, probably because it was associated manorially with East Stoke.

Hyde Heath and House (in Bere Regis) *Hyde* 1285, *Hide* 1288, *La Hyde* 1316, *the Hyde* 1476. Identical in origin with the previous two names.

Hydes (in Lydlinch) *Hydes* 1431. Named from the family of Roger *de la Hide* 1268, from Old English *hīd* as in previous names. In medieval times called alternatively *Lydlinch Baret* from a family called *Baret* which also had lands here.

Ibberton *Abristetone* 1086 (Domesday Book), *Hedbredinton* 1212, *Edbrightinton* 1288, *Ibrigton* 1291. 'Farm called after a man named Ēadbeorht', from Old English -*ingtūn* and an Old English personal name.

Iford (in Bournemouth) *Huver* 12th century, *Uvre* 1272, *Uvere* 13th century, *Iver* 1540. From Old English *yfer* 'a slope'. The alteration to Iford is probably quite recent.

Ilsington (in Puddletown) *Elsangtone* 1086 (Domesday Book), *Ilsington* 1257, *Elsinton* 1260, *Ilssyngton* 1331. Probably 'farm called after a man named Aelfsige', from Old English -*ingtūn* and an Old English personal name.

Innsacre (in Shipton Gorge) *Insaker* 13th century, *Insacre* 14th century, *Insacr* 1454, *Innesacr* 1469. Probably 'plot of arable or cultivated land belonging to a man called Ine', from Old English *aecer* and an Old English personal name.

Ivy Cross (in Shaftesbury) *Ivy Crosse* 1574. Self-explanatory, from Old English *īfig* and *cros*.

Iwerne, River an old Celtic river-name, first recorded in the 10th century and probably meaning 'the yew river'; it gives its name to three parishes on its banks.

Iwerne Courtney or Shroton *Werne* 1086 (Domesday

Book), *Yuern Curtenay* 1244, *Schyreuetone* 1337, *Iwerne Courteney alias Shyrevton* 1403. 'Estate on the River Iwerne belonging to the Courtenay family'; the *Courtenays*, Earls of Devon, were here from the early 13th century. The alternative name Shroton means 'sheriff's farm or estate', from Old English *scīr-rēfa* and *tūn*; the Domesday Book manor belonged to Baldwin of Exeter, *sheriff* of Devon.

Iwerne Minster *Ywern* 877 (in a later copy of an Anglo-Saxon charter), *Evneminstre* 1086 (Domesday Book), *Iwerne Ministre* 1280. Named from the River Iwerne which rises here. The addition is Old English *mynster*, perhaps in the sense 'church of a monastery' in allusion to its early possession by Shaftesbury abbey, or simply 'large church' if the church here was particularly important even by the time of Domesday Book.

Iwerne Steepleton *Werne* 1086 (Domesday Book), *Stepleton* 1234, *Stupelton* 1244, *Iwernestapleton* 1346. 'Village on the River Iwerne with a church steeple', from Old English *stīepel* and *tūn*.

Jordon Hill (near Preston) *Churdon* 1452, *Cherdoun* 1461, *Jordayne* 1531, *Jorden* 1617. Probably 'hill at the turn or bend', from Old English *cierr* and *dūn*, with reference to the course taken by the River Jordon (which is named from the hill) as it rounds the east side of the hill.

Jumpers Common (in Christchurch) named from a family called *Jumper* recorded in the 16th century.

Kendalls, The (in Gillingham) recorded as two fields called *Kendle* in 1839, but possibly to be associated with *Kynhull* 1280 which may be 'royal hill' from Old English *cyne-* and *hyll*, or 'cows' hill' if the first element is Middle English *kyne* 'cows'.

Kershay Farms (in Netherbury) *Kyrseheye* 1306, *Curseheygh* 1332, *Curseyah* 1340, *Kersey* 16th century. Second element is Old English *haeg* 'enclosure', first element is possibly a surname.

Keysworth Farm (in Wareham) *Kaerswurth* 1227, *Kares-*

worthe 1309, *Kisworthe* 1469, *Kesworthe* 1575. Probably 'cress enclosure', from Old English *caerse* and *worth*. The farm is near the River Piddle or Trent.

Kimmeridge *Cameric, Cuneliz* 1086 (Domesday Book), *Kimerich* 1212, *Kymerygge* 1489. Probably 'convenient track', from Old English *cȳme* and *ric*, perhaps an allusion to the fact that the road through Kimmeridge seems to afford the only easy access to the sea for two miles in either direction.

King Barrow (in Alderholt) *Kyngbor'ghe* 1404, *Kingbarowe* 17th century. From Old English *cyning* 'king' and *beorg* 'barrow, hill'. This is a natural mound, not a tumulus, so 'king' perhaps alludes simply to its size.

Kingcombe, Higher and Lower (in Toller Porcorum) *Chimedecome* 1086 (Domesday Book), *Kendecumb* 1212, *Kentecumb* 1288, *Keincombe* 1303. 'Valley where wall-germander grows', from Old English *cymed* and *cumb*.

King Down (in Pamphill) *the Kinges Downe* 1591. Self-explanatory, from Old English *cyning* and *dūn*. It lay within the former royal manor of Kingston Lacy.

King's Court Wood (in Motcombe) named from the former 'King's Court Palace' first recorded in the 13th century and reputed to have been a royal hunting lodge.

Kingsettle Farm (in Motcombe) *Kyngesettl* 1268, *Kinges-settle* 1285, *Kynsettle* 1369, *Kyngsetell* 1441. Literally 'king's seat', from Old English *cyning* and *setl*, perhaps used as a hill-name since the farm lies on the lower slopes of a hill that reaches 800 feet. On the other hand the name may have referred to a royal hunting lodge or the like in the old forest of Gillingham.

Kingsland (in Netherbury) *Kingesland* 1237, *Kyngeslond* 1332. Self-explanatory, from Old English *cyning* and *land*.

King's Mill Bridge (in Marnhull) *Kingesmolne* 1268, *Kyngesmulle* early 14th century. Self-explanatory, from Old English *cyning* and *myln*.

Kingstag (in Lydlinch) *Kingestake* 1337, *Kingstake brydg* 16th century. 'King's stake or boundary post', from Old

English *cyning* and *staca*. The boundaries of three parishes meet here on the bridge over the River Lydden.

Kingston (in Corfe Castle) *Chingestone* 1086 (Domesday Book), *Kingeston* 1212, *Kynggeston* 1288, *Kyngston* 1512. 'The king's farm, the royal manor', from Old English *cyning* and *tūn*. In an Anglo-Saxon charter dated 948, Eadred king of Wessex granted land here to the abbess of Shaftesbury.

Kingston (in Hazelbury Bryan) *Kingeston* 1580, *Kinston* 1605, *Kinson* 1774. Identical in origin with the previous name.

Kingston Lacy Hall (in Pamphill) *Kingestune* 1170, *Kynggestone Lacy* 1319, *Kyngeston Lacy* 1337, *Kingeston-Haul* 16th century. Identical in origin with the previous names; the manorial addition is from John *de Lacy*, earl of Lincoln, to whom the manor was granted in 1230. The present 17th century hall replaced an earlier house; it was called simply *Kingston Hall* until the early 19th century.

Kingston Maurward (in Stinsford) *Kingeston* 1244, *Kyngeston Marlevard* 1280, *Kyngeston Marleward* 1303, *Kyngeston Maureward* 1329. Identical in origin with the previous names. The manorial addition is from the family of Geoffrey *Mauregard* who is mentioned here in 1247.

Kingston Russell *Kingeston* 1212, *Kyngeston Russel* 1284, *Kynggestun* 1285, *Kyngeston Russell* 1375. Identical in origin with the other Kingstons. The addition is manorial, from the family of John *Russel* who held it of the king in 1212.

Kingswood Farm (in Studland) *Kyngeswode* 1397, *Kynswood* 1546. 'The king's wood', from Old English *cyning* and *wudu*.

Kington Farm, Little (in West Stour) *Chintone* 1086 (Domesday Book), *Parva Kynton* 1238, *Little Kyngton* 1272. The addition is Latin *parva* 'small', distinguishing this place from Kington Magna.

Kington Magna *Chintone* 1086 (Domesday Book), *Kinton* 1203, *Magna Kington* 1243, *Great Kington* 1290. 'Royal manor', from Old English *cyne-* and *tūn*. The addition is Latin *magna* 'great', distinguishing this place from Little Kington.

Kinson   *Chinestanestone* 1086 (Domesday Book), *Kyne-stanton* 1231, *Kinestaneston* 1238, *Kyneston* 1431. 'Farm belonging to a man called Cynestān', from Old English *tūn* and an Old English personal name.

Kitford Bridge (in Folke)   *Kytefordbrygge* 1484. 'Bridge at the ford frequented by kites', from Old English *cȳta, ford* and *brycg.*

Knaps Hill farm (in Buckland Newton)   *Knapshill* 1675. Named from the family of Thomas *Cnap* who had lands here in the 14th century.

Knighton (in Beer Hackett)   *Knythteton* 1288, *Knyghteton* 1352, *Knyghton* 1362. 'Farm belonging to the thanes or retainers', from Old English *cniht* and *tūn*, although if the name originated after the Norman Conquest of 1066, *cniht* may have its later sense 'knight'.

Knighton (in Canford Magna)   *Knyghteton* 1288, *Knyghton* 1348. Identical in origin with the previous name.

Knighton, East (in Winfrith Newburgh)   *Knytteton* 1244, *Knihtteton* 1254, *Knyghteton* 1313, *Knyghton* 1440. Identical in origin with the previous two names.

Knighton House (in Durweston)   *Knicteton* 1212, *Knyhteton* 1243, *Knytteton* 1277, *Knyghton* 1346. 'Farm of the thanes or retainers', from Old English *cniht* and *tūn*. This manor was held by five thanes in the 11th century.

Knighton, West (parish)   *Chenistetone* 1086 (Domesday Book), *Cnititon* 1208, *Knighton* 1222, *Knyghteton* 1288. 'Farm of the thanes or retainers', from Old English *cniht* and *tūn*. This manor was held by two thanes or retainers of a high personage at the time of Domesday Book.

Knitson Farm (in Langton Matravers)   *Knyghtwyneston* 1309, *Knyghneston* 14th century, *Knyghteston* 1366, *Knightsen* 1586. 'Farm or estate belonging to a man called Cnihtwine', from Old English *tūn* and an Old English personal name.

Knob's Crook (in Woodlands)   not in the early records, but possibly an allusion to the sharply curved ridge here, from Middle English *knob* 'a knoll' and Old English *crōc* 'a bend'.

95

Knoll (in Buckland Newton)   *Knolle* 1268, *Cnolle* 1291, *Knoll* 1481. From Old English *cnoll* 'hill-top, summit of a large hill, hillock'.

Knoll, The (in Corfe Mullen)   *La Cnolle* 1228. Identical in origin with the previous name.

Knowle   see Church Knowle.

Knowle Hall (in Woodlands)   *Cnolle* 1212, *Knol* 1242, *Knolle* 1244, *Knoll-Hill farm* 1650. From Old English *cnoll* 'hill-top, hillock', with the later addition of *hyll*. The hill rises to over 250 feet, and gives name to Knowlton.

Knowlton (in Woodlands)   *Chenoltune* 1086 (Domesday Book), *Cnolton* 1212, *Knolton* 1242. 'Farm by the hillock', from Old English *cnoll* (i.e. Knowle Hill) and *tūn*.

Lackington, White   see White Lackington.

Lake Farm (in Thornford)   *Lake* 1563. From Old English *lacu* 'a stream, a watercourse'.

La Lee Farm (in Winterborne Whitechurch)   *la Le* 1244, *La Lee* 1280, *La Leye* 1291, *Laley* 1560. 'The wood' or 'the clearing in the wood', from Old English *lēah* with the French definite article, the survival of which suggests strong French influence (the manor was held in medieval times by Milton Abbey).

Lambrook (in Netherbury)   *Lambrok* 1268, *Lambroke* 1288, *Lambrouk* 1332. 'Brook by which lambs are pastured', from Old English *lamb* and *brōc*.

Langbourne (in Langton Long Blandford)   not on early record, but no doubt 'long stream' from Old English *lang* and *burna*.

Langdon Farm (in Beaminster)   *Langedon* 1244, *Langeden* 1268, *Langgedon* 1332. 'Long hill or down', from Old English *lang* and *dūn*.

Langford Farm (in Stratton)   *Langeford* 1086 (Domesday Book), *Langford* 1332, *Longford* 1811. 'Long ford', from Old English *lang* and *ford*. The ford was across Sydling Water, a tributary of the River Frome.

Langham (in Gillingham)   *Langeham* 1156, *Langham* 1159,

Langenham 1280, *Langnam* 1501. 'The long enclosure or river-meadow', from Old English *lang* and *hamm*.

Langton Herring *Langetone* 1086 (Domesday Book), *Langetun* 1221, *Langeton Heryng* 1336, *Langton Herynge* 1406. 'Long farm or estate', from Old English *lang* and *tūn*. The manorial addition is from the family of *Harang*, here from the 13th century; the same family gave its name to Chaldon Herring, Herrison and Winterborne Herringston.

Langton Long Blandford *Bleneford* 1086 (Domesday Book), *Longeblaneford* 1242, *Langeton* 1273, *Blaneford Langeton* 1280, *Langton Long Blandford* 1598. Originally distinguished from the other Blandfords by Old English *lang* 'long', then by its alternative name Langton, 'long farm or estate' from Old English *lang* and *tūn*. In medieval times different manors here were known as *Langeton Botiller* and *Langeton Latyle* from the surnames of the families possessing them.

Langton Matravers *Langeton* 1165, *Langeton Mawtravers* 1428, *Langton Matrevers* 1497. 'Long farm or estate', from Old English *lang* and *tūn*. The manorial addition is from the *Mautravers* family, here from the 13th century.

Lankham Bottom (in Cattistock) *Langcum* 1317. 'Long valley', from Old English *lang* and *cumb*.

Laverstock Farm (in Stoke Abbott) *Laurechestocam* 12th century, *Larkestok* 1244, *Lauerekestok* 1268, *Laverkstok* 1285. 'Farm frequented by larks', from Old English *lāwerce* and *stoc*. This name also occurs in Wiltshire and Hampshire.

Lazerton Farm (in Stourpaine) *Werne* 1086 (Domesday Book), *Lasceton* 1244, *Lazereton* 1270, *Iwernelazerton* 1346. Originally named from the River Iwerne on which it stands. Lazerton is possibly 'farm of the leech gatherers', from Old English *lǣcere* and *tūn*.

Leeson House (in Langton Matravers) *Lesinton* 1224, *Lesseton* 1243, *Leston* 1288, *Leaston* 1623. Probably 'farm called after a man named Lēofsige', from Old English *-ingtūn* and an Old English personal name.

Leigh (parish) *Lega* 1228, *Legh* 1244, *Leghe* 1288, *Leyghe*

1327. 'The wood or the clearing in a wood', from Old English *lēah*.

Leigh (in Colehill) *Lege* 1086 (Domesday Book), *Leye* 1280, *Leygh* 1297, *Lye* 1369. Identical in origin with the previous name.

Leigh Park (in Wimborne Minster) *Leye park* 1348, *Leigh'park* 1374, *Leyghparke* 1463, *Lye parke* 1477. Named from Leigh in Colehill; there was a medieval deer-park here.

Lenthay (in Sherborne) *Lentehay* 1454, *Lenthey* 1461. 'Enclosure used at Lent or in Spring', from Old English *lencten* and *haeg*.

Letton (in Pimperne) *Litten* 1784, possibly *Latton* 1327, *Lacton* 1332. Perhaps Old English *lēac-tūn* 'herb garden'.

Lewcombe (in East Chelborough) *Leuecumbe* 1268, *Leucumbe* 1297, *Lucombe* 1535. 'Sheltered valley', or 'valley with a shelter', from Old English *hlēo* or *hlēow* and *cumb*.

Lewell Farms (in West Knighton) *Lewelle, Liwelle* 1086 (Domesday Book), *Lywolle* 1285. Probably 'well or spring with a shelter', from Old English *hlēo* or *hlēow* and *wella*.

Leweston *Leweston, Leuston* 1244, *Leuweston* 1288, *Leueston* 1346. Probably 'farm belonging to a man called Lēofwīg', from Old English *tūn* and an Old English personal name.

Lillington *Lilletone* 1166, *Lillington, Lullinton* 1200, *Lyllinton* 1285. 'Farm called after a man named Lylla', from Old English *-ingtūn* and an Old English personal name.

Lilliput (in Poole) *Lillypute* 1783, *Lilliput* 1811. A literary name, like the nearby Branksome. Lilliput is the name of the imaginary country peopled by pygmies in Jonathan Swift's *Gulliver's Travels* (1726). It is probably no coincidence that in the 18th century there was a prominent family in these parts called *Gulliver*!

Lily Farm (in Charmouth) *Lidleghe* 1240, *Lydlege* 1327, *Lydeley* 1399. Probably 'wood or clearing on a slope', from Old English *hlith* and *lēah*.

Lim, River see Lyme Regis.

Limbury Farm (in Netherbury) *Lymbury* 1288, *Lymbry*

1608. 'Hill where flax is grown', from Old English *līn* and *beorg*.

Linton Hill (in Abbotsbury) *Lyndone* 1332, *Lyndon* 1383, *Lymdon* 1404. 'Hill or down where flax is grown', from Old English *līn* and *dūn*.

Lions Hill (in St Leonards and St Ives)   Named from a family called *Lyne*, here in the 16th century.

Littledown (in Bournemouth)   *le Lytildoune* 13th century. Self-explanatory, from Old English *lȳtel* and *dūn* 'hill, down'.

Little Mayne Farm (in West Knighton)   *Maine* 1086 (Domesday Book), *Parva Maene* 1202, *Lyttlemayne* 1306. 'Little' (Old English *lȳtel* and Latin *parva*) to distinguish this manor from Fryer Mayne and Broadmayne (see under the latter for the meaning of Mayne).

Littlemoor (in Broadwey)   *Lytilmore* 1431, *Litulmore* 1445. From Old English *lȳtel* 'little' and *mōr* 'moor, marshy ground'.

Little Puddle Farm and Hill (in Piddlehinton)   *Litele Pudele* 934 (in a later copy of an Anglo-Saxon charter), *Pidre* 1086 (Domesday Book), *Litelepidele* 1212. 'Little estate on the River Piddle', from Old English *lȳtel*.

Littleton (in Blandford St Mary)   *Liteltone* 1086 (Domesday Book), *Litletun* 1220, *Littleton* 1243, *Lytylton* 1428. 'Little farm or estate', from Old English *lȳtel* and *tūn*, so named to distinguish it from Langton (Long Blandford) on the opposite bank of the River Stour.

Littlewindsor (in Broadwindsor)   *Windresorie* 1086 (Domesday Book), *Parua Windesoria* 1189, *Parva Windlesor* 1209, *Little Windesore* 1279, *Petite Wyndesore* 1327. Old English *lȳtel* 'little', alternating with Latin *parva* and French *petit*, distinguishes this manor from Broadwindsor, which see for the origin of the name.

Little Wood (in Chettle)   *littlen wde* 935 (in a 15th century copy of an Anglo-Saxon charter). Self-explanatory, and virtually unchanged after a thousand years, from Old English *lȳtel* and *wudu*.

Litton Cheney *Lideton* 1204, *Lidinton* 1212, *Ludeton* 1232, *Lutton* 1258. Probably 'farm by a torrent or noisy stream', from Old English *hlȳde* and *tūn*. The manorial addition, only appearing relatively late, is from the *Cheyne* family, here from the late 14th century.

Locketts Farm (in Hazelbury Bryan) *Lockets* 1697. From the family of John *Locket*, first mentioned at the end of the 14th century.

Lodden, River probably an old Celtic river-name, identical in origin with the River Lydden; it is first recorded in the 13th century.

Loders *Lodre, Lodres* 1086 (Domesday Book), *Loddre, Loddres* 1244, *Loderes* 1291. This may originally have been the old name of the river here, which is now called the Asker (from Askerswell further upstream). If so, it was probably a Celtic river-name meaning 'pool stream' (containing the words found in Cornish as *lo* and *dour*).

Lodmoor (near Melcombe Regis) *lodomor* 984 (in a 14th century copy of an Anglo-Saxon charter), *Lodemor* 1297, *Lodemoure* 1452, *Lodmore* 1460. Possibly 'muddy tract of marshy land', from Celtic *lutā* 'mud' and Old English *mōr*.

Longbury (in Gillingham) *Langborowe* 1609. 'Long barrow', from Old English *lang* and *beorg*.

Longcombe Bottom (in Fontmell Magna) *Langencumb* 932 (in a later copy of an Anglo-Saxon charter). 'Long valley', from Old English *lang* and *cumb*.

Longfleet (in Poole) *Langeflete* 1230, *Langflete* 1463, *Langefleatte* 1543, *Longflete* 1575. 'Long inlet or creek', from Old English *lang* and *flēot*.

Longham (in Hampreston) *Longeham* 1541, *Longham* 1575. 'Long enclosure or river-meadow', from Old English *lang* and *hamm*.

Long Lane Farm (in Holt) *Langlanne* 1524, *Longe Lane* 1591. Self-explanatory, from Old English *lang* and *lane*.

Longmoor Farm (in Gillingham) *Longmore* 1650. Self-explanatory, from Old English *lang* and *mōr* 'marshy ground'.

Look Farm (in Puncknowle) *Luk* 1212, *Luca* 1279, *Louke* 1336, *Luke* 1350. Possibly from an Old English word *lūce* meaning 'enclosure'.

Lorton (in Broadwey) not in early records, but possibly 'dirty farm', from Old English *lorte* and *tūn*.

Loscombe (in Powerstock) *Loscum* 1244, *Loscumbe* 1288, *Loscomb* 1356, *Loscombe* 1418. 'Valley with a pig-sty', from Old English *hlōse* and *cumb*.

Loverley Farm (in Gussage All Saints) *Loverlay, Luverlay* 12th century, *Loverlee* 1288, *Louerleygh* 1341. Probably 'wood or clearing belonging to a woman called Lēofwaru', from Old English *lēah* and an Old English personal name.

Lowbrook Farm (in Okeford Fitzpaine) *Lollebrok* 1264, *Lollebrouk* 1346, *Lullebrouk* 1358. Probably 'brook belonging to a man called Lulla', from Old English *brōc* and an Old English personal name.

Lox Lane Farm (in Gillingham) *Lockslane* 1599, *Lox Lane* 1839. From a surname *Lock*.

Loxtree Farm (in Evershot) *Lokestrewe* 1268, *Loxtrowe* 1361. 'Tree belonging to a man called Locc', from Old English *trēow* and an Old English personal name.

Luccombe Farms (in Milton Abbas) *Loucome* 1317. Probably identical in origin with the next name.

Luccombe Farm (in Netherbury) *Leucom* 1251, *Leucumbe* 1260. 'Sheltered valley', or 'valley with a shelter', from Old English *hlēo* or *hlēow* and *cumb*.

Luckford Lake (a tributary of the River Frome) *Luggeford* 1381. Possibly 'the ford of a man called Lugga', from Old English *ford* and an Old English personal name. However the first element may alternatively be an old river-name of Celtic origin.

Lulworth, East and West *Lulvorde, Loloworde* 1086 (Domesday Book), *Lulleworth* 1199, *Westlullewrth* 1258, *Estlolleworth* 1268. 'Enclosure belonging to a man called Lulla', from Old English *worth* and an Old English personal name.

Luscombe Valley (in Poole)   *Loscomb* 1822. 'Valley with a pig-sty', from Old English *hlōse* and *cumb*.

Luton Farm and Down (in Tarrant Monkton)   *Loueton, Tarante Loueton* 1280, *Loveton* 1283, *Tarant Loveton* 1435, *Lovetowne* 1618. Probably 'farm (on the River Tarrant) belonging to a man called Lufa', from Old English *tūn* and an Old English personal name. *Tarrant* was only finally dropped from the name in the 17th century.

Lutton (in Steeple)   *Lutton* 1280, *Lutteton* 1288, *Luton* 1376. 'Farm belonging to a man called Lutta', from Old English *tūn* and an Old English personal name.

Lydford Farm (in Cann)   *Glideford* 1280, *Glidford* 1289, *Lydford* 1502. 'Ford frequented by the kite or other bird of prey', from Old English *glida* and *ford*. The loss of initial G- from the 16th century is unusual.

Lydden, River   an old Celtic river-name, first recorded in the 10th century and probably meaning 'the broad one'; it gives its name to Lydlinch.

Lydlinch   *Lidelinz* 1182, *Lideling* 1205, *Lidelinch* 1285. 'Ridge by, or bank of, River Lydden', from Old English *hlinc*.

Lymburgh's Farm (in Marnhull)   *Linberg, Limberghe* 1244, *Lymbergh* 1268, *Lymbres* 1597. Either 'lime-tree hill' from Old English *lind* and *beorg*, or 'hill where flax is grown' if the first element is Old English *līn*.

Lyme Regis   *Lim* 774 (in a later copy of an Anglo-Saxon charter), *Lime, Lym* 1086 (Domesday Book), *Lyme Regis* 1285. This place and Uplyme in Devon take their name from the River Lim. This is an old river-name of Celtic origin meaning simply 'stream'.

Lynch Farm (in Corfe Castle)   *hlinc* 956 (in a later copy of an Anglo-Saxon charter), *La Linche* 1254, *Lynch* 1545. 'The ridge or bank', from Old English *hlinc*.

Lyscombe Farm (in Cheselbourne)   *Liscombe* 934 (in a later copy of an Anglo-Saxon charter), *Liscome* 1086 (Domesday Book), *Liscumb* 1212, *Lyscumb* 1288. 'Valley where reeds grow', from Old English *lisc* and *cumb*.

Lytchett Matravers   *Lichet* 1086 (Domesday Book), *Lichet Mautrauers* 1280, *Lychet Mautrauers* 1288, *Litchett Matreevers* 1673. The Lytchett in this and the neighbouring Lytchett Minster is an old Celtic name meaning 'grey wood' from Celtic *lēd* and *cēd*. The woodland here is mentioned in Domesday Book. The manorial addition is from the family of Hugh *Maltrauers* who held the manor in 1086; the same family gave its name to Langton Matravers.

Lytchett Minster   *Licheminster* 1244, *Lechet Ministre* 1269, *Lychet Minystre* 1280, *Luchet Mynstre* 1314. For the meaning of Lytchett, see Lytchett Matravers. The addition Minster is from Old English *mynster* 'large church', probably with reference to the church at Sturminster Marshall, of which Lytchett Minster was once a chapelry. In the 16th century Lytchett Minster was sometimes known as *South Lytchett* (in relation to Lytchett Matravers) or *Bere Lytchett* (from Bere Farm in this parish).

Madjeston (in Gillingham) *Malgereston* 1205, *Magerston* 1256, *Maugereston* 1266, *Maggeston* 1342. 'Farm belonging to a man called Malger', from Old English *tūn* and a Continental Germanic personal name.

Magiston Farm (in Sydling St Nicholas)   *Mageston* 1390. Perhaps identical in origin with Madjeston in Gillingham.

Maiden Castle (in Winterborne St Martin)   *Mayden Castell* 1607. The same name is applied to a number of other prehistoric earthworks in Britain besides this Iron Age hillfort. The meaning may be 'fortification thought never to have been taken, one that looks impregnable', or simply refer to the fact that this was a place frequented by maidens. Maiden Castle is probably the city of *Dunium* (from Celtic *dūno* 'a fort') referred to by the Greek geographer Ptolemy in the 2nd century, but this is more likely the fort at Hod Hill.

Maiden Newton   *Newetone* 1086 (Domesday Book), *Maydene Neweton* 1288, *Mayden Nywton* 1303, *Maydene Newenton* 1325. 'New farm', from Old English *nīwe* and *tūn*. The addition means 'of the maidens', from Old English *maegden*; the exact allusion is obscure, but it could suggest that the manor was once owned by nuns.

Main Down (in Tarrant Gunville) *la Menedon* 1397, *Menedone* 1398. 'The common hill or down', from Old English *māene* and *dūn*.

Mandeville Stoke Farm (in Whitchurch Canonicorum) *Stoches* 1086 (Domesday Book), *Stok Maundeuyl* 1288. From Old English *stoc* 'secondary settlement', the later manorial addition being from the *Mandeville* family, here from the 13th century. Part of the original estate was known in medieval times as *Stoke Waleys*, so named from another family.

Mangerton (in Netherbury) *Mangerton* 1207, *Mangereston* 1274, *Mangertone* 1285, *Manggerton* 1333. 'Farm belonging to the traders', from Old English *mangere* and *tūn*.

Mannington (in Holt) *Manitone* 1086 (Domesday Book), *Manyton, Maninton* 1244, *Manington* 1279. 'Farm called after a man named Mann or Manna', from Old English *-ingtūn* and an Old English personal name.

Manor Farm (in Motcombe) earlier called Woodsend Farm, a name that goes back to the 13th century *Wodesende*, meaning 'end of the wood', from Old English *wudu* and *ende*.

Manor Hill (in Tarrant Gunville) *Manewodehulle* 1397, *Mamewoodhill* 1541. 'Hill at the common wood', from Old English *māene, wudu* and *hyll*.

Manston *Manestone* 1086 (Domesday Book), *Manneston* 1196, *Manston* 1268. 'Farm belonging to a man called Mann', from Old English *tūn* and an Old English personal name.

Manswood (in Moor Crichel) *Mangewood* 1774. Perhaps from the word *mange* 'a cutaneous disease of animals caused by a parasite', used of a wood thought diseased, or of a wood thought to harbour the parasite.

Mappercombe Manor (in Powerstock) *Mepercumbe* 1285, *Mopercumbe* 1288, *Mopercome* 1318, *Mapercombe* 1636. The second element is Old English *cumb* 'valley', the first is uncertain.

Mapperton (parish) *Malperetone, Maperetone* 1086 (Domesday Book), *Mapeldoreton* 1236, *Maperton* 1244. 'Maple-tree farm', from Old English *mapuldor* and *tūn*.

Mapperton (in Sturminster Marshall)   *Mapeldertune* 943 (in a 15th century copy of an Anglo-Saxon charter), *Mapledretone* 1086 (Domesday Book), *Maperton* 1212, *Mapellerton* 1316. Identical in origin with the previous name.

Mappowder   *Mapledre* 1086 (Domesday Book), *Mapoldre* 1189, *Maupodre* 1227, *Mapoudre* 1303. From Old English *mapuldor* 'a maple-tree'.

Margaret Marsh   *Margaretysmerschchurche* 1395, *Margret marshe* 1575, *Margetsmarshe* 1581. Self-explanatory, from Old English *mersc* 'marsh'. *Margaret* may be from the dedication of the church, but it is probably more likely to have been the name of an early owner of the ground itself, as in the nearby Guy's Marsh. It belonged to Shaftesbury Abbey, so perhaps the *Margaret* in question was one of the two 14th century abbesses so named. The church dedication would then have followed at a later date.

Marley Wood (in Winfrith Newburgh)   *Muryle* 1390, *Meriley* 1456, *Merley* 1474. 'Pleasant wood or clearing', or 'wood or clearing where merry-making took place', from Old English *myrge* and *lēah*.

Marnhull   *Marnhulle* 1267, *Marenhull* 1274, *Marenil* 1291, *Marnell* 1426. The second element is Old English *hyll* 'hill', but the first element is uncertain. It may be an Old English personal name *Mearna*, or an Old English noun *mearn* referring to the soft stone or marl found here.

Marshalsea (in Marshwood)   *Maskylsay* 1448, *Marshalshay* 1637. 'Enclosure belonging to a family called *Maskell* or *Marshal*', from Old English *haeg*.

Marsh Farm (in Bloxworth)   *Mersch* 1327, *Mershe* 1332, *Marsh* 1661. Self-explanatory, from Old English *mersc* 'marsh'.

Marsh Farm (in Ibberton)   *le Merche* 1327, *Marsh* 1672. Identical in origin with the previous name.

Marsh Farm (in Stalbridge) *the Mersch* 1327. Identical in origin with the previous names.

Marshwood *Merswude* 1188, *Merswde* 1201, *Mershwod* 1288, *Marshwode* 1358. 'Wood by a marsh', from Old English *mersc* and *wudu*. This place gives its name to Marshwood Vale, first recorded in the 14th century (*Merswodeuaal* 1319), from Middle English *vale* 'a wide valley'.

Martinstown see Winterborne St Martin.

Matravers (in Loders) at first this place was called simply *Lodre* in 1086 (Domesday Book), then *Lodres Luttone* as in 1285, later *Lodres Mautravers* as in 1356. For the meaning of the original name, see under Loders. The earlier addition *Luttone* is from Litton Cheney, with which there must have been some manorial connection. The later addition *Mautravers* is from the family of this name, here from the 14th century.

Matterley Cottages (in Woodlands) *mapoldor lea* 1033 (in a 12th century copy of an Anglo-Saxon charter), *Materlie* 1551. 'Maple-tree wood or clearing', from Old English *mapuldor* and *lēah*.

Maumbury (in Dorchester) *Memburi* 1333, *Mambury*, *Maumbiry* 1382, *Malmebury* 1553. The second element is Old English *burh*, here in the sense 'pre-English earthwork' since Maumbury is a 'henge monument' of Neolithic date which later served as a Roman amphitheatre. The first element is possibly Old English *mealm* 'sandy or chalky soil', but it could alternatively be Old English *māene* 'common' or Celtic *main* 'a rock or stone'.

Meerhay (in Beaminster) *Merehey* 1516, *Meerehaie* 1629. 'Enclosure by a pool', from Old English *mere* and *haeg*.

Melbury Abbas *Meleburge* 956 (in a later copy of an Anglo-Saxon charter), *Meleberie* 1086 (Domesday Book), *Melbury Abbatisse* 1291, *Mellebury Abbatisse* 1428. Probably 'multi-coloured fortified place', from Old English *māele* and *burh*. The addition is a reduced form of Latin *abbatissa* 'abbess', since this manor, like Compton Abbas, belonged to Shaftesbury abbey from 956. The group of Melbury names in the west of the county have the same origin as this name.

Melbury Bubb *Meleberie* 1086 (Domesday Book), *Melebir Bubbe* 1244, *Bubbe Melebur* 1284, *Maleburi Bobbe* 1290. One of a group of names in the west of the county identical in origin with Melbury Abbas. The manorial addition distinguishing this place from the neighbouring parishes of Melbury Osmond and Melbury Sampford, is from the *Bubbe* family, here from the early 13th century.

Melbury Osmond *Melesberie* 1086 (Domesday Book), *Meleberi Willelmi filii Osmundi* 1202, *Melebur Osmund* 1283, *Melbury Osmond* 1316. See Melbury Bubb. The addition is manorial, from the 'William son of Osmund' who presumably held this manor in or before 1202. The dedication of the church here to St Osmond must have come later.

Melbury Sampford *Meleberie* 1086 (Domesday Book), *Melebury Saunford* 1312, *Melbury Sandford* 1361, *Melbury Samford* 1386. See Melbury Bubb. The addition is manorial, from the *Saunford* family here from the late 13th century. In medieval times this place was often alternatively called *Melbury Turberville*, from the family of that name.

Melcombe Bingham see Bingham's Melcombe.

Melcombe Horsey *Melecumb* 1205, *Mellecumbe* 1244, *Milecumb* 1268, *Melcombe Horsey* 1535. Probably 'milk valley', i.e. 'valley where milk was produced, fertile valley', from Old English *meoluc* and *cumb*. The manorial addition is from the *Horsey* family, here in the 16th century. In medieval times this place was often called *Upmelcombe* or *Overmelcombe*, from Old English *upp* 'upper' and *uferra* 'higher', to distinguish it from Bingham's Melcombe.

Melcombe Regis *Melecumb* 1223, *Melecomb* 1268, *Melcoumb* 1280, *Melcoumbe Regis* 1336. Identical in origin with Melcombe Horsey. Melcombe was anciently royal demesne, hence Latin *regis* 'of the king'.

Melplash (in Netherbury) *Melpleys* 1155, *Meleplays* 1288, *Melepleisch* 1312, *Meleplash* 1337. Probably 'multicoloured pool', from Old English *mǣle* and *plaesc*.

Merritown (in Hurn) *Merrytown alias Funk Town* 1682, earlier *Fonketon* in the 14th century. *Merrytown* may be ironical (from Old English *myrge* 'pleasant'), since *Fonketon* may have as its first element Middle English *fonke* 'a spark (of fire)', perhaps alluding to a smithy.

Merry Field Hill (in Colehill) *Meriefelde* 1595. 'Pleasant field' or 'field where merry-making took place', from Old English *myrge* and *feld*.

Middlebere Farm and Heath (in Arne) *Middlebere* 1291, *Middelbere* 1376, *Middelbeare* 1468. 'Middle wood or woodland pasture', from Old English *middel* and *bearu* or *bǣr*.

Middlemarsh (in Minterne Magna) *Middelmersh* 1227, *Middelmers* 1244, *Midelmersh* 1318. Self-explanatory, from Old English *middel* and *mersc*.

Milborne St Andrew *Muleburne* 934 (in a later copy of an Anglo-Saxon charter), *Meleburne* 1086 (Domesday Book), *Muleburne St Andrew* 1294, *Milborne Seint Andrewe* 1391. Named from the stream on which it stands, 'mill stream', from Old English *myln* and *burna*. The addition *St Andrew* is from the dedication of the church to distinguish this place from Milborne Stileham.

Milborne Stileham *Meleburne, Meleborne* 1086 (Domesday Book), *Muleburn* 1258, *Milborn Stylam* 1431. Named from the same stream as Milborne St Andrew. The distinguishing addition Stileham may be a place-name meaning 'enclosure at the stile or steep ascent', from Old English *stigel* and *hamm*. In medieval times this place was alternatively known as *Milborne Bek*, from its possession by the Benedictine abbey of Bec-Hellouin in Normandy.

Mill Down (in Pimperne) *Mulledoune* 1382. Self-explanatory, from Old English *myln* and *dūn*. The mill referred to, called *Whitecliff Mill*, was on the River Stour just south of Nutford Farm.

Milton Abbas *Middeltone* 934 (in a later copy of an Anglo-Saxon charter), *Mideltune* 1086 (Domesday Book), *Middelton Abbatis* 1268, *Middelton Abbas* 1456. 'Middle farm or estate', from Old English *middel* and *tūn*. The addition is Latin *abbas* 'an abbot', with reference to the abbey here.

Milton on Stour (in Gillingham) *Mideltone* 1086 (Domesday Book), *Middelton* 1236, *Milton on Stoure* 1397, *Mylton super Stowre* 1512. Identical in origin with Milton Abbas, 'middle' perhaps alluding to its position between Gillingham and Silton. It is on the River Stour.

Milton, West (in Powerstock) *Mideltone* 1086 (Domesday Book), *Midelton* 1212, *Middelton* 1288, *Mylton* 1303. Identical in origin with Milton Abbas, from which it is distinguished by *West*.

Minchington (in Sixpenny Handley) *Munecheneton* 1307, *Mynchyndon* 1499, *Minchenton* 1500. 'Farm belonging to the nuns', from Old English *myncen* and *tūn*, alluding to the possession of this manor by the Benedictine nunnery of Shaftesbury. In medieval times this place was often known as 'Gussage Minchington' from its proximity to Gussage St Andrew.

Minterne Magna *Minterne* 987 (in a later copy of an Anglo-Saxon charter), *Mynterne* 1268, *Great Mynterne* 1363, *Mynterne Magna* 1596. 'House near the place where mint grows', from Old English *minte* and *aern*. The addition is Latin *magna* 'great' to distinguish this place from Minterne Parva.

Minterne Parva (in Minterne Magna) *Minterne Parva* 1314, *Parva Minterne* 1340. The addition is Latin *parva* 'small' in contrast to Minterne Magna.

Miz Maze (in Leigh) not on record before the 19th century, but from *mizmaze* 'a maze or labyrinth'.

Mogers Leaze (in Clifton Maybank) *Mogers lease* 1563. From Old English *lǣs* 'pasture', with the name of the *Moger* family, here in the 16th century.

Monastery Farm (in East Lulworth) so called because it was originally built in 1795 as a monastery for some refugee Trappist monks.

Monkton Up Wimborne (in Wimborne St Giles) *Winburne* 1086 (Domesday Book), *Vpwimburn Abbatis* 1268,

Wymborne Monkton 1504, *Mounckton Up Wimborne* 1617. For the significance of *Up* and *Wimborne*, see Wimborne St Giles. *Monkton* means 'estate of the monks' from Old English *munuc* and *tūn*, an allusion to the possession of this manor by the abbey of Tewkesbury (the alternative *Abbatis* is Latin for 'of the abbot').

Monkton Wyld   see Wyld Farms (in Wootton Fitzpaine).

Monkwood (in Marshwood)   *Munkewode* 1244, *Monekwode* 1317, *Monkwode* 1399. Identical in origin with the next name.

Monkwood Hill Farm (in Piddletrenthide)   *Munkewode* 1244, *Monekwode* 1327, *Monkwode* 1332. 'Wood belonging to the monks', from Old English *munuc* and *wudu*, probably with reference to the monks of Glastonbury Abbey.

Monmouth's Ash (in Woodlands)   in a field called *Monmouths Field* in 1840, named from the Duke of Monmouth, illegitimate son of Charles II, who was captured hiding in an ash-tree here (no longer standing) after his defeat at the battle of Sedgemoor in 1685.

Moorbath (in Symondsbury)   *Mordaat* 1086 (Domesday Book), *Morba* 1200, *Morbath* 1244, *Mourebathe* 1409. 'Bathing-place in marshy ground', from Old English *mōr* and *baeth*. Morebath in Devon is identical in origin.

Moor Court Farm, Moorside (in Marnhull)   *Mora* 13th century, *la More* early 14th century, *More* 1412, *Moorecorte alias Mooreside* 1597. Old English *mōr* 'moor, marshy ground', with the later addition of *court* 'large house' and *sīde* 'side'.

Moorcourt Farm (in Sturminster Marshall)   *Moreis* 1204, *Moors Court* 1346, *Morescourte* 1469, *Moorecourte* 1626. An early manorial name, meaning 'the manor-house of a family called *More*', from Middle English *court*.

Moor Crichel   see Crichel.

Moordown (in Bournemouth)   *Mourdon* late 13th century, *Mourden* 1300, *Moredown* 1759. Probably identical in origin with Morden.

Moors River   a recent name for the river, from East and West Moors.

Morden *Mordune, Mordone* 1086 (Domesday Book), *Morden* 1196, *Mourdone* 1340. 'Hill in marshy ground', from Old English *mōr* and *dūn*. The two manors of East and West Morden are recorded early, *Estmorden* from 1250, *Westmorden* fom 1275.

Morcombelake (in Whitchurch Canonicorum) *Morecomblake* 1558. 'Stream in the marshy valley', from Old English *mōr, cumb* and *lacu*.

Moreton *Mortune* 1086 (Domesday Book), *Moreton* 1195, *Mourton* 1332, *Mowreton* 1414. 'Marshland farm', from Old English *mōr* and *tūn*.

Mosterton *Mortestorne* 1086 (Domesday Book), *Mortesthorn* 1209, *Mostreton* 1354, *Musterton* 1431. 'Thorn-tree belonging to a man called Mort', from Old English *thorn* and an Old English personal name.

Motcombe *Motcumbe, Motecumb* 1244, *Mottecumbe* 1288, *Modecumbe* 1371. 'Valley where meetings are held', from Old English *mōt* and *cumb*. This may well have been the meeting-place of the old medieval hundred of Gillingham.

Mount Ararat (in Verwood) probably a recent name, although this remote hill in Boveridge Heath is named after the mountain on which Noah's ark is said to have rested!

Muckleford (in Bradford Peverell) *Mukelford* 1244, *Mukleford, Mokeleford* 1268, *Muckleford* 1635. 'Ford belonging to a man called Mucela', from Old English *ford* and an Old English personal name. The ford was across the River Frome.

Mude, River a late back-formation from Mudeford.

Mudeford (in Christchurch) *Modeford* 13th century, *Muddiford* 1826. Probably 'muddy ford', from Middle English *mode, mudde* 'mud' and *ford*. The river-name Mude is a back-formation from this name.

Mupe Bay and Rocks (in West Lulworth) *Mewup hill* 1753, *Muop's Bay* 1774. Perhaps 'small bay frequented by seagulls', from Old English *māew* and *hōp*.

Muscliff (in Bournemouth) *Museclive* 1242, *Museclyve*

1314, *Moseclyve* 1317. 'Cliff or slope frequented by mice', from Old English *mūs* and *clif*.

Muston Farm (in Piddlehinton) *Mostereston* 1270, *Mustreston* 1412, *Muserton* 1539. 'Farm or estate belonging to the *de Musters* family', like Winterborne Muston, from Old English *tūn*.

Mythe Hill (in Mapperton) *Methe* 1423, *Meath* 1589. From Old English *mȳthe* 'a confluence of rivers'.

Nash Court (in Marnhull) *Esse* 1303, *Asshe* 1347, *Aysshcourt* 1482, *Naishe* 16th century, *Nasshe Court* 1564. '(Place at) the ash-tree', from Old English *aesc*, with the later addition of *court* 'large house'. The initial *N-* is all that remains of Middle English *atten* 'at the'.

Nash Farm (in Marshwood) *Nayssh* 1351, *Nash* 1590. This was no doubt the home of Roger *Attenasshe* 1319, that is 'Roger living at the ash-tree'. This name is thus identical in origin with Nash Court.

Netherbury *Niderberie* 1086 (Domesday Book), *Nutherbir* 1226, *Nitherbury* 1285, *Netherbury* 1288. 'Lower fortified place', from Old English *neotherra* and *burh*.

Netherhay (in Broadwindsor) *Netherhey* 1244, *Nethereheye* 1252, *Nitherhegh* 1355, *Nethirhay* 1496. 'Lower enclosure', from Old English *neotherra* and *haeg*. Named in contrast to a place in the same parish now lost called *Uphay*, from Old English *upp* 'higher up'.

Netherstoke (in Halstock) *Nitherstoc* 1145, *Netherestok* 1208, *Nitherstok* 1244. 'Lower outlying farmstead', from Old English *neotherra* and *stoc*, 'lower' in relation to Halstock.

Nettlecombe (in Powerstock) *Netelcome* 1086 (Domesday Book), *Netlecumb* 1206, *Nettelcumbe* 1244, *Netylcombe* 1421. 'Valley where nettles grow', from Old English *netel* and *cumb*.

New Cross Gate (in Shillingstone) not recorded before the 19th century, with *cross* in the sense 'cross-roads'.

Newland (in Glanvilles Wootton) *Newelond* 1396, *Neulonde* 1409, *Newlond* 1439. 'Newly cleared land, land newly brought into cultivation', from Old English *nīwe* and *land*.

Newlands Farm (in Batcombe) *Neulond* 1274, *Nywelond* 1327, *Nulond* 1428. Identical in origin with the previous name.

New Mills Heath (in Corfe Castle) *Neumulle* 1334, *le Nuwemulle, Newemylles* 1586. 'The new mill(s)', from Old English *nīwe* and *myln*. The Corfe River is nearby, but there is no mill now.

Newnham Farms (in Broadwindsor) *Newenham* 1227, *Niweham* 1244, *Neweham* 1252, *Nywenham* 1316. 'New enclosure', from Old English *nīwe* and *hamm*.

Newton (in Sturminster Newton) see Sturminster Newton.

Newton (in Studland) *Nyweton* 1404, *Newton* 1575. 'New farm or village', from Old English *nīwe* and *tūn*. In 1286 there was an ambitious proposal to start a 'new town' here, but it was probably never more than a tiny hamlet.

Newton Farm (in Hilton) *Niwton, Newton* 1400. Identical in origin with the previous name.

Newton Farm (in Lytchett Minster) *Niweton* 1332, *Newton* 1420, *Newtown* 1811. Identical in origin with the previous names.

Newton Peveril (in Sturminster Marshall) *Neuton* 1260, *Neweton Peverel* 1306, *Neuton by Stouremynstre Marchall* 1375, *Newton Peverell* 1583. Identical in origin with the previous names. The addition is manorial, from the *Peverel* family, here in the 13th century; the same family gave its name to Bradford Peverell.

New Town (in Witchampton) the site of a new village built in the late 18th century to rehouse the displaced inhabitants of Moor Crichel.

Norden Farm and Heath (in Corfe Castle) *Northdon* 1291, *Nordone* 1381. 'North hill or down', from Old English *north* and *dūn*.

Normandy Farm (in Winterborne Stickland) perhaps commemorating the possession of one of the manors here at the time of Domesday Book (1086) by the Norman abbey of

Coutances, but probably only a name of recent origin.

Norris Mill (in Puddletown)   first recorded in 1625, named from a family called *Norris*.

Northbourne (in Bournemouth)   a recent name for a modern district of the town, contrasted with Southbourne and Westbourne.

Northbrook (in Puddletown)   *Bynorthebrouk* 14th century, *Northebrook* 1580. '(Place) to the north of the brook', from Old English *northan* and *brōc*.

North Haven Point (in Poole)   *Northavensford* 1341, *le Northauen forde* 1364, *Northe Havyn Poynt* 1539. From Old English *haefen* 'harbour', with *ford* and *point*; it is opposite South Haven Point in Studland, at the entrance to Poole Harbour. It is clear from the early spellings that there was once a ford here where there is now a ferry.

North Hayes Farm (in Motcombe)   *le Northhey* 1317, *Northayes* 1501, *Northehaies* 1609. 'Northern enclosures', from Old English *north* and *haeg*.

Northport (in Wareham)   *Northeport* 1370, *Northport* 1381. Probably '(place) to the north of the town', from Old English *northan* and *port*.

Northwood Farm (in Manston)   *Northwode* 1332, *North Wood* 1667. Self-explanatory, from Old English *north* and *wudu*, from its situation at the northern end of the parish.

Nothe, The (in Weymouth)   *Waymouthe Northe* 1604. From Old English *hnoth* 'knoll, hill', as in White Nothe which is also a coastal promontory.

Nottington (in Broadwey)   *Notinton* 1212, *Notington* 1234. 'Farm called Hnotta', OE *-ingtūn* and personal name.

Notton (in Maiden Newton)   *Natton* 1350, *Neton* 1370, *Notton* 1527. 'Cattle farm', from Old English *nēat* and *tūn*.

Nutford Farm (in Pimperne)   *Nortforde* 1086 (Domesday Book), *Nutford* 1189, *Nutteford* 1228, *Notforde* 1338. 'Ford where nuts grow', from Old English *hnutu* and *ford*; the ford is over the River Stour. In medieval times it was sometimes known as *Blakenotford*, from Old English *blaec* 'black, dark', probably to distinguish this place from the adjacent *Notford-locky*, now France Farm, in Stourpaine.

Nyland (in Kington Magna)   *Iland* 1086 (Domesday Book), *Liland* 1212, *la Ilond* 1380, *Nilonde* 1581. 'The island', i.e. 'the dry ground in a marsh', from Old English *īeg-land*. The earlier initial *L-* is from the French definite article *le* or *la*, the later initial *N-* is all that remains of Middle English *atten* '(place) at the'.

Oakers Wood (in Affpuddle)   *Wolgariswode* 1465, *Aulgers Wood* 1694, *Okerswood* 1795. 'Wood belonging to a man called Wulfgār', from Old English *wudu* and an Old English personal name.

Oakford Farm (in Marshwood)   *Okford* 1268, *Okeford* 1399. 'Ford by the oak-tree', from Old English *āc* and *ford*.

Oakley (in Canford Magna)   *Ocle* 1327, *Ocley* 1463, *Okleye* 1360. 'Oak-tree wood or clearing', from Old English *āc* and *lēah*.

Oakley Down and Farm (in Wimborne St Giles);   *ac lee* 956 (in a 14th century copy of an Anglo-Saxon charter), *Ockeleghe* 1280, *Ocleye* 1288, *Okeley* 1618. Identical in origin with the previous name.

Oborne   *Womburnan* 975 (in a later copy of an Anglo-Saxon charter), *Wocburne* 1086 (Domesday Book), *Woburn* 1212, *Oburne* 1479. '(Place at) the crooked or winding stream', from Old English *wōh* and *burna*.

Ogden Down Farm (in Gussage St Michael)   *Hocken Down* 1842. 'Down where young sheep are pastured', from a dialectal plural form of *hogg*.

Okeford, Child   *Acford* 1086 (Domesday Book), *Childacford* 1227, *Childocford* 1236, *Childehokeford* 1262. 'Oak-tree ford', from Old English *āc* and *ford*, one of a group of three parishes which share this name, the others being Okeford Fitzpaine and Shillingstone (earlier called *Okeford Shillyng*). The addition is Old English *cild* 'son of a royal or noble family', though the particular reference is obscure.

Okeford Fitzpaine   *Acford* 939–46, *Adford* (for *Ac-*) 1086

(Domesday Book), *Acford* 1236, *Ocford Fitz Payn* 1321, *Acford filii Pagani* 1340. See Child Okeford. The manorial addition is from the family of *Fitz Payn* ('son of Payn', Latinized as *filius Pagani*), here from the 13th century, see Wootton Fitzpaine. In early medieval times the manor was sometimes known as *Acford Alvredi* or *Aufrey* because in the 12th century it belonged to the great landowner Alvred or Aufrey de Lincoln.

Old Harry (in Studland)   a sea-stack of chalk first recorded with this name in the 18th century, *old harry* being a familiar name for the devil. A second sea-stack called Old Harry's Wife collapsed in 1896.

Old Lawn Farm (in Pamphill)   recorded as *Old Land* in the 16th and 19th centuries from Old English *eald* 'old' (here in the sense 'long used', or 'formerly used') and *land* 'tract of land, arable land'.

Orchard, East and West (parishes)   *Archet* 939 (in a later copy of an Anglo-Saxon charter), *Orchet* 1330, *West Orchard* 1427, *Estorchard* 1575. This is an old Celtic name containing Celtic *cēd* 'wood' (= Welsh *coed*), with *ar* 'beside, facing', and meaning '(place) beside the wood'.

Orchard, East and West (in Church Knowle)   *Horcerd* 1086 (Domesday Book), *Orcharde* 1291, *Est Orchard, West Orchard* 1399. 'The orchard or garden', from Old English *orceard*. The orchard here is actually mentioned in Domesday Book.

Organ Ford (in Lytchett Minster)   *Argent* 1194, *Argente* 1196, *Organforde* 1593, *Orgayne alias Organt* 1600. Probably a name of French origin transferred from the place called Argent in the French département of Cher; a 12th century owner of this Dorset estate may have originated from the French place and given it the same name.

Osehill Green (in Glanvilles Wootton)   *Oswaldeshulle* 1270, *Osweldeshulle* 1315, *Ouseleshull* 1405, *Ossedshill* 1617. 'Hill belonging to a man called Ōsweald', from Old English *hyll* and an Old English personal name.

Osmington   *Osmyntone, Osmingtone* 934 (in later copies of

116

Anglo-Saxon charters), *Osmentone* 1086 (Domesday Book), *Osmyngtone* 1291. Probably 'farm called after a man named Ōsmund', from Old English *-ingtūn* and personal name.

Overcombe (in Preston)   from *uferra* 'higher' and *cumb*.

Ower (in Corfe Castle)   *Ore* 934 (in a later copy of an Anglo-Saxon charter), *Oure* 1316, *Owre* 1512. '(Place at) the bank or shore', from Old English *ōra*. This place on the shore of Poole Harbour was at one time a quay for the shipping of stone.

Owermoigne   *Ogre* 1086 (Domesday Book), *Our* 1219, *Ore* 1288, *Oure Moyngne* 1314, *Ovre Moigne* 1375. Probably 'the wind-gap(s)' from a Celtic *ogrodrust-*, referring to gaps in the chalk hills funnelling winds off the sea. Second part is manorial, for the manor was held by the family of *Moigne* from the beginning of the 13th century. The same family gave name to Shipton Moyne in Gloucestershire.

Pallington (in Affpuddle)   *Palliton, Palinton* 1244, *Palyngton* 1316, *Pallington* 1589. 'Farm called after a man named Paelli', from Old English *-ingtūn* and an Old English personal name.

Pamphill   *Pamphilla* 1168, *Pemphull* 1323, *Peympehull* 1332, *Pymphill* 1496. The second element is clearly Old English *hyll* 'hill', but the first is difficult. It may be an Old English word *pamp* or *pempe* meaning 'hill', or an Old English personal name *Pampa* or *Pempa*.

Park Farm (in Gillingham)   named from a medieval deer park within the royal forest of Gillingham; both park and forest are mentioned as early as the 13th century.

Park Farm (in Marshwood)   *la Parroc* 13th century, *Parrok* 1412. From Old English *pearroc* 'a small enclosure, a paddock'.

Parkstone (in Poole)   *Parkeston* 1326, *Parkestone* 1494, *Parkyston* 1529, *Parkson* 1774. 'The park stone', probably with reference to a stone marking the boundary of a medieval deer park, from Middle English *park* and Old English *stān*.

Parley, East (in Hurn)   *Estperle, Est Purle* 1280. Sharing its origin with the following name, with Old English *ēast* to distinguish it.

Parley, West *Perlai* 1086 (Domesday Book), *Parlea* 1194, *Westperele* 1305, *West Perleygh* 1431. 'Wood where pear-trees grow', from Old English *peru* and *lēah*, with *west* to distinguish it from East Parley.

Parnham (in Beaminster) *Perham* 1228, *Perhamme* 1413, *Parnham* 1431, *Parham* 1436. 'Enclosure where pear-trees grow', from Old English *peru* and *hamm*.

Parrett, River see Perrott.

Paynthouse Farm (in Cann) not recorded before the 19th century, but probably from the word *penthouse* 'an outhouse or shed with sloping roof'.

Peacemarsh (in Gillingham) *Pesemershe* 1535, *Peasemarsh* 1628, *Peace Marsh* 1811. 'Marshy land where peas are grown', from Old English *pise* and *mersc*.

Pegg's Farm (in Iwerne Minster) *Pegges* 1346, *Pegges Farme* 1664. Named from the family of John and Robert *le Peg* who had lands here in 1317.

Penbury Knoll (in Pentridge) only recorded from the 18th century, the name for the summit of Pentridge Hill. It is from the Celtic *penn* 'hill' (see Pentridge), Old English *burh* 'fortified place' (with reference to the hill-fort here) and Old English *cnoll* 'hill-top'.

Pen Hill (in Sutton Waldron) earlier called *Seaxpenn* 932 (in a later copy of an Anglo-Saxon charter), meaning 'hill of the Saxons', from Old English *Seaxe* and Celtic *penn*. The hill may have marked an ancient Saxon boundary. It was also an old hundred meeting place, giving its name *Sexpene* to a Domesday Book hundred that was later combined with Handley hundred to form the hundred of Sixpenny Handley. 'Sixpenny', from *Sexpene* through folk etymology, is now found as the name of nearby Sixpenny Farm in Fontmell Magna as well as in the name of Sixpenny Handley parish.

Penn (in Wootton Fitzpaine) *la Penne* 1244, *Penne* 1577.

From Celtic *penn* 'hill' or Old English *penn* 'pen, enclosure for animals'.

Pentridge *Pentric* 762 (in a 13th century copy of an Anglo-Saxon charter), *Pentric* 1086 (Domesday Book), *Pencriz* 1187, *Pentrich* 1264. A very old name of Celtic origin, probably 'the hill of the boar', from Celtic *penn* and *tyrch*. The hill referred to is Pentridge Hill which rises to 600 feet.

Perrott, South *Pedret* 1086 (Domesday Book), *Suthperet* 1268, *Suthperette* 1275, *Southperot* 1424. Named from the River Parrett, a Celtic name, 'four fords'. *South* to distinguish this place from North Perrott in Somerset.

Perry Copse and Farm (in Alderholt) *Purie* 1324, *La Purye* 1404, *Perrye* 17th century. 'The pear-tree', from Old English *pyrige*.

Petersham Farm (in Holt) *Pitrichesham, Petrishesham* 1086 (Domesday Book), *Piterichesham* 1263, *Petrisham* 1398. 'Homestead or enclosure belonging to a man called Peohtrīc', from Old English *hām* or *hamm* and a personal name.

Peveril Point (in Swanage) from 1539, the surname *Peverel*.

Philliols Farm (in Bere Regis) *Pillols* 1617, *Filloles* 1646, *Filiols* 1774. Named from the *Filiol* family, which had lands in this area from the 14th century.

Picket Farm (in South Perrott) *Pikyate* 1236, *Pikiete* 1285, *Pykeyate* 1399, *Pikat* 1425. 'Gate or pass by a pointed hill', from Old English *pīc* and *geat*.

Piddle, River a river-name of Old English origin, from *pidele* 'a marsh, a fen'. It is recorded from the 10th century and gives its name to Piddletrenthide, Piddlehinton, Puddletown, Tolpuddle, Affpuddle and Turners Puddle. The discrepancy between Piddle- and Puddle- in these names reflects alternative spellings for the river-name even in very early times, and one is not really more 'correct' than the other, but for local sensitivity on the matter, see Puddletown. The River Piddle is sometimes called Trent, but this only dates from the 16th century, and probably arose through a misunderstanding of the name Piddletrenthide.

Piddlehinton   *Pidele* 1086 (Domesday Book), *Hinepidel, Pidel Hineton* 1244, *Pudele Hynton* 1368. 'Estate on the River Piddle belonging to a religious community', from Old English *hīwan* and *tūn*. Piddlehinton belonged to the French abbey of Marmoutier in the late 11th century.

Piddles Wood (in Sturminster Newton)   *Puttekwurth* 1244, *Putteleswurthe* 13th century, *Puttelesworthe* 1337, *Pittelesworth* 1340. Probably 'enclosure belonging to a man called Pyttel', from Old English *worth* and an Old English personal name, but the first element may alternatively be the Old English noun *pyttel* 'a hawk, a mousehawk' (surviving in Dorset dialect as *dun-piddle*), replaced by Old English *puttoc* 'a kite' in the first spelling.

Piddletrenthide   *Uppidelen* 966 (in a later copy of an Anglo-Saxon charter), *Pidrie* 1086 (Domesday Book), *Pidele Trentehydes* 1212, *Pydle Trenthide* 1288. 'Estate on the River Piddle assessed at thirty hides' (its assessment in Domesday Book), from French *trente* 'thirty' and Old English *hīd* 'a hide of land', and with Old English *upp* 'higher up' in the earliest spelling. In medieval times it was sometimes referred to as *Pidelthirtihide* using the English word for the number.

Pilford (in Colehill)   *Pilforde* 1583. Probably 'ford marked by a stake', from Old English *pīl* and *ford*, but alternatively the first element may be Old English *pyll* 'a pool in a river, a small stream'.

Pilsdon   *Pilesdone* 1086 (Domesday Book), *Pillesdun* 1168, *Pilesdon* 1196, *Pillisdon* 1236. Probably 'hill with a peak', or 'hill marked by a stake', from Old English *pīl* and *dūn*. The reference is to Pilsdon Pen, the highest hill in Dorset (908 feet above sea level), Pen representing the old Celtic word *penn* 'a hill'.

Pimperne   *Pimpern* 935 (in a 15th century copy of an Anglo-Saxon charter), *Pinpre* 1086 (Domesday Book), *Pimpre* 1179, *Pymperne* 1285. This is a difficult name. It may be an old Celtic name meaning 'five trees' from *pimp* 'five' and *prenn* 'tree', or it may be of Old English origin, with a meaning 'place among hills', from a derivative of a word *pimp* 'hill'.

Pinford (in Castleton) *Pinefort* 1160, *Pinford* 1264, *Pyneford* 1285. From Old English *ford* 'a ford'. The first element may be Old English *pīn* 'pine-tree', *pinn* 'pin or peg', or an Old English personal name *Pinna*.

Pipsford Farm (in Corscombe) *Pippeseia* 1197, *Pipesie* 1203, *Pippesye* 1337, *Pipsford* 1802. 'Well-watered land belonging to a man called Pipp', from Old English *ēg* and an Old English personal name. The change of the second element to -*ford* seems to be quite recent.

Pistle Down (in Edmondsham) not recorded before the 19th century, possibly from *epistle* with reference to a reading from the scriptures during the beating of the bounds, since this place is in the extreme east corner of the parish.

Pithouse Farm (near Hurn) *Pyttehouse* 1544. Self-explanatory, from Old English *pytt* and *hūs*.

Pitt Farm (in Whitchurch Canonicorum) *la Putte* 1240, *la Pitte* 1244, *Pytte* 1318. From Old English *pytt* 'a pit or hollow'.

Plumber Manor (in Lydlinch) *Plumbere* 1086 (Domesday Book), *Plumber* 1243, *Plomber* 1303, *Plumbeare* 1412. 'Wood where plum-trees grow', from Old English *plūme* and *bearu*.

Plush (in Piddletrenthide) *Plyssch, Plissh* 891 (in a later copy of an Anglo-Saxon charter), *Plys* 1268, *Plysse* 1288, *Plussh* 1412. From Old English *plysc* 'a pool'.

Pokesdown (in Bournemouth) *Pokesdoune* 1300, *Pokesdon* 1333, *Pokesdowne* 1540. Probably 'hill or down haunted by a puck or goblin', from Old English *pūca* and *dūn*. However, if the name is a very old one, the first element could be the Old English personal name *Poc* suggested for Poxwell.

Poole *Pole* 1183, *la Pole* 1220, *la Poule* 1347, *Poole* 1392. 'The pool or creek', from Old English *pōl*, with reference to Poole Harbour.

Poorton, North and South *Powrtone, Pourtone* 1086 (Domesday Book), *Northportun, Suthporton* 1288. From Old

English *tūn* 'farm, estate' with an obscure first element which may be an old river-name, see Powerstock.

Portesham *Porteshamme* 1024 (Anglo-Saxon charter), *Portesham* 1086 (Domesday Book), *Portsham* 1653. 'Enclosure belonging to the port or town', from Old English *port* and *hamm*, the town referred to probably being Abbotsbury.

Portland, Isle of *Port* 9th century (Anglo-Saxon Chronicle), *Portlande* 862 (in a 14th century copy of an Anglo-Saxon charter), *Portlaund* 1244, *Portlond* 1280. 'Land or estate attached to *Port* ('the harbour')', from Old English *port* and *land*. The Bill of Portland, referring to the tapering southern promontory of the island, is mentioned from 1649 and is from Old English *bile* 'a bill, a beak'.

Poterne Farm (in Verwood) *Poterne* 1280, *Poternne* 1340, *Wymbourne Poterne* 1384, *Wymborne Poterne* 1430. 'Building where pots are made, a pottery', from Old English *pott* and *aern*. The addition *Wimborne-*, found up to the 19th century, is from the association of this manor with Monkton Up Wimborne.

Poundbury Camp (in Dorchester) *Ponebury* 1333, *Pumrie* 1590, *Pumberry* 1650. Probably 'pre-English earthwork associated with a man called Pūna', from Old English *burh* and an Old English personal name. Poundbury is an Iron Age hill-fort.

Povington (in Tyneham) *Povintone* 1086 (Domesday Book), *Povincton* 1205, *Povington* 1285. Probably 'farm called after a man named Pēofa', from Old English *-ingtūn* and an Old English personal name.

Powerstock *Povrestoch* 1086 (Domesday Book), *Pourstoke* 1195, *Porestoc* 1217, *Porstok* 1224. The second element is Old English *stoc* 'place, secondary settlement, outlying farmstead'. However the first element, which this name shares with North and South Poorton, is obscure, although it may be an old river-name.

Poxwell *Poceswylle* 987 (in a 13th century copy of an Anglo-Saxon charter), *Pocheswelle* 1086 (Domesday Book),

Pokeswell 1285, *Poxwell* 1535. There are two possible meanings. It could mean 'the steeply rising ground belonging to a man called Poca', from Old English *swelle* and a personal name, or 'the spring of a man called Poc', from Old English *wella* and a different personal name.

Poyntington *Ponditone* 1086 (Domesday Book), *Puntintuna* 1122, *Puntinton* 1206, *Pointyngton* 1440. 'Farm or estate called after a man named Punt', from Old English *-ingtūn* and an Old English personal name.

Preston (parish) *Prestun* 1228, *Prestone* 1285, *Preston* 1291. 'Priest farm', from Old English *prēost* and *tūn*. It was an old prebend of Salisbury cathedral.

Preston Farm (in Tarrant Rushton) *Prestetune* 1086 (Domesday Book), *Presteton* 1268, *Preston Tarente* 1280, *Tarente Preston* 1318. 'The farm belonging to the priests on the River Tarrant', from Old English *prēost* and *tūn*.

Preston Hill and House (in Iwerne Minster) *Prestone* early 12th century, *Preston* 1332. 'Priest farm', from Old English *prēost* and *tūn*.

Puckstone (in Studland) not on record before the 18th century, but the meaning is 'goblin's stone', from Old English *pūca* and *stān*.

Puddletown *Pitretone* 1086 (Domesday Book), *Pideleton* 1212, *Pudeleton* 1280, *Pudultoune* 1349. 'Farm on the River Piddle', from Old English *tūn*. The name was the subject of local controversy in 1956, when Dorset County Council sought to change it to Piddletown. Fierce local protest against the change, mainly on the grounds of the expense involved but also because Puddletown sounded 'nicer', eventually won the day!

Pulham *Poleham* 1086 (Domesday Book), *Puleham* 1130, *Pullam* 1212, *Pulham* 1244. 'Homestead or enclosure by the pools or streams', from Old English *pull* or *pōl* with either *hām* or *hamm*.

Pulston Barn (in Charminster) *Cerna Pulli* 1166, *Pulleinston* 1236, *Puleyneston* 1244, *Pollyston* 1546. 'Manor or estate of the

Pulein family', from Old English *tūn*. This family was here from the middle of the 12th century. Pulston is one of the several manors called *Cerne* or *Cernel* in Domesday Book (from its situation on the River Cerne).

Puncknowle *Pomacanole* 1086 (Domesday Book), *Pomecnolle* 1268, *Pomcnolle* 1303, *Pompknolle* 1391. The second element is Old English *cnoll* 'a hill-top, a hillock'. The first is either Old English *plūme* 'a plum-tree' (with early loss of the *l*), or an Anglo-Saxon personal name *Puma*.

Purbeck, Isle of *Purbicinga* 948 (in a later copy of an Anglo-Saxon charter), *Porbi* 1086 (Domesday Book), *Purbik* 1221, *Purbek* 1380. 'Beak-shaped ridge frequented by the bittern or snipe', from Old English *pūr* and *bic*. The name originally referred to the prominent central chalk ridge which crosses the Isle of Purbeck from west to east. In the earliest spelling the name is combined with a form of Old English *-ingas* meaning 'dwellers in'.

Purcombe (in Marshwood) *Piricume* 13th century, *Pirecome* 1310. 'Pear-tree valley', from Old English *pyrige* and *cumb*.

Purcombe Farm (in Whitchurch Canonicorum) *Pirecumbe* 13th century, *Pirycumbe* 1275. Identical in origin with the previous name.

Purewell (in Christchurch) *Perewull* 1300, *Pirewolle* 1327, *Purwell* 1680. 'Spring or stream by the pear-tree', from Old English *peru* and *wella*.

Purse Caundle see Caundle.

Pussex Farm (in Hurn) perhaps to be identified with a place called *Possochulle* recorded at the beginning of the 14th century, from Old English *hyll* 'hill' and (possibly) an Old English personal name *Possuc*.

Putton (in Chickerell) *Podinton* 1237, *Pudington* 1288, *Podington* 1293, *Putton* 1430. 'Farm called after a man named Puda', from Old English *-ingtūn* and an Old English personal name.

Pymore (in Allington) *Pimore* 1236, *Pymore* 1244, *Pymor* 1275, *Pymowre* 1456. 'Marshy ground infested by gnats or other insects', from Old English *pīe* and *mōr*. The place is low-lying by the River Brit.

Quarleston Farm (in Winterborne Stickland) *Winterburn Quarel* 1232, *Quarellyston* 1268, *Quarleston* 1280, *Wynterburne Quareleston* 1288. Originally 'estate on the River Winterborne held by the *Quarel* family', here in the 13th and 14th centuries, with Old English *tūn* 'manor, estate'.

Queen Oak (in Bourton) *Queene Oake Close* 1609. No doubt named from one of the Queens of England who at different dates possessed the manor of Gillingham.

Radipole *Retpole* 1086 (Domesday Book), *Redpole* 1166, *Radepol, Radipol* 1237, *Radipole* 1594. 'Reed pool', from Old English *hrēod* and *pōl*, with reference to Radipole Lake at the north end of which Radipole is situated.

Rampisham *Ramesham* 1086 (Domesday Book), *Rammesham* 1238, *Rammysham* 1288, *Rampsham* 1401. The second element is probably Old English *hamm* 'enclosure, river-meadow'. The first element is probably Old English *ramm* 'a ram' or a personal name *Ram*, but Old English *hramsa* 'wild garlic' is also possible.

Ranston (in Iwerne Courtney) *Iwerne* 1086 (Domesday Book), *Iwerne Randelleston* 1257, *Randolveston* 1274, *Randolston* 1362. At first named from the River Iwerne, but then 'Randulf's manor or estate', from Old English *tūn* and a Norman French personal name.

Rawlsbury Camp (in Hilton) *Raulesbury* 1400. Perhaps 'Radulf's fortification', from Old English *burh* and a Continental Germanic personal name. This is an Iron Age hill-fort.

Redcliff Farm (in Arne) *Radeclive* 1256, *Redclyffe* 1545. '(Place at) the red cliff', from Old English *rēad* and *clif*.

Red Hill (in Bournemouth) self-explanatory, so called from the 18th century.

Rempstone Hall (in Corfe Castle) *Rameston* 1280, *Remston, Rymeston* 1288, *Rempston* 1435. Probably 'farm where wild garlic grows', from Old English *hramsa* and *tūn*.

Renscombe Farm (in Worth Matravers) *Hreminescumbe*

987 (in a later copy of an Anglo-Saxon charter), *Romescumbe* 1086 (Domesday Book), *Remescumb* 1275, *Rennscumbe* 1291. 'Raven's valley', from Old English *hremn* and *cumb*, although alternatively the first element could be the Old English personal name *Hremn*.

Revels Inn Farm (in Buckland Newton) *the land of Rivell* 1264, *Ryvell* 1510. Named from a family called *Ryvel* here in the 13th and 14th centuries.

Rew (Hill and Manor) (in Winterborne St Martin) *La Rewe* 1283, *Rewe* 1528. 'The row (of houses or trees)', from Old English *rāew*.

Ridge (in Arne) *Rygge* 1431, *Rydge* 1632. From Old English *hrycg* 'a ridge or bank, a long narrow hill'.

Ridge (in Hazelbury Bryan) first recorded at the end of the 16th century, identical in origin with the previous name.

Ridge Cliff (in Chideock) named from *La Rhigge* 13th century, *le Rygge* 1469, *Chidiock Rygge* 1495. Identical in origin with the previous names.

Ridge Farm (in Wootton Fitzpaine) *Rugge* 1431. Identical in origin with the previous names.

Ridge Hill (in Buckland Newton) *La Rigge* 14th century. Identical in origin with the previous names.

Ridgeway Hill (in Bincombe) first recorded in 1680, named from the Roman road between Dorchester and Weymouth, from Old English *hrycg* and *weg*.

Ringmoor (in Turnworth) *Hringmere* early 13th century. 'Pool near the circular enclosure', from Old English *hring* (referring to one of the ancient earthworks north of the village) and *mere*. For a similar change of *-mere* to *-moor*, see Ashmore.

Ringstead Bay (in Owermoigne) named from the lost medieval village of Ringstead in Osmington. This was *Ringestede* 1086 (Domesday Book), *Ryngstede* 1276, *Ringsteed* 1634, from Old English *hring* 'ring' and *stede* 'place or site'. The 'ring' was perhaps a stone circle, or a circular enclosure or other feature.

Rockley (in Poole) *Rodeclyve* 1341, *Redecliue* 1364, *Radcliff* 1626, *Rockly* 1774. 'The reedy bank', from Old English *hrēod* and *clif*. The late development of *-cliff* to *-ley* occurs also in Catsley.

Rodden (in Abbotsbury) *Raddun* 1221, *Raddon* 1244, *Roddon* 1420, *Rodden* 1637. 'Red hill or down', from Old English *rēad* and *dūn*. The soil here is a rich red clay.

Rodmore Farm (in Lydlinch) *Rodmor* 1318, *Rodmore* 1424. 'Moor or marshy ground where reeds grow', from Old English *hrēod* and *mōr*.

Rollington (in Corfe Castle) *Ragintone* 1086 (Domesday Book), *Radelinton* 1236, *Redlyngton* 1291, *Rollyngton* 1435. Probably 'farm called after a man named Rǣdel', from Old English *-ingtūn* and an Old English personal name.

Romford (in Edmondsham) *Runford* 1268, *Rungeford* 1308, *Rongford* 1403, *Rumford* 1618. 'Ford marked by a pole', from Old English *hrung* and *ford*. The Cranborne-Ringwood road crosses the River Crane here.

Rushmore Farm (in Cranborne) *Rushmore* 1620. 'Marshy ground where rushes grow', from Old English *rysc* and *mōr*.

Rushton (in East Stoke) *Riston* 1086 (Domesday Book), *Ruston* 1304, *Risshton* 1313, *Rushton* 1318. 'Farm or enclosure where rushes grow', from Old English *rysc* and *tūn*.

Ryall (in Whitchurch Canonicorum) *Rihull* 1240, *Rioll* 1468, *Ryolle* 1478, *Ryalle* 1494. 'Hill where rye is grown', from Old English *ryge* and *hyll*.

Ryme Intrinseca *Rima* 1160, *Ryme* 1229, *Rime* 1244, *Ryme Intrinsica* 1611. From Old English *rima* 'a rim, an edge, a border', with reference to its situation either on the slope of a ridge or near the county boundary. The Latin addition *intrinseca* 'inner, lying within the bounds' distinguished this place from the former manor of Ryme *Ex*trinseca in Long Bredy.

St Alban's or St Aldhelm's Head (in Worth Matravers) *the foreland of Seynt Aldem* 1500, *Sainct Aldelmes Point* 1543, *St Albans Head* 1826. Named from the small Norman chapel, standing on this promontory, dedicated to St Aldhelm, first bishop of Sherborne. It will be noted that the alternative modern form of the name is historically incorrect and dates only from the 19th century.

St Andrew's Farm (in West Lulworth)   *St Andrew* 1284, *Lulleworth St Andrew* 1302, *Seynt Andrewes* 1412. There was once a church here dedicated to St Andrew.

St Catherine's Hill (near Hurn)   near a ford on the River Stour called *Catelineford* in the 14th century, from Old English *ford* and the personal name *Cateline*, an old French form of Catherine. However *Saint* in the modern name is probably a recent addition.

St Ives   *Iuez* 1167, *Yuez* 1187, *Yvetis* 1212, *Ivese* 1248, *Ivettis* 1250. Probably from an Old English word *īfet* 'a clump of ivy, a place overgrown with ivy'. *Saint* was only added in recent times, partly because of the association with St Leonards (which is a genuine saint's name), partly no doubt on the model of the St Ives in Cornwall and Cambridgeshire.

St James (in Shaftesbury)   *parochia Sancti Jacobi* 1297, *the paryshe of Sayncte James* 1566. From the dedication of the church here, *James* usually being written *Jacobus* in Latin documents.

St Leonards   named from a medieval religious house or hospital dedicated to St Leonard and first recorded in 1288 as *domus Sancti Leonardi de Russeton* 'the house of St Leonard at *Russeton*'. The exact whereabouts of *Russeton* ('rush farm' from Old English *rysc* and *tūn*) is not known but it was probably near the River Crane. A chapel called *Sct. Leonarde* is marked on Saxton's map of 1575.

St Leonard's Bridge and Farm (in West Moors)   the bridge is recorded from the 17th century, the farm from the 19th century, both, like St Leonards parish, named from the medieval religious house of St Leonard.

Salterns (in Poole)   *Salterns* 1811. From Old English *salt-aern* 'a building where salt is made or sold'.

Salwayash (in Netherbury)   *Shallways Ash* 1682.

Sandbanks (in Poole)   not recorded before about 1800, and self-explanatory.

Sandford (in Wareham)   *Sanford* 1606, *Sampford* 1671, *Sandford* 1811. 'Sandy ford', from Old English *sand* and *ford*.

Sandford Orcas   *Sanford* 1086 (Domesday Book), *Sandford* 1243, *Sandford Horscoys* 1372, *Samford Orescoys* 1427. Identical in origin with the previous name. The manorial addition is from the family of *Orescuils*, here from the 12th century.

Sandhills (in Holwell)   *Sandhulle* 13th century, *Sandehull* 1353. Self-explanatory, from Old English *sand* and *hyll*.

Sandley (in Gillingham)   *Sandhull* 1292, *Sandehull* 1329, *Saundell* 1501, *Sandley* 1609. 'Sandy hill', from Old English *sand* and *hyll*. The development of *-hill* to *-ley* is due to the lack of stress on the second element.

Sandpit (in Broadwindsor)   *Sandpitte* 1244, *Sampite* 1252, *Sandputte* 1256, *Sandpit* 1268. Self-explanatory, from Old English *sand* and *pytt*.

Sandsfoot Castle (in Weymouth)   *Sandfot castel* 16th century, *the Castell of Sandysfoote* 1553, *Sansfoote Castle* 1646. 'The castle at the foot of the sandy shore', from Old English *sand, fōt* and *castel*.

Sandway (in Bourton)   *Sandweye* 1292. Self-explanatory, from Old English *sand* and *weg*.

Seaborough   *Seveberge* 1086 (Domesday Book), *Seveberugh* 1256, *Seuenbergh* 1306. 'Seven hills or barrows', from Old English *seofon* and *beorg*.

Seacombe Cliff (in Worth Matravers)   *Secombe* 1306. 'Valley opening on to the sea', from Old English *sǣ* and *cumb*.

Seatown (in Chideock)   *Setowne* 1469, *Seeton* 1470, *See towne* 1494, *Zetowne* 1508. 'Farm or estate by the sea', from Old English *sǣ* and *tūn*. The spelling with *Z-* represents a local dialect pronunciation. Seaton in Devon is identical in origin.

Shade House Farm (in Stour Provost)   *Shardehowse* 1570,

Sherdehowse 1577. 'House at a cleft or gap', from Old English *sceard* and *hūs*.

Shaftesbury *Sceaftesburi* 877 (in a later copy of an Anglo-Saxon charter), *Sceftesberie* 1086 (Domesday Book), *Schaftebir* 1200, *Shaftesbyry* 1258. Probably 'fortified place belonging to a man called Sceaft', from Old English *burh* and an Old English personal name. Alternatively the first element may be the Old English noun *sceaft* 'a shaft, a pole', used either of some actual pole or figuratively of the steepsided, prominent hill on which the town stands. In medieval times the place was often referred to as *Shafton*, probably a reduced form of the Latinized *Shaftonia* (the first part of the English name and a Latin ending *-onia*). The pronunciation *Shaston* still in use seems to originate in the misreading of *f* as *s* in old documents.

Shapwick *Scapeuuic* 1086 (Domesday Book), *Sapewic* 1170, *Shepwyk* 1238, *Schapwyk* 1244. 'Sheep farm', from Old English *scēap* and *wīc*.

Shatcombe Farm (in Beaminster) *Shotecumbe* 1306, *Shotecombe, Shatecombe* 1412, *Shotcombe* 1486. 'Valley at a corner or angle of land', from Old English *scēat* and *cumb*. The nearby White Sheet Hill probably contains the same word.

Shatcombe Farm (in Wynford Eagle) *Shapcumbe* 1473. 'Valley where sheep are kept', from Old English *scēap* and *cumb*.

Shave Cross (in Marshwood) *la Sahe* 13th century, *la Schaghe* 1325, *Schaue* 1399, *Shawe* 1456. From Old English *sceaga* 'a small wood, a copse', with the later addition of *cross*.

Shave Hill (in Buckhorn Weston) *Shawe* 1647. From Old English *sceaga* 'a small wood, a copse'.

Sherborne *Scireburnan* 864 (in a later copy of an Anglo-Saxon charter), *Scireburne* 1086 (Domesday Book), *Schireburn* 1193, *Shereburn* 1288. '(Place at) the bright or clear stream', from Old English *scīr* and *burna*.

Sherborne Causeway (in Motcombe) *Sherbourne causeway* 1568, *the Cawsey leadinge to Sherborne Common* 1609. From

Middle English *cauce* 'raised way across marshy ground', this being part of the road from Shaftesbury to Sherborne.

Sherford (in Morden)   *Sireford* 1244, *Shyreford* 1311, *Schyreford* 1408, *Sherford* 1473. 'Bright or clear ford', from Old English *scīr* and *ford*. The site of the original ford was no doubt where the road to Wareham crosses Sherford River at Sherford Bridge.

Shillingstone   *Alford* (an error for *Acford*) 1086 (Domesday Book), *Akeford Skelling* 1220, *Ocford Sculling* 1280, *Okeford Shillyng* 1355, *Skillyng Okeford* 1407, *Shillyngeston* 1444. Originally sharing its name with Child Okeford and Okeford Fitzpaine, later distinguished from them by the name of the man who held the manor at the time of Domesday Book, one *Schelin*. The modern form Shillingstone, dating only from the 15th century, is 'Schelin's estate', from Old English *tūn*.

Shilvinghampton (in Portesham)   *Scilfemetune, Silfemetone* 1086 (Domesday Book), *Shelfhamton* 1253, *Schilfamtun* 1285. 'Farm of the dwellers by the shelf or slope', from Old English *scylf, hǣme* and *tūn*.

Shipstal Point (in Arne)   *Shepstall* 1586. 'The sheepfold', from Old English *scēap* and *steall*.

Shipton Gorge   *Sepetone* 1086 (Domesday Book), *Sipton* 1214, *Scepton* 1268, *Shipton Gorges* 1594. 'Sheep farm', from Old English *scēap* or *scīep* and *tūn*. The manorial addition is from the family of Ralph *de Gorges*, here from the late 13th century. In medieval times it was alternatively known as *Shipton Maureward*, from another family with lands here in the early 13th century.

Shitterton (in Bere Regis)   *Scetre* 1086 (Domesday Book), *Schitereston* 1285, *Shyterton* 1332, *Shitterton* 1687. 'Farm at the stream used as a sewer', from Old English *scitere* and *tūn*. For reasons of prudishness the name now sometimes appears as Sitterton.

Shroton   see Iwerne Courtney.

Silkhay Farm (in Netherbury)   *Selkeheye* 1332, *Sylkey*

1510. 'Enclosure belonging to a family called *Selk*', from Old English *haeg*.

Silton   *Seltone* 1086 (Domesday Book), *Salton* 1268, *Silton* 1332, *Sylton* 1361. Probably 'farm where sallows or willows grow', from Old English *sealh* and *tūn*.

Simene, River   *Simen* 1577. Formed from the name Symondsbury.

Sixpenny Farm (in Fontmell Magna)   see Pen Hill in Sutton Waldron.

Sixpenny Handley   *Hanlee* 877 (in a later copy of an Anglo-Saxon charter), *Hanlege* 1086 (Domesday Book), *Henle* 1182, *Handeleygh* 1496, *Sexpennyhanley* 1575. 'The high wood or clearing', from Old English *hēah* and *lēah*. Note that the -*d*- only appears at the end of the 15th century, and that 'Sixpenny' is first added in the 16th century (from the name of the hundred of Sixpenny Handley, see Pen Hill in Sutton Waldron for the origin of 'Sixpenny').

Slait Barn (in Silton)   named from *Sheep Slait* 1837 which is from Old English *slaeget* 'a sheep pasture'.

Slape House (in Netherbury)   *Slepa* 1226, *Slepe* 1263, *Slape* 1291. From Old English *slāep* 'a slippery muddy place'.

Slaughtergate Farm (in Gillingham)   named from *Slaunders Yate* 1609, *Slanders Gate* 1642, which is from Old English *geat* 'gate' and a surname. The modern form of the name arose through the popular association of this place with the slaughter of the Danish Vikings at the battle of Penselwood in 1016.

Sleep Bottom and Brook (in Alderholt)   not on early record, but probably from Old English *slāep* 'a slippery, muddy place', with *botm* 'valley'.

Sleight (in Corfe Mullen)   *Sleyte* 1327. From Old English *slaeget* 'a sheep pasture'.

Sleight Buildings (in Winfrith Newburgh)   *Sleight* 1641, *Slight* 1682. Identical in origin with the previous name.

Slepe (in Arne)   *Slepe* 1244, *Sleape* 1584. 'The slippery, muddy place', from Old English *slāep*.

Slepe (in Lytchett Minster)   *Slape* 1315, *Slepe* 1327. Identical in origin with the previous name.

Small Mouth (in Wyke Regis)   *Smalemue* 1244, *Smalemouth* 1328, *Smalemuth* 1379, *Smallemouth* 1526. 'The narrow mouth', from Old English *smael* and *mūtha*, alluding to the estuary of East Fleet. There was a ferry here across to the Isle of Portland until 1839 when the bridge called Ferry Bridge was built.

Smedmore Hill and House (in Kimmeridge)   *Metmore* 1086 (Domesday Book), *Smethemore* 1242, *Smedemore* 1244, *Smedmour* 1387. 'Smooth or level moor', from Old English *smēthe* and *mōr*. The Domesday Book spelling is rather erratic – the Norman scribes sometimes had difficulty even with comparatively straightforward names of Anglo-Saxon origin!

Smetherd Farm (in Fifehead Neville)   *Smitheard* 1744. Perhaps 'smithy yard', from Old English *smethe* and *geard*.

Snelling Farm (in Turners Puddle)   *Snellyng* 1415, *Snelling* 1533, *Snellinge* 1565. 'Place belonging to a man called Snell', from Old English *-ing* and an Old English personal name.

Snow's Down (in Langton Long Blandford)   from the family of George *Snow* who held the manor of Langton Long Blandford in the 18th century.

Somerford (in Christchurch)   *Sumerford* 12th century, *Somerford* 1280. 'Ford that can be used only in summer', from Old English *sumor* and *ford*. The ford was on the River Mude.

Sopley Common (in Hurn)   named from Sopley in Hampshire, which is *Sopelie* 1086 (Domesday Book), *Soppele* 1263, meaning 'wood or clearing belonging to a man called Soppa', from Old English *lēah* and an Old English personal name.

Southbourne (in Bournemouth)   like Northbourne and Westbourne, a name of recent invention for a district of the town.

Southbrook (in Bere Regis)   *Suthebrok* 1300, *Southbrouk* 1375, *Sudbrooke* 1617, *Sowthbrooke* 1627. '(Place to) the south of the brook', from Old English *sūthan* and *brōc*. The brook is that which gives name to Shitterton.

Southcombe Valley (in Piddletrenthide) *Suthcombe* 1557. 'South valley', from Old English *sūth* and *cumb*.

South Down Farm (in Owermoigne) *Suddon* 1327, *Sudden* 1340, *Sooden Farme* 1664. 'South hill or down', from Old English *sūth* and *dūn*.

South Haven Point (in Studland) *Sowthe Havyn Poynte* 1539. See North Haven Point (in Poole).

Southover (in Frampton) *Southover* 1670. 'South bank', from Old English *sūth* and *ōfer*, with reference to its position on the River Frome.

Southover Heath and House (in Tolpuddle) *Southouere* 1400, *Southover* 1546. Identical in origin with the previous name, here probably with reference to its position on the River Piddle.

Southwell (on Isle of Portland) *Southwelle, Southwool* 1608, *Southwell* 1650. 'South well, spring or stream', from Old English *sūth* and *wella*.

Sovell Down (in Gussage St Michael) probably to be associated with *la Southfelde* 1367, from Old English *sūth* 'south' and *feld* 'open country'.

Spetisbury *Spehtesberie, Spesteberie* 1086 (Domesday Book), *Spectebury* 1291, *Spectesbury* 1294. 'Pre-English earthwork frequented by the green woodpecker', from Old English *speoht* or *speht* and *burh*. Alternatively the first element could be the same word used as a personal name, perhaps that of the Anglo-Saxon who came to possess the earthwork or who was associated with it in some other way. The reference is to the Iron Age hill-fort known as Crawford Castle or Spetisbury Rings.

Springbourne (in Bournemouth) a name of recent invention for a district of the town.

Stafford, West *Stanford, Staford* 1086 (Domesday Book), *Stafford* 1212, *West Stafford* 1285. 'Stony ford', from Old English *stān* and *ford*, alluding to a crossing of the River Frome. There was formerly an East Stafford in the neighbouring parish of West Knighton.

Stake Ford Cross (in Yetminster)   *Stakyforde* 1350, *Stake-ford* 1398. 'Ford marked out by stakes', from Old English *staca* and *ford*. The stakes may well have marked the boundary between the three parishes that meet here.

Stalbridge   *Stapulbreicge* 998 (in a later copy of an Anglo-Saxon charter), *Staplebrige* 1086 (Domesday Book), *Stapel-brigge* 1212, *Stalbriggh* 1346. 'Bridge built on posts or piles', from Old English *stapol* and *brycg*.

Stalbridge Weston (in Stalbridge)   *Westune* 933 (in a later copy of an Anglo-Saxon charter), *Westone* 1086 (Domesday Book), *Weston* 1212. 'West farm', from Old English *west* and *tūn*. *Stalbridge* (from the parish) was added to the name in the 17th century.

Stallen (in Nether Compton)   *Stawell* 1244, *Stanwell* 1290, *Stale* 1575. '(Place at) the stony spring or stream', from Old English *stān* and *wella*. The final *-n* in the modern form of the name is curious.

Stanbridge (in Hinton Parva)   *Stanbrig* 1230, *Stanbrugg* 1254, *Stambrigge* 1262, *Stanebrigg* 1297. 'Stone bridge', from Old English *stān* and *brycg*, although *brycg* here probably has the alternative medieval sense 'causeway, raised track through marshy ground', since the Wimborne road crosses low-lying land by the River Allen here.

Stanbridge Mill Farm (in Horton)   named from a medieval stone bridge across the River Allen, referred to in Latin as *pontem petre* as early as 1280, and as *la Stanebrigge* in 1311, from Old English *stān* and *brycg*.

Stancombe Farm (in Litton Cheney)   *Stancombe* 1337, *Stankombe* 1412. 'Stony valley', from Old English *stān* and *cumb*.

Stanpit (in Christchurch)   *Stanpeta* 1086 (Domesday Book), *Stanputta* 12th century, *Stamputte* 1331. 'Stone pit', from Old English *stān* and *pytt*.

Stanton St Gabriel   *Stantone* 1086 (Domesday Book), *Staunton* 1268, *Staunton Gabriell* 1434, *Staunton Gabriel* 1465.

'Farm on stony ground', from Old English *stān* and *tūn*. St Gabriel is from the dedication of the church.

Stapehill (in Hampreston)　*Staphill* 1583. Apparently 'steep hill', from Old English *stēap* and *hyll*; since there is only a low hill here, the name is possibly ironical.

Steeple　*Stiple* 1086 (Domesday Book), *Stuple* 1204, *Stepel* 1222, *Steple* 1262. 'Steep place', from Old English *stīepel*. The word can also mean 'steeple, tower' but the topographical meaning is more likely here.

Steepleton Iwerne　see under Iwerne.

Sterte (in Poole)　*Strette* 1520, *Stert* 1822. Probably from Old English *steort* 'tail of land'.

Stinsford　*Stiteford, Stincteford* 1086 (Domesday Book), *Stinteford* 1236, *Stintesford* 1244, *Stynsford* 1270. 'Ford frequented by the sandpiper or dunlin', from Old English *stint* and *ford*. The ford was no doubt across the River Frome or some branch of it.

Stoborough (in Arne)　*Stanberge* 1086 (Domesday Book), *Stabergh* 1253, *Stoburgh* 1315, *Stoughborough* 1515. 'Stony hill or barrow', from Old English *stān* and *beorg*. As in many similar names, the second element has been replaced by *burh* 'fortification'.

Stockbridge Farm (in Lillington)　*Stokbrigg* 1244, *Stokbrigge* 1327, *Stokebrugge* 1386. 'Bridge made of logs', from Old English *stocc* and *brycg*.

Stock Gaylard House (in Lydlinch)　*Stoches* 1086 (Domesday Book), *Stok* 1268, *Stoke Coilard* 1305, *Stoke Gaillard* 1316. 'Outlying farm buildings, a secondary settlement', from Old English *stoc*. The addition is probably manorial, but a family called *Coilard* have not been noted here.

Stock Hill (in Gillingham)　neighbouring places are *Stokkefeld* 1441, *Stokford* 1501, *Stock waye* 1626. All are from Old English *stocc* 'tree-stump' or *stoc* 'secondary settlement'.

Stock Hill (in Glanvilles Wootton)　*Stochullane* 1441, *Stokhillane* 1445. '(Lane by) the hill where there are tree-stumps', from Old English *stocc*, *hyll* and *lane*.

Stockley Farms (in Bere Regis) *Stocle* 1308, *Stockley* 1403, *Stokkele* 1415, *Stokeley* 1546. 'Clearing characterized by tree-stumps', from Old English *stocc* and *lēah*.

Stockwood *Stocwode* 1223, *Stokwud* 1224, *Stokewod* 1265, *Stokkewode* 15th century. 'Wood belonging to a secondary settlement', from Old English *stoc* and *wudu*. In medieval times the place was alternatively known as *Stoke St Edwold* from the dedication of the church.

Stoke Abbott *Stoche* 1086 (Domesday Book), *Stok Abbatis* 1273, *Stoke Abbots* 1275, *Stoke Abbot* 1348. 'Secondary settlement belonging to the abbot', from Old English *stoc* with Latin *abbatis* 'of the abbot' alternating with Middle English *abbat*. This manor originally belonged to the abbey of Sherborne.

Stoke, East *Stoches* 1086 (Domesday Book), *Stok* 1284, *Estok* 1316, *East Stoake* 1664. 'Outlying farm buildings, a secondary settlement', from Old English *stoc*. 'East' perhaps in relation to Bindon Abbey in Wool.

Stokeford (in East Stoke) *Stokford* 1244, *Stokeford* 1355, *Stokkeford* 1445. 'The ford near Stoke', from Old English *ford*.

Stoke Wake *Stoche* 1086 (Domesday Book), *Stok* 1212, *Stoke Wake* 1285, *Stoke Wak* 1316. From Old English *stoc* 'secondary settlement, outlying farmstead'. The addition is manorial, from the *Wake* family, here from the 13th century.

Stone (in Pamphill) *la Stane* 1268, *Stone* 1280, *la Stone* 1288, *Stoune* 1523. From Old English *stān* 'a stone', perhaps originally with reference to a boundary stone.

Stour, River an Old English river-name, first recorded in the 10th century and probably meaning 'the strong or powerful one'. Rivers with the same name occur in Kent, Essex, Worcestershire and Staffordshire. The Dorset river gives its name to East and West Stour, Stourpaine, Stour Provost, and Sturminster Marshall and Sturminster Newton.

Stour, East and West *Sture* 1086 (Domesday Book), *Sturewestouere* 1268, *Stoure Estouere* 1371, *East Stower, West Stower* 1664. Named for their situation on the River Stour.

The earlier additions *Estouere* and *Westouere* mean 'east bank' and 'west bank' respectively, from Old English *ōfer*. In medieval times these places were sometimes known as *Stour Cosin* and *Stour Wake*, from two families who had lands here.

Stourpaine *Sture* 1086 (Domesday Book), *Stures Paen* 1243, *Sture Payn* 1280, *Stoure Payn* 1303. 'Estate on the River Stour held by the *Payn* family', here during the 13th and 14th centuries.

Stour Provost *Stur* 1086 (Domesday Book), *Sture Preauus* 1270, *Stowr Preves* 1517, *Stowr Provost* 1549. Named from the River Stour. The earlier addition is from the abbey of St Leger at *Préaux* in Normandy which possessed this manor during the 12th and 13th centuries. The addition was changed to *Provost* after the manor was given by Edward IV (1461–83) to the Provost of King's College Cambridge.

Stourton Caundle *Candel, Candelle* 1086 (Domesday Book), *Caundelhaddon* 1275, *Candel Haddon* 1285, *Stourton Candel* 1709. For the name Caundle, see Bishop's Caundle. The addition *Stourton* is from the Lords *Stourton* who held the manor from the 15th century. The earlier addition *Haddon* is from the *Haddon* family, here from the 13th century.

Stratton *Stratton* 1212, *Stratone* 1270, *Strathon* 1291, *Stretton* 1348. 'Farm on a Roman road', from Old English *strǣt* and *tūn*. The Roman road from Dorchester to Ilchester was joined here by a branch from Stinsford.

Strode (in Netherbury) *Strode* 1225, *Strod* 1253, *la Strode* 1268, *Stroud* 1412. From Old English *strōd* 'marshy land overgrown with brushwood'.

Stroud Bridge (in Bloxworth) named from *Stroda* 1303, *Strode* 1332, *Stroude* 1340, *Stroode* 1544. Identical in origin with the previous name.

Stroud Farm (in Lydlinch) *Stroude* 1340, *Strode* 1621. Identical in origin with the previous two names.

Stubhampton (in Tarrant Gunville) *Stibemetune* 1086 (Domesday Book), *Stubhamtune* 1262, *Stibampton* 1268, *Stubbehamton* 1541. Probably 'farm of the dwellers by the tree-stump', from Old English *stybb, hǣme* and *tūn*. In medieval times it was sometimes known as *Tarente Stubhampton* because the River Tarrant rises here.

Studland   *Stollant* 1086 (Domesday Book), *Stodland* 1210, *Stoudlond* 1327, *Studlond* 1512. 'Tract of land where a herd of horses is kept', from Old English *stōd* and *land*.

Sturminster Marshall   *Sture minster* 9th century (in a later copy of an Anglo-Saxon charter), *Sturminstre* 1086 (Domesday Book), *Sturministre Marescal* 1268, *Sturmenstre Marchal* 1327. 'The church on the River Stour', from Old English *mynster*. The manorial addition is from the *Marshals*, earls of Pembroke, of whom William *Mareschal* was here in 1204.

Sturminster Newton   *Nywetone, at Stoure* 968 (in a later copy of an Anglo-Saxon charter), *Newentone* 1086 (Domesday Book), *Stourminstr* 1244, *Sturminstr Nyweton* 1291. Newton is 'new farm or estate', from Old English *nīwe* and *tūn*, Sturminster is 'church on the River Stour', from Old English *mynster*. Newton is on the opposite side of the river to Sturminster, but its name was added to distinguish this place from Sturminster Marshall.

Sturthill, Higher and Lower (in Shipton Gorge)   *Sterte* 1086 (Domesday Book), *Stertel* 1212, *Upsteortel* 1268, *Nithersturtel* 1329. From Old English *steortel* 'small projecting piece of land'. The additions *Up-* and *Nither-*, from Old English *upp* 'higher up' and *neotherra* 'lower', earlier denoted Higher and Lower Sturthill respectively.

Sugar Hill (in Bloxworth)   not on early record, but possibly 'hill frequented by robbers', from Old English *scēacere* and *hyll*. The name applies to a stretch of the road from Wareham to Bere Regis where it crosses Bloxworth Heath.

Sutton Holms (in Wimborne St Giles)   *Suddon* 1226, *Suthdun* 1241, *Sudden* 1407, *Sutton Holms* 1811. 'South hill or down', from Old English *sūth* and *dūn*. The relatively recent addition *Holms* is from Dorset dialect *holm* 'holly'.

Sutton Poyntz (near Preston)   *Suttone* 891 (in a 14th century copy of an Anglo-Saxon charter), *Sutone* 1086 (Domesday Book), *Sutton Pointz* 1314, *Sutton Poyns* 1412. 'South farm or estate', from Old English *sūth* and *tūn*. *Poyntz* is a manorial addition, since the manor was held by the family of this name from the 13th century.

Sutton Waldron *Suttune* 932 (in a later copy of an Anglo-Saxon charter), *Sudtone* 1086 (Domesday Book), *Sutton Walerand* 1297, *Sutton Walron* 1545. 'South farm or estate', from Old English *sūth* and *tūn*, 'south' perhaps in relation to Fontmell Magna. The manorial addition is from *Waleran* the huntsman, who held this manor at the time of Domesday Book, or from his descendants who inherited his name.

Swalland Farm (in Kimmeridge) *Swanlond* 1376, *Swalland* 1545, *Swallonde* 1590. 'Land of the herdsmen or peasants', from Old English *swān* and *land*.

Swanage *Swanawic* 9th century (Anglo-Saxon Chronicle), *Swanwic, Sonwic* 1086 (Domesday Book), *Swanwyche* 1244. Probably 'dairy farm of the herdsmen or peasants', from Old English *swān* and *wīc*. Alternatively, if the first element is Old English *swan* 'a swan', the meaning would be 'farm where swans are reared, swannery'.

Swineham (in Wareham) *Swynham* 1650, *Swineham* 1675. Probably 'water-meadow where swine are kept', from Old English *swīn* and *hamm*.

Swyre *Suere* 1086 (Domesday Book), *Swere* 1196, *Suure* 1275, *Swyre* 1288. From Old English *swēora* or *swȳra* 'a neck of land, a col'.

Swyre Head (in Chaldon Herring) not recorded before 1811, but from Old English *swȳra* 'a neck of land' and *hēafod* 'headland'. It is a worn-down coastal promontory.

Swyre Head (in Corfe Castle) *swuren* 955 (in a later copy of an Anglo-Saxon charter), *Swyer hill* 1590. Identical in origin with the previous name.

Sydling St Nicholas *Sidelyng* 934 (in a later copy of an Anglo-Saxon charter), *Sidelince* 1086 (Domesday Book), *Sideling* 1212, *Brodesideling* 1288. '(Place at) the large ridge', from Old English *sīd* and *hlinc*, referring to one of the hills above the village. In medieval times it was often called *Brodesideling* (from Old English *brād* 'broad') to distinguish it from Up Sydling. The later addition is from the dedication of the church.

Sydling, Up (in Sydling St Nicholas) *Upsidelinch* 1230, *Upsideling* 1244, *Upsidelyng* 1311. The addition is Old English *upp* 'up, higher up' to distinguish it from *Brodesideling*, the earlier name of Sydling St Nicholas.

Symondsbury *Simondesberge* 1086 (Domesday Book), *Simunisberge* 1212, *Symundesberg* 1237, *Symondesburgh* 1340. 'Hill or barrow of a man called Sigemund', from Old English *beorg* and an Old English personal name. The river here is now called Simene, a back-formation from Symondsbury.

Tadden (in Pamphill) probably to be identified with *Tadhavene* 1327, *Taddehauene* 1332, which means 'haven or place of shelter for toads', from Old English *tāde* and *haefen*. The name was perhaps originally intended to be jocular or may refer literally to the marshy ground here.

Tadnoll Dairy and Mill (in Chaldon Herring) *Tadenhole* 1281, *Tadenoll* 1394, *Tadynollesmyll* 1463, *Tadnoll Mill* 1663. The meaning of this name is not certain, but it is probably 'toad-infested hollow', from Old English *tāde* and *hol*.

Talbot Village (in Bournemouth) district named c.1860 after the local landowners, the *Talbot* sisters.

Tarrant, River an old Celtic river-name, first recorded in the 10th century, a variant of the name Trent. Its meaning was probably 'the trespasser', i.e. 'river liable to floods'. The Tarrant gives its name to no less than eight different parishes on its banks.

Tarrant Crawford *Tarente* 1086 (Domesday Book), *Tarrent* 1237, *Little Craweford* 1280, *Lyttle Craford within Tarrant* 1598, *Tarrant Crawford or Little Crawford* 1795. Originally named from the River Tarrant. *Little Crawford* comprised a large part of the present parish and was so called to distinguish it from *Great Crawford* in Spettisbury on the opposite bank of the River Stour; the name means 'crow ford', from Old English *cráwe* and *ford*.

Tarrant Gunville   *Tarente* 1086 (Domesday Book), *Tarente Gundevill* 1233, *Tarrente Gundevill* 1247, *Tarente Gondevill* 1263. 'Estate on the River Tarrant held by the *Gundeville* family', here in the 12th and 13th centuries.

Tarrant Hinton   *Terente* 9th century (in a later copy of an Anglo-Saxon charter), *Tarente* 1086 (Domesday Book), *Tarente Hyneton* 1280, *Tarente Hynton* 1340. 'Estate on the River Tarrant belonging to a religious community'. Hinton is from Old English *hīwan* and *tūn*. The religious community referred to is Shaftesbury Abbey, which was granted this manor in Anglo-Saxon times.

Tarrant Keynston   *Tarente* 1086 (Domesday Book), *Tarente Kahaines* 1225, *Kayneston* 1278, *Tarente Keyneston* 1303. 'Estate on the River Tarrant held by the *Cahaignes* family', here from the end of the 12th to the end of the 14th century: *-ton* is from Old English *tūn* 'manor, estate'.

Tarrant Launceston   *Tarente* 1086 (Domesday Book), *Tarente Loueweniston* 1280, *Tarente Lowyneston* 1288, *Tarent Launston* 1397. 'Estate on the River Tarrant held by a man called *Lēofwine* or a family called *Lowin*'; *-ton* is from Old English *tūn* 'manor, estate'.

Tarrant Monkton   *Tarente* 1086 (Domesday Book), *Tarenta Monachorum* 12th century, *Tarent Moneketon* 1280, *Tarente Monketon* 1288, *Tarente Munketon* 1367. 'Estate on the River Tarrant belonging to the monks', from Old English *munuc* and *tūn*, with reference to the possession of this manor by the priory of Cranborne and the abbey of Tewkesbury. The alternative Latin addition *Monachorum*, found up to the 16th century, means 'of the monks'.

Tarrant Rawston   *Tarente* 1086 (Domesday Book), *Tarente Antyoche* 1288, *Antiocheston* 1428, *Tarrant Rawston alias Antyocke* 1535. The earlier name, 'estate on the River Tarrant held by the *Antioch* family', was in use until the 16th century; this family held the manor in the 13th and 14th centuries. The later addition *Rawston* probably means 'Ralph's estate', though the man in question has not been traced; *-ton* is from Old English *tūn* 'manor, estate'.

Tarrant Rushton　*Tarente* 1086 (Domesday Book), *Tarente Russeus* 1280, *Russcheustone* 1283, *Tarente Russcheweston* 1307. 'Estate on the River Tarrant held by the *de Rusceaus* family'; this family held the manor in the 13th century. The form *Rushton* (from the family name and Old English *tūn*) appears to have been influenced by the common place-name Rushton from Old English *rysc* 'a rush', like Rushton in East Stoke. In medieval times Tarrant Rushton was sometimes known as *Tarente Vilers*, from the lords of the manor in the 12th century.

Tatton Farm and House (in Chickerell)　*Tatetun, Tatentone* 1086 (Domesday Book), *Tattun* 1212, *Tatton* 1262. 'Farm of a man called Tāta', from Old English *tūn* and an Old English personal name.

Terrace Farm (in Stour Provost)　'Terrace' is a folk etymology of 'Terry's', found in *Terryeslane* 1420, *Tyrryestherne, Tarryescrofte* 1439, all of them named from a family called *Terry* which had lands here from the 14th century, with Old English *lane* 'lane', *thyrne* 'thorn bush' and *croft* 'small enclosed field'.

Thickthorn Down (in Long Crichel)　not recorded before the 18th century, and self-explanatory.

Thorncombe (parish)　*Tornecoma* 1086 (Domesday Book), *Tornecumba* 12th century, *Thorncumbe* 1236, *Thornecombe* 1399. 'Valley where thorn-trees grow', from Old English *thorn* and *cumb*. This parish was in Devon until 1844.

Thorncombe (in Blandford St Mary)　*Tornecome* 1086 (Domesday Book), *Thorncumbe* 1236, *Tornecoumbe* 1325. Identical in origin with previous name. Now Thornicombe.

Thorney Down Farm (in Sixpenny Handley)　*la Thornedowne* 1503, *Thorneydowne* 1575. 'Hill or down growing with thorn-trees', from Old English *thornig* and *dūn*.

Thornford　*Thornford* 951 (in a later copy of an Anglo-

Saxon charter), *Torneford* 1086 (Domesday Book), *Thorneford* 1249. 'Ford where thorn-trees grow', from Old English *thorn* and *ford*.

Thorngrove (in Gillingham) *Thorngraue* 1292, *Thorngroue* 1301, *Thornegraue* 1415, *Thornegrove* 1609. 'Thorn-tree copse', from Old English *thorn* and *grāf*. This estate was alternatively known as Queen's Farm in the 18th century, no doubt a reference to one of the Queens of England who at different dates possessed the manor of Gillingham.

Thornhill (in Stalbridge) *Thornhill* 1244, *Thornhull* 1268. 'Hill where thorn-trees grow', from Old English *thorn* and *hyll*.

Thornhill Farm (in Broadwey) *Thornhulle* 1431, *Thornehill* 1445. Identical in origin with the previous name.

Thorn Hill Farm (in Holt) *Tornehelle* 1086 (Domesday Book), *Thornhill* 1212. Identical with previous names.

Thornicombe (in Blandford St Mary) see Thorncombe.

Thorton Farm (in Marnhull) *Thorntune* 958 (in a later copy of an Anglo-Saxon charter), *Torentone* 1086 (Domesday Book), *Thornton* 1212, *Thorneton* 1244. 'Thorntree farm', or 'thorn enclosure', from Old English *thorn* and *tūn*.

Three Legged Cross (in Verwood) recorded from the 16th century, perhaps with reference to a T-junction (with *cross* meaning cross-roads) or to a gallows (which was nicknamed *three legged mare*).

Throop (in Bournemouth) *la Throup, la Trope* 12th century, *la Thrope* 1274, *Throppe* 1540. From Old English *throp* 'an outlying farm or secondary settlement'.

Throop (in Turners Puddle) *la Trop* 1237, *Thrope* 1268, *le Thrope* 1386, *Throope* 1609. Identical in origin with the previous name.

Throop Dairy House (in Maiden Newton) *la Thrope* 1268, *Thrope* 1288, *Throupe* 1348. Has the same origin as the two previous names.

Thurnwood Farm (in Mappowder) *Thurnwodd* 1567,

Thurnwood 1632. 'Thorn-bush wood', from Old English *thyrne* and *wudu*.

Tiley (in Buckland Newton) *Tylly* 1244, *Tyleye* 1299, *Tilleye* 1315, *Tyley* 1325. 'Wood or clearing where tiles are made', from Old English *tigel* and *lēah*.

Tilly Whim Caves (in Swanage) this name for the remains of an ancient stone quarry is not recorded before 1811, but the first element is probably the Dorset surname *Tilly*, the second element the word *whim* 'a windlass, a winding gear' (no doubt used for lowering stone to boats).

Tincleton *Tincladene* 1086 (Domesday Book), *Tyncleden* 1268, *Tinckledenne* 1280, *Tynkelton* 1535. Probably 'valley of the small farms', from Old English *tȳnincel* and *denu*. The alteration of the ending -*den* to -*ton* is relatively recent.

Todber *Todeberie* 1086 (Domesday Book), *Totebera* 1194, *Toteberge* 1212, *Toddebir* 1228. Probably 'hill or grove belonging to a man called Tota', from Old English *beorg* or *bearu* and an Old English personal name. However the first element may be Old English *tōte* 'a look-out'.

Tollard Farnham (in Farnham) *Toulard Fernham* 1282, *Tollard Farneham* 1500. This part of Farnham was held in the 13th century by the family of Brian *de Tollard* (from the neighbouring parish of Tollard Royal in Wiltshire), hence the manorial addition.

Tollerford (in Frome Vauchurch) *Tolreforde* 1086, *Tolreford* 1244. 'Ford over the River Toller', from Old English *ford*. Toller, the original name of the River Hooke, is probably an old Celtic river-name meaning 'hollow stream, stream running in a deep valley'. The modern name of the river, Hooke, is taken from the place called Hooke higher upstream.

Toller Fratrum and Toller Porcorum *Tolre* 1086 (Domesday Book), *Tollre* 1244, *Tolre Fratrum, Tolre Porcorum* 1340. Named from the river on which they stand, earlier called the *Toller*, now called the River Hooke, see Tollerford. The two Latin additions are humorously contrasting, *Fratrum*

145

meaning 'of the brethren' because this manor once belonged to the Knights Hospitallers, *Porcorum* meaning 'of the pigs' because the place was renowned for its herds of swine! In fact in medieval records Toller Porcorum is usually referred to in more homely fashion as *Swyne Tolre*, from Old English *swīn*.

Toller Whelme (in Corscombe) *Tollor aewylman* 1035 (in a later copy of an Anglo-Saxon charter), *Tolre* 1086 (Domesday Book), *Tollre Euulme* 1268, *Tolreewelme* 1334. 'Source of the River Toller', from Old English *āewielm* 'river-spring'. Toller is the old name of the River Hooke, see Tollerford.

Tolpuddle *Pidele* 1086 (Domesday Book), *Tollepidele* 1210, *Tolepidele* 1212, *Tollepudele* 1285. 'Estate on the River Piddle belonging to a woman called Tola'. The woman in question, the Danish widow of King Edward the Confessor's house-carl, gave all her lands including Tolpuddle to Abbotsbury abbey before 1066.

Totnell (in Leigh) *Totenhulle* 1327, *Totnell* 1601. Probably 'look-out hill', from Old English *tōte* and *hyll*, although the first element could alternatively be an Old English personal name *Tota*.

Tout Hill (in East Stoke) not in early records, but the meaning is 'look-out hill', from Old English *tōt-hyll*.

Townsend (in Bournemouth) *Tounesende* 1300. Self-explanatory, with reference to the south end of Holdenhurst, from Old English *tūn* and *ende*.

Trent *Trente* 1086 (Domesday Book), *Trenta* 1163, *Trent* 1486. Originally the name of the stream here (now called Trent Brook), an old Celtic river-name found elsewhere in England and possibly originally meaning 'the trespasser', i.e. 'river liable to floods'.

Trickett's Cross (in West Moors) not in the early records, but from *cross* in the sense 'cross-roads' with a surname.

Trigon Farm and Hill (in Wareham) first recorded in the mid-19th century, probably from *trigon* 'a triangle' describing the shape of the farm or the hill, or from a family so called.

Trill Bridge (in Fifehead Magdalen) probably named from

Trul 1268, *Tril* 1316, which may originally have referred to the small tributary of the River Stour rising in Stour Provost. This stream-name has the same origin as the next name.

Trill Farm (in Beer Hackett) *Tril* 1012, *Trelle* 1086 (Domesday Book), *Trulle* 13th century, *Tryll* 1316. Named from the stream here, a tributary of the River Yeo, from Old English *tyrl* 'the rolling or turning one'.

Troy Town Farm (in Puddletown) not recorded before the 19th century, but from *troy town* 'a maze'.

Tuckton (in Bournemouth) *Tuketon* 1248, *Tocketon* 1300, *Toketon* 1397, *Tucketon* 1540. 'Farm belonging to a man called Tucca or Tocca', from Old English *tūn* and an Old English personal name.

Turners Puddle *Pidele* 1086 (Domesday Book), *Tunerepidel* 1242, *Tonerespydele* 1268, *Tournerspedyll* 1428. 'The estate on the River Piddle held by the *Toner* family'; this family held the manor from the time of Domesday Book.

Turnworth *Torneworde* 1086 (Domesday Book), *Turnewrd, Thurneworda* early 13th century, *Turnewurth* 1234. 'Thorn-bush enclosure, enclosure formed by thorn-bushes', from Old English *thyrne* and *worth*.

Tut Hill Farm (in Caundle Marsh) not recorded before the 19th century, but from Old English *tōt-hyll* 'a look-out hill'.

Twinwood Coppice (in Hinton St Mary) *Twynwoode, Twinwodd* 16th century. '(Land) between the woods', from Old English *betwēonan* and *wudu*.

Twofords Bridge (in Lydlinch) *bridge called Twyforde* 1496. Identical in origin with the next name. The road to Sturminster Newton crosses two streams here.

Twyford (in Compton Abbas) *Tweyford* 1395, *Twyforde* 1564, *Twiford* 1575. 'Double ford', from Old English *twī-* and *ford*, a common place-name found in several English counties. The road here crossed two streams, one called Twyford Brook, the other unnamed.

Tyneham *Tigeham, Tingeham* 1086 (Domesday Book),

Tynam 1244, *Tynham* 1280. Probably 'goat's enclosure', from Old English *tige* and *hamm*.

Uddens House (in Holt) *udding* 956 (in a 14th century copy of an Anglo-Saxon charter), *Uddyng* 1313, *Uddynge* 1331, *Uddinges* 1598. Probably 'Udd(a)'s place', from an Old English masculine personal name *Udd* or *Udda* and *-ing*.

Ulwell (in Swanage) *Holewell* 1236, *Hulewlle* 1268, *Oulewell* 1291, *Ulewel* 1315. 'Well, spring or stream frequented by owls', from Old English *ūle* and *wella*.

Uploders (in Loders) *Lodre* 1086 (Domesday Book), *Uppelodres* 1445, *Uplodre* 1446, *Uplodres* 1467. For the meaning of the original name, see Loders. The addition *Up-* means 'higher upstream', from Old English *upp*.

Uppington (in Hinton Martell) not recorded before the 19th century, but probably '(land) higher up in the village', from Old English *upp, in*, and *tūn*, this being the highest part of the parish.

Upton (in Lytchett Minster) *Upton* 1463, *Uppon* 1522. Identical in origin with the next name.

Upton (in Osmington) *Upton* 1361, *Vpton* 1447, *vppertowne* 1664. 'Higher farm', or 'higher part of the village', from Old English *upp* and *tūn*. Upton now lies in a valley, but the name must originally have referred to the higher ground to the south.

Upwey *Wai(e)* 1086 (Domesday Book), *Uppeweie* 1241, *Upeweye* 1311, *Upwaye* 1327. 'The upper or higher manor on the River Wey', from Old English *upp*; the river actually rises here.

Vale Acre Farm (in Alderholt) *Vellak* 1314, *Fenlak* 1324, *Fellake* 1404, *Velacre* 1508. Probably 'fen stream', from Old English *fenn* and *lacu*, with *V-* for *F-* characteristic of the Dorset dialect. The reshaping of the name through folk etymology is relatively recent.

Vearse Farm (in Symondsbury) *Vearse* 1668, *Vears* 1674. Named from a family called *Veer*, here from the 13th century, see also the nearby Watton in the same parish.

Venn Farm (in Stoke Abbott)   *Venne* 1327, *Wenne* 1340. From Old English *fenn* 'fen, marshland', here with the old dialect pronunciation.

Verne Yeates (on Isle of Portland)   *Ferne* 1321, *Fearne yates, Verne yates* 1608. Probably from Old English *fergen* 'mountain, wooded hill'; this is the highest part of the island, rising to nearly 500 feet. *Yeates* is from Old English *geat* 'gate', referring either to actual gates, or to gaps or passes on the main route between Fortuneswell and Easton.

Verwood   *Beuboys* 1288, *Fairwod* 1329, *Fayrwode* 1404, *Ferwood* 1614. 'Beautiful wood', from Old English *faeger* and *wudu*, the modern form reflecting the Dorset dialect pronunciation with *V-* for *F-*. The 13th century spelling shows a French version of the name, from Old French *beu* and *bois*.

Waddock Farm (in Affpuddle)   *Waddoke* 1564, *Waddock* 1612, *Wadduck* 1674. Probably 'oak-tree near the ford', from Old English *waed* and *āc*.

Waddon, Friar Waddon, Little Waddon (in Portesham) *Wadone* 1086 (Domesday Book), *Waddun* 1194, *Waddon* 1201, *Little Waddone* 1305, *Frerenwaddon* 1384. 'Hill or down where woad grows', from Old English *wād* and *dūn*. The addition *Friar* (earlier *Freren* 'of the Friars') refers to the possession of lands here by the Knights Hospitallers. Friar Waddon was more usually called *Brodewaddon* in medieval times, from Old English *brād* 'broad', to distinguish it from Little Waddon.

Waddon Hill (in Loders)   *Waddon* 1463. Identical in origin with the previous name.

Wadmill Farm (in Stour Provost)   *Wabenhull* 1300, *Wapenell* 1444, *Wabnell* 1570, *Wadmell* 1841. Probably 'hill belonging to a man called Waba', from Old English *hyll* and an Old English personal name. There was apparently never a mill here, the comparatively recent alteration of the name being due to folk etymology.

Wakeham (on Isle of Portland)   *Wacombe* 1608, *Wacum* 1650. The second element is Old English *cumb* 'valley', the first may be Old English *wacu* 'a watch, a wake'.

Walditch (in Bothenhampton) *Waldic* 1086 (Domesday Book), *Waudich* 1236, *Waldich* 1268, *Waldysche* 1416. 'Ditch with a wall or embankment', the second element being Old English *dīc*, the first being either Old English *weall* or *walu*.

Walford Bridge and Farm (in Wimborne Minster) *Walteford* 1086 (Domesday Book), *Waltford* 1323, *Waltefford* 1409, *Walford* 1535. Probably 'shaky, unsteady ford, i.e. ford difficult to cross', from Old English *wealt* and *ford*. The road from Cranborne into Wimborne crosses the River Allen here.

Walkford (in Christchurch) *Walkeforde* 1280, *Walkford* 1397. The first element may be the old name of the stream here, now called Walkford Brook. This might have been Old English *Wealce*, meaning 'the rolling one', with Old English *ford*.

Wall Farm (in Stoke Abbott) *Walle* 1332. Self-explanatory, from Old English *weall*.

Walton Elm (in Marnhull) *Walton* 13th century, *Waltone* early 14th century, *Walton Elm* 1811. Old English *tūn* 'farm, estate', with either *weald* 'woodland' or *weall* 'wall'. *Elm*, presumably from some conspicuous elm-tree, is only added from the early 19th century.

Wantsley Farm (in Broadwindsor) *Wantesleghe* 1244, *Wantesleye* 1326, *Wantysle* 1441. 'Wood or clearing belonging to a man called Want', from Old English *lēah* and an Old English personal name.

Wareham *Werham* 9th century (Anglo-Saxon Chronicle), *Warham* 1086 (Domesday Book), *Wharam* 1340, *Wareham* 1476. 'Homestead by a weir', from Old English *wer* or *waer* and *hām*. There was no doubt a weir and fishery here on the River Frome at an early date.

Warmwell *Warmewelle, Warmwelle* 1086 (Domesday Book), *Wermewelle* 1205, *Warmell* 1440. 'The warm spring', from Old English *wearm* and *wella*. There is a spring just north of the village.

Warren (in Bere Regis) *Warame* 1546, *Rabbit Warren* 1845.

The game preserve (Middle English *wareine*) from which this place takes its name belonged to the abbess of Tarrant.

Warren Hill (in Bournemouth)   named from *The Warren* recorded in the 17th century.

Watercombe *Watrecome* 1086 (Domesday Book), *Watercumbe* 1204, *Watercome* 1280, *Watercum* 1288. 'Wet valley', from Old English *waeter* 'water' and *cumb*.

Watcombe Bottom (in Alton Pancras)   *Whetecombe* 891 (in a later copy of an Anglo-Saxon charter). 'Valley where wheat is grown', from Old English *hwǣte* and *cumb*.

Waterloo Farm (in Gillingham)   no doubt a transferred name commemorating the famous battle of 1815.

Waterston (in Puddletown)   *Pidere* 1086 (Domesday Book), *Walterton* 1227, *Pydele Waltereston* 1268, *Waterston* 1658. Originally named from the River Piddle on which it stands, but later 'Walter's farm', from Old English *tūn*.

Watton (in Symondsbury)   *Wotton Ver* 1304, *Watton* 1329, *Vereswatton* 1371, *Wattone* 1412. Probably 'farm on the River Woth', from Old English *tūn*. *Woth* is the old name of the River Brit, see Wooth Grange. The manor was held at an early date by the *Veer* family, see also the nearby Vearse Farm in the same parish.

Waytown (in Netherbury)   the home of John *atte Weye* 1327, 'at the way or road', from Old English *weg*, later with the addition of *town*.

Weathergrove (in Sandford Orcas)   *wederangrafe* 938 (in a later copy of an Anglo-Saxon charter), *Weregrave* 1086 (Domesday Book), *Wedergraue* 1378, *Wethirgrave* 1454. Probably 'grove belonging to a man called Wedera', from Old English *grāf* and an Old English personal name.

Week Common and Farm (in St Leonards and St Ives) *Wike* 1327, *Week* 1759. 'The dairy farm', from Old English *wīc*.

Week Street Down (in Gussage St Michael)   the stretch of the Salisbury to Blandford Forum road flanked by the down is referred to in an Anglo-Saxon charter dated 935 as *wic* *herepàth*, that is 'highway to the dwelling or dairy farm', from Old English *wīc* and *here-paeth*.

Wellwood (in Beaminster) *Welle* 1285, *Well* 1483. From Old English *wella* 'spring or stream', with the later addition of *wood*.

West Bay (in Bridport) a modern name.

Westbourne (in Bournemouth) like Northbourne and Southbourne, a name of recent invention for a district of the town.

Westbrook Farm (in Gillingham) *Westbrooke* 1609. Named from West Brook, a small tributary of the River Stour.

Westbrook House (in Upwey) *Westebroke* 1285, *Westbrook* 1428. '(Place) to the west of the brook', from Old English *westan* and *brōc*, describing its situation by the River Wey.

Westbury Farm (in Tarrant Gunville) *Westbury* 1414. 'West manor house', from Middle English *bury*, distinguished from Eastbury House in the same parish.

Westcombe Coppice (in Hooke) *Westcombe* 1510. 'West valley', from Old English *west* and *cumb*.

Westfields (in Mappowder) *Westfyldes* 1536. Self-explanatory, from Old English *west* and *feld*.

Westford Farm (in Thorncombe) *Westforde* 1291, *Westford* 1322. Self-explanatory, 'west' in relation to the ford that gave name to Forde Abbey in this parish.

West Hall (in Folke) *Westhalle* 1352, *Westall* 1353, *West Halle* 1491. Self-explanatory, though Old English *heall* here probably has the sense 'manor house'.

Westley Wood (in Sturminster Marshall) *Westleye* 1306, *Westlee* 1325, *Westley* 1593. 'The west wood or woodland glade', from Old English *west* and *lēah*. It lies west of the village.

West Moors *La More* 1310, *Moures* 1407, *Mores* 1489, *West Moors* 1591. 'The marshy ground(s)', from Old English *mōr*, with *west* to distinguish it from East Moors Farm.

Weston (on Isle of Portland) *Westone* 1324, *Weston* 1608.

'West farm or village', from Old English *west* and *tūn*, in contrast to Easton.

Westover Farm (in St Leonards and St Ives)   *Westover* 1638. '(Place on) the west river-bank', from Old English *west* and *ōfer*. The farm is situated by the River Avon.

Westover Farm (in Wootton Fitzpaine)   *Westouer* 1332. Identical in origin with the previous name.

Westport House (in Wareham)   *Bywesteport* 1264, *Westeport* 1274. Probably '(place) to the west of the town', from Old English *bī*, *westan* and *port*.

West Wood (in Ashmore)   *Westewode* 1280, *West Wood* 1590. Self-explanatory, from Old English *west* and *wudu*.

Westworth Farm (in Edmondsham)   *Worth* 1268, *Worthe* 1575. From Old English *worth* 'enclosure', with the addition of *west* from the 18th century to distinguish this farm from Eastworth Farm in Verwood.

Wey, River   see under Broadwey.

Weymouth   *Waimouthe* 934 (in a later copy of an Anglo-Saxon charter), *Waymue* 1244, *Weymuth* 1248, *Weyemouthe* 1371. 'The mouth of the River Wey', from Old English *mūtha*.

Whatcombe (in Winterborne Whitechurch)   *Watecumbe, Whatecumbe* 1288, *Watecombe* 1332, *Watcoumbe* 1363. Probably 'wet valley', from Old English *wāet* and *cumb*, though the first element may be Old English *hwāete* 'wheat'. In earlier times it was sometimes called *Winterborne Whatcombe* because of its location on the River Winterborne.

Whatcombe Down (in Kingston Russell)   *Whatecome* 1340. Identical in origin with the other Whatcombe.

Whatley Farm (in Broadwindsor)   *Hwatelegh* 13th century, *Watelegh* 1271, *Whatley* 1811. 'Clearing where wheat is grown', from Old English *hwāete* and *lēah*.

Whistley Farm (in Gillingham)   not on record before the 19th century, from Old English *west* 'west' and *lēah* 'wood, clearing'.

Whitchurch Canonicorum   *Witcerce* 1086 (Domesday

Book), *Witechurch* 1231, *Whytchyrche* 1242, *Whitchurch Canonicorum* 1262. 'White church', that is probably 'stone church', from Old English *hwīt* and *cirice*. The Latin addition *Canonicorum* means 'of the canons (of Salisbury)'. Church dedication to Candida (St Wite) may be from place-name.

Whitcombe *Widecome* 934 (in a later copy of an Anglo-Saxon charter), *Widecome* 1086 (Domesday Book), *Wydcombe* 1461, *Whitcombe* 1573. 'Wide valley', from Old English *wīd* and *cumb*.

Whitecliff Farm (in Swanage) *Witeclive* 1086 (Domesday Book), *Whyteclive* 1251, *Witeclyf* 1315, *Whiteclife* 1339. '(Place at) the white cliff', from Old English *hwīt* and *clif*, with reference to the chalk cliff near here.

Whitefield (in Morden) *Whytewell* 1422, *Whitewell* 1671, *Whitefield* 1811. 'White spring or stream', from Old English *hwīt* and *wella*, with reference to the springs or stream here.

White Lackington (in Piddletrenthide) *Wyghtlakynton* 1354. 'Farm called after Wihtlāc', OE *ingtūn* and personal name.

White Mead (in Puddletown) *la Wytemede* 1270, *Whytmede* 1539. 'White meadow', from Old English *hwīt* and *māed*.

White Mill (in Shapwick) *Wytemull* 1341, *la Whitemulle* 1389, *Whitemull* 1429, *Wytemylle* 1550. Self-explanatory, from Old English *hwīt* and *myln*. It gives name to White Mill Bridge in Sturminster Marshall.

White Nothe (in Owermoigne) *the White North* 1649, *White Nore* 1811. From Old English *hwīt* 'white' (here referring to the chalk cliffs) and *hnoth* 'knoll or hill'.

White Sheet Hill (in Holt) *White Shite Heth* 1547, *Whiteshitte Heath* 1591. The middle element is probably Old English *scyte* '(steep) slope or hill', with *hwīt* 'white' (probably alluding to soil colour) and (earlier) *hāeth* 'heath'.

Whiteway (in Tyneham) *Whitewey* 1327, *Whitway* 1451. 'White way', from Old English *hwīt* and *weg*, referring to a road over the chalk hill.

Whiteway Farm (in Church Knowle) *Wyteweye* 1284, *Whyteweye* 1290. Identical in origin with the previous name.

154

Whitey Top (in Pentridge)   named from *Whiteway* 1838, which is self-explanatory from Old English *hwīt* and *weg*.

Whitfield Farm (in Bradford Peverell)   *Whitewell, Wittewell* 1195, *Witewell* 1201, *Whytewelle* 1300. 'White spring', from Old English *hwīt* and *wella*, in allusion to a spring which breaks out at the bottom of a chalky hill. The modern alteration of the name to -*field* is due to confusion with Frome Whitfield to which manor it once belonged.

Whitfield Farm (in Lillington)   *Whitefeld* 1309, *Whittefeld* 1474, *Whytefeld* 1566. Apparently self-explanatory, from Old English *hwīt* and *feld*, but probably signifying 'unwooded open country, dry open pasture'.

Wick (in Bournemouth)   *la Wych* 12th century, *Wyke* 1263, *la Wyk* late 13th century. 'The dairy farm', from Old English *wīc*.

Wigbeth (in Horton)   recorded only from the 19th century, and of uncertain origin.

Wilkswood Farm (in Langton Matravers)   *Wilceswde, Wilchesode* 1086 (Domesday Book), *Wylcheswode* 1305, *Wilkeswood* 1585. Probably 'wood belonging to a man called Willic', from Old English *wudu* and an Old English personal name.

Wilksworth Farm (in Colehill)   *Wedechesworde* 1086 (Domesday Book), *Wudekesworth* 1244, *Wodekesworthe* 1280, *Wilkesworth* 1508. Probably 'enclosure belonging to a man called Wuduc', from Old English *worth* and an Old English personal name.

Wimborne Minster   *Winburnan* 9th century (Anglo-Saxon Chronicle), *Winburne* 1086 (Domesday book), *Wymburne-minstre* 1236, *Wymborn Ministre* 1285. 'Meadow stream', from Old English *winn* and *burna*, originally the name of the river here, now called the River Allen. The addition *Minster* is from Old English *mynster* '(the church of) a monastery', originally with reference to the nunnery which was founded here by Queen Cūthburh of Wessex at the beginning of the 8th century.

Wimborne St Giles   *Winburne* 1086 (Domesday Book), *Up*

Wimburn 12th century, *Vpwymburn Sancti Egidij* 1268, *Upwymbourne St Giles* 1399. Like Wimborne Minster, named from the river here, now called Allen. *Up* means 'higher up (the river)', from Old English *upp*. *St Giles* (Latin *Egidius*) is from the dedication of the church. In medieval times this place was also known as *Upwymburne Malemayns* or *Upwymburn Pleycy*, from two families who held the manor in the 13th century.

Winfrith Newburgh   *Winfrode* 1086 (Domesday Book), *Winfrot* 1195, *Wynefred Neuburgh* 1288, *Wynfreth Neuburgh* 1431. This is an old Celtic river-name, meaning 'white or bright stream', from *winn* and *frud*. It was originally the name of the River Win, a tributary of the River Frome. *Newburgh* is the name of the family which held the manor from the 12th century onwards. The first part of Wynford Eagle has the same origin as Winfrith.

Winkton (in Christchurch)   *Weringetone* 1086 (Domesday Book), *Wineketon* 1236, *Wyneketon* 1256, *Wynketon* 1280, *Winketon* 1347. 'Farm belonging to a man called Wineca', from Old English *tūn* and an Old English personal name.

Winspit (in Worth Matravers)   not recorded before the 18th century, but possibly an old name meaning 'stone pit with a winch', from Old English *wince* and *pytt*.

Winterborne, River   there are two rivers called Winterborne in Dorset, each of them giving name to several villages along their banks. The South Winterborne is a tributary of the River Frome, the more northerly Winterborne is a tributary of the River Stour. The name means 'winter stream', that is one that flows most strongly in winter, from Old English *winter-burna*.

Winterborne Came   *Wintreburne* 1086 (Domesday Book), *Winterburn Caam* 1280, *Wynterborne Cam* 1288, *Wynterborn-came* 1437. One of the several places named from the South Winterborne river. The addition *Came* is from the possession of this manor by the abbey of St Stephen at *Caen* (in Normandy) from the time of William the Conqueror.

Winterborne Clenston *Wintreburne* 1086 (Domesday Book), *Winterborn Clench* 1243, *Clenchton* 1268, *Wynterburn Clencheston* 1303. 'Estate on the River Winterborne held by the *Clench* family', here from the 13th century; *-ton* is from Old English *tūn* 'manor, estate'.

Winterborne Herringston *Wintreburne* 1086 (Domesday Book), *Winterborn Harang* 1243, *Wynterburne Heringeston* 1288, *Heryngeston* 1464. Named from the same river as Winterborne Came. The addition is from the family of *Harang*, which possessed the manor from the 13th century, with Old English *tūn* in the sense 'estate, village'. For the same family, see also Chaldon Herring, Herrison, and Langton Herring.

Winterborne Houghton *Wintreburne* 1086 (Domesday Book), *Winterborn Hueton* 1246, *Wynterburn Hugheton* 1288, *Wynterbourne Houtone* 1302. 'Estate on the River Winterborne held by Hugh', with Old English *tūn* 'manor, estate'. The man in question is probably one *Hugh de Boscherbert* who held a manor here at the time of Domesday Book.

Winterborne Kingston *Wintreburne* 1086 (Domesday Book), *Kingeswinterburn* 1194, *Kingeston* 1244, *Wynterbourn Kyngeston* 1280, *Wynterborn Regis* 1312. Named from the same river as Winterborne Clenston. Kingston is 'farm or estate belonging to the king', from Old English *cyning* and *tūn*; it was held by the king from at least as early as the time of King John.

Winterborne Monkton *Wintreburne* 1086 (Domesday Book), *Wynterburn Moneketon* 1268, *Wynterburne Munketon* 1288, *Wyntreborne Monketon* 1397. Named from the same river as Winterborne Came. The addition *Monkton* means 'estate or village of the monks', from Old English *munuc* and *tūn*, since this place belonged to the Cluniac priory of Le Wast near Boulogne from the early 13th century. In medieval times it was sometimes referred to as *Winterborne Wast*.

Winterborne Muston (in Winterborne Kingston) *Wintreburne* 1086 (Domesday Book), *Winterborn Musters* 1243, *Winterborne Mousterston* 1310, *Wynterbourne Musterestone* 1317.

Named from the same river as Winterborne Clenston. *Muston* means 'farm or estate belonging to the *de Musters* family', from Old English *tūn*; this family was here from the 13th century, see also Muston in Piddlehinton. In medieval times this place (or part of it) was known as *Winterborne Turberville*, from the *Turberville* family who also had lands here.

Winterborne St Martin *Wintreburne* 1086 (Domesday Book), *Wynterburn Sancti Martini* 1244, *Wynterburn Seynt Martyn* 1280, *Martyn towne* 1494. Named from the same river as Winterborne Came. 'St Martin' is from the dedication of the church. Martinstown is an alternative modern name, first found at the end of the 15th century.

Winterborne Stickland *Winterburne* 1086 (Domesday Book), *Winterburn Stikellane* 1203, *Wynterborne Stykelane* 1288, *Wynterburne Stikelland* 1311. 'Estate on the River Winterborne with a steep lane', from Old English *sticol* and *lane*. Lanes climb the hills to east and west out of the deep valley of the River Winterborne in which the village lies. The word *stickle* 'steep' survives in Dorset dialect.

Winterborne Tomson *Winterburne* 942 (in a 15th century copy of an Anglo–Saxon charter), *Wintreburne* 1086 (Domesday Book), *Winterborn Thom'* 1243, *Wynterbourn Thomaston* 1280. 'Estate on the River Winterborne held by someone called Thomas', although the man in question has not been traced; the final *-ton* (from Old English *tūn* 'manor, estate') is found weakened to *-on* from the 16th century.

Winterborne Whitechurch *Wintreburne* 1086 (Domesday Book), *Winterburn Albi Monasterii* 1201, *Winterburn Blancmustier* 1212, *Wynterborn Wytecherch* 1268. 'Estate on the River Winterborne with a white church', from Old English *hwīt* and *cirice* (alternating respectively in medieval times with Latin *albus* and *monasterium* and Old French *blanc* and *moustier*). 'White church' may suggest a church built of stone as distinct from a wooden one.

Winterborne Zelstone *Wintreborne* 1086 (Domesday Book), *Wynterburne Malreward* 1230, *Winterborn Maureward*

1285, *Wynterbourn Selyston* 1350, *Winterborne Zelston* 1626. Named from the more northerly River Winterborne. The earlier manorial addition is from the family of *Malreward* or *Maureward*, here from the 12th to 16th centuries (for the same family name see Kingston Maurward). The later addition is from a family called *de Seles*, combined with Old English *tūn* 'estate'.

Winterbourne Abbas *Winceburnan* 987 (in a later copy of an Anglo-Saxon charter), *Wintreburne* 1086 (Domesday Book), *Wynterburn Abbatis* 1244, *Wynterburn Abbots* 1297. Named from the same river as Winterborne Came. The addition is Latin *abbas* 'abbot' because this manor belonged to the Abbey of Cerne. In medieval times it was sometimes known as *Watreleswyntreburn*, from Old English *waeter-lēas* 'waterless', from the dryness of the South Winterborne river here in some seasons.

Winterbourne Steepleton *Wintreburne* 1086 (Domesday Book), *Stipelwinterburn* 1199, *Stepelton* 1219, *Wynterburn Stepilton* 1244. Named from the same river as Winterborne Came. Steepleton means 'village with a church steeple', from Old English *stīepel* and *tūn*.

Winterhays (in Yetminster) *Wynterhey* 1327, *Wynterheie* 1328, *Winterhays* 1577. 'Enclosure used in winter', from Old English *winter* and *haeg*.

Winton (in Bournemouth) district named from Earl of Eglinton created also Earl of *Winton* in 1859, a kinsman of the Talbot sisters, see Talbot Village.

Witchampton *Wichemetune* 1086 (Domesday Book), *Wichamton* 1216, *Wichehampton* 1271, *Whichampton* 1280. Probably 'farm of the dwellers at a place called *Wīchām*', that is at 'a village associated with a Romano-British settlement', from Old English *wīc, hǣme* and *tūn*. There are extensive Roman remains here.

Withyhook Mill (in Leigh) *Widihoc* 1197, *la Wytheoc* 1283, *Wydihok* 1325. 'Spit of land growing with willows', from Old English *wīthig* and *hōc*.

Wolfeton (in Charminster) *Wolueton* 1231, *Wulveton* 1236, *Wulfeton* 1279, *Wolfeton* 1303. 'Farm of a man called Wulfa', from Old English *tūn* and an Old English personal name.

Wolfridge Farm (in Motcombe) *Wolfridge* in 1811, but probably to be identified with *Welrigge* 1292, *Wilrygge* 1327, *Wolrig* 1411, 'ridge where there is a spring or stream', from Old English *wella* and *hrycg*, probably with reference to the higher ground to the east. *Wolf-* in the modern form is due to folk etymology.

Wonston (in Hazelbury Bryan) *Wolmerston* 1280, *Womeston* 1580, *Womston* 1607. 'Farm belonging to a man called Wulfmǣr', from Old English *tūn* and an Old English personal name.

Woodbridge (in Fontmell Magna) *wde bricge* 932 (in a later copy of an Anglo–Saxon charter), *Wodebrygge* 1395, *Woodbridge* 1618. 'The wooden bridge', from Old English *wudu* and *brycg*.

Woodbridge (in Holwell) *Wudebrige* 1194, *la Wudebrug* 1251, *la Wodebrigg* 1268. Identical in origin with the previous name.

Woodbury Hill (in Bere Regis) *Wudebur* 1254, *Wodeburi* 1287, *Wodbury* 1456, *Wodebery hill* 1476. 'Fortification by the wood', from Old English *wudu* and *burh*. There are remains of an earthwork here.

Woodcutts (in Sixpenny Handley) *Wodecote* 1244, *Wode-cotys* 1456, *Woodcotes* 1575. 'Cottages in a wood', from Old English *wudu* and *cot*.

Woodcutts Farm (in Hinton Martell) *la Wodecote* 1290, *Wodecote* 1300, *Woodcutts* 1811. Identical in origin with the previous name.

Woodhouse Cross (in Gillingham) *Woodhowse Crosse* 1609. 'House in the wood', or 'house made of wood', from Old English *wudu* and *hūs*, with *cros* 'a cross'.

Woodlake (in Bloxworth) first recorded in the 17th century. 'Woodland stream', from Old English *wudu* and *lacu*.

Woodlands *Wodelande* 1244, *Wodelond* 1268, *Wodlond* 1394, *Wudlond* 1486. 'Wooded estate or tract of land', or 'land cleared for cultivation near or within a wood', from Old English *wudu* and *land*. The final *-s* in the name, representing a plural form, only appears in the 18th century.

Woodrow (in Fifehead Neville) *Woderove* 14th century. 'Row of trees', from Old English *wudu* and *rāw*.

Woodrow (in Hazelbury Bryan) *Woodrowe* 1580. Identical in origin with the previous name.

Woodrow Farms (in Stourton Caundle) *Woderewe* 1327, *Woodrow* 1709. 'Row of trees, narrow wood', from Old English *wudu* and *rāew*.

Woodsford *Werdesford, Wardesford* 1086 (Domesday Book), *Wyrdesford, Wodesforde* 1280. 'The ford of a man called Weard', from Old English *ford* and a personal name.

Woodstreet Farm (in Wool) *Windestorte* 1086 (Domesday Book), *Wudestort, Wodestort* 1234, *Wodestrete* 1279. 'Tail of land by a wood', from Old English *wudu* and *steort*. The spelling in Domesday Book is rather erratic, and the second element was confused at an early date with *strǣt* 'street'.

Woodville (in Stour Provost) *Wodefeld* 1444. 'Wood field', from Old English *wudu* and *feld*.

Woodyates, East and West (in Pentridge) *Wdegeate, Wudegate* 9th century (in later copies of Anglo-Saxon charters), *Odiete* 1086 (Domesday Book), *Wudiete* 1199. '(Place at) the gate or gap in the wood', from Old English *wudu* and *geat*. The gate or gap may have been at Bokerly Junction, where Bokerly Ditch was breached by the road from Blandford Forum to Salisbury. The final *-s* in the name, representing a plural form, only appears in the 16th century.

Wool *Wille, Welle* 1086 (Domesday Book), *Welles* 1166, *Woll* 1249, *Wull* 1251. '(Place at) the spring or springs', from Old English *wella*. There are several springs south of the village. This name preserves the genuine West Saxon dialect form of the word *well*.

Wool Bridge, Woolbridge Heath (in East Stoke)

Wullebrigg 1244, *Wolbrigg* 1288, *Wellebrigge* 1318, *Wollebrigge* 1343. 'The bridge near Wool', from Old English *brycg*. This is an important crossing of the River Frome.

Woolcombe (in Melbury Bubb) *Wellecome* 1086 (Domesday Book), *Wulecumb* 1219, *Wollecumbe* 1286, *Wolecumbe* 1303. 'Valley with a spring or stream', from Old English *wella* and *cumb*.

Woolcombe Farm (in Toller Porcorum) *Wellacome, Wilecome* 1086 (Domesday Book), *Wllecumba* 1265, *Wollecumbe* 1285. Identical in origin with the preceding name.

Woolgarston (in Corfe Castle) *Orgarestone* 1086 (Domesday Book), *Wulgareston* 1213, *Wolgareston* 1256, *Wolston* 1528. 'Farm belonging to a man called Wulfgār', from Old English *tūn* and an Old English personal name.

Woolland *Wennland* 833 (in a later copy of an Anglo-Saxon charter), *Winlande* 1086 (Domesday Book), *Wuland* 1212, *Wollond* 1268. 'Pasture or meadow land', from Old English *wynn* and *land*.

Wools Bridge, Woolsbridge (in Verwood) *Woolles bridge* 1618. Probably from Old English *wella* 'spring, stream' (with reference to Moors River) and *brycg*.

Wooth Grange (in Netherbury) originally called *Woth Fraunceys* 1276, *Wothfrances* 1382, *Wooth Fraunces* 1405. *Woth* is the old name of the River Brit and probably meant 'sound, melody'. An estate here was held by a family called *Fraunceys*.

Wootton Fitzpaine *Wodetone, Odetun* 1086 (Domesday Book), *Wudeton* 1244, *Wodeton Roberti filii Pagani* 1316, *Wotton Fitz Payn* 1392. 'Farm in or by a wood', from Old English *wudu* and *tūn*. The manorial addition is from the family of *Fitz Payn*, as in Okeford Fitzpaine. In the 1316 spelling the Latinized addition means 'of Robert son of Payn'.

Wootton Glanville see Glanvilles Wootton.

Wootton North *Wotton* 1180, *Wuttun* 1226, *Wottoune* 1491. Identical in origin with Wootton Fitzpaine; 'north' in relation to Glanvilles Wootton.

Worbarrow (Bay and Tout) (in Tyneham) *Wyrebarowe*

1462, *Wyrbarow* 1500, *Worthbarow* 1575, *Warbarrow Tout* 1841. Probably 'hill where watch was kept', from Old English *weard* and *beorg*, obviously with reference to the conical hill here which provides good views to east and west along the coast. The meaning of the name is confirmed by the later addition of Tout, which is from Old English *tōte* 'look-out hill'.

Worgret (in Arne) *Vergroh, Weregrote* 1086 (Domesday Book), *Wergerod* 1202, *Worgret* 1575. 'The gallows for criminals', from Old English *wearg-rōd*. Worgret is one mile out of Wareham on the road to Dorchester.

Worth Matravers *Orde, Wirde* 1086 (Domesday Book), *Wurthe* 1220, *Worth Matrauers* 1664. 'The enclosure', from Old English *worth*. The manorial addition is from the *Mautravers* family, here from the 14th century.

Wrackleford House (in Stratton) *Wrakylford, Wrakylsford* 1544, *Wrekelsford* 1546, *Wrackleford* 1606. 'Ford belonging to a man called Wrǣcwulf', from Old English *ford* and an Old English personal name. The ford was no doubt across the River Frome.

Wraxall *Brocheshale* 1086 (Domesday Book, a mistake for *Wrocheshale*), *Wrokeshal* 1196, *Wroxhale* 1253, *Wraxhale* 1483. 'Nook of land or secluded hollow frequented by the buzzard or other bird of prey', from Old English *wrocc* and *healh*.

Wych (in Bothenhampton) *la Wiche* 1481, *le Wyche* 1496, *Wyche* 1539. From Old English *wīc* 'dairy farm', or *wice* 'wych-elm'.

Wyke Farm (in Castleton) *Wica* 1125, *Wike* 1212, *Wyke* 1290, *Wyk* 1355. 'The dairy farm', from Old English *wīc*.

Wyke Farm and Down (in Gussage All Saints) *Wyke* 1276, *Wike* 1596, *Wick* 1811. Identical in origin with the previous name.

Wyke Farm (in Halstock) *Wika* 1236, *la Wike* 1244, *la Wyk* 1268, *Week* 1596. Identical in origin with the previous names.

Wyke Marsh (in Gillingham) first recorded in the 18th

century, named from *Wyke* 1244, *Week* 1609, identical in origin with the previous names.

Wyke Oliver House (near Preston) *Wyke* 1327, *Wike* 1332, *Weeke Oliver* 1616. 'The dairy farm', from Old English *wīc*. John *Oliver* held lands here in 1640, but his family must have been here even earlier.

Wyke Regis *Wike* 984 (in a 14th century copy of an Anglo-Saxon charter), *Wick* 1220, *Kingeswik* 1242, *Wyke Regis* 1407. In this name the Old English word *wīc* may have the meaning 'specialized farm' or 'harbour, fishery'. It was anciently royal demesne, hence the Latin addition *Regis* 'of the king'.

Wyke Wood (in Abbotsbury) *Wyke, Wike* 1269, *Wyke Wodde* 1495, *Wyke Woodde* 1550. 'Wood by the dairy farm', from Old English *wīc* and *wudu*.

Wyld Farms, Monkton Wyld (in Wootton Fitzpaine) *La Uilla* 1189, *Wila* 1204, *Wyle* 1316, *Monkynwyll* 1535. From Old English *wīl* 'a wile, a trick', probably denoting 'a trap or a snare'. The spelling with *-d* is quite a recent development. *Monkyn-*, later altered to Monkton, means 'of the monks', alluding to the possession of lands here by Forde Abbey.

Wynford Eagle *Wenfrot* 1086 (Domesday Book), *Winfrot Gileberti de Aquila* 1204, *Wynford Aquile* 1275, *Wynfrod Egle* 1288. An old Celtic name, originally applied to the stream on which Wynford stands, and identical in origin with the first part of Winfrith Newburgh. The manorial addition is from the family of Gilbert *del Egle* (latinized as *de Aquila*) who came from Laigle in France.

Wytch Farm and Heath (in Corfe Castle) *Wicha* 12th century, *Wyche* 1498. These places take their name from the River Wych, now called the Corfe River, although its estuary in Poole Harbour is still called Wych Channel. The river-name Wych, on record from the 10th century, is from Old English *wice* 'wych-elm or other tree with pliant branches'.

Wytherstone Farm (in Powerstock) *Wytheston* 1269, *Witherston* 1285, *Wythereston* 1288, *Witheston* 1336. Either 'farm belonging to a man called Wither', from Old English *tūn* and an Old English personal name, or 'stone near which willows grow', from Old English *wīthig* and *stān*.

Yard Dairy (in Rampisham) *Le Yerde* 13th century, *La Yurd* 1360, *Yarde* 1510. From Old English *gierd* 'a measure of land consisting of about thirty acres'.

Yardgrove Farm (in Marnhull) *Gerdegrave* 1258, *Yerdgrave* 1270, *Yerdegrove* 1342. Probably 'grove or copse where rods or spars are obtained', from Old English *gerd* and *grāf*.

Yellowham Hill and Wood (in Puddletown) *Golwham* 1270, *Yolweham* 1404, *Yelweham* 1427, *Yeleuham* 1492. 'Yellow enclosure', from Old English *geolu* and *hamm*. 'Yellow' may allude to the soil or to yellow flowers.

Yetminster *Etiminstre* 1086 (Domesday Book), *Eteministr* 1214, *Yateminstre* 1226, *Yeteministr* 1252. 'Church of a man called Ēata', from Old English *mynster* and an Old English personal name.

Yewstock (in Hinton St Mary) *Hevedstokke* early 14th century, *la Hevedstocke* 1340, *Hewstock* 1811. 'The head post', i.e. 'the post on which the head of a beheaded criminal was exposed', from Old English *hēafod-stocc*. The cottage of this name stands on the parish boundary.

Yondover (in Loders) *Endouer* 1454, *Yendover* 1498, *Yandover* 1535, *Endover* 1545. '(Land) beyond the river-bank', from Old English *begeondan* and *ōfer*.

GLOSSARY OF THE ELEMENTS FOUND IN DORSET PLACE-NAMES

In this list, OE stands for Old English, ME for Middle English, and ModE for Modern English. The Old English letters 'ash' and 'thorn' have been rendered *ae* and *th* throughout in order to make the information more readily accessible to the general reader.

abbas (Latin) 'abbot'. Abbott's Wootton, Bradford Abbas, Cerne Abbas, West Compton, Milton Abbas, Stoke Abbott, Winterbourne Abbas.

abbat (ME) 'abbot'. Stoke Abbott.

abbatissa (Latin) 'abbess'. Compton Abbas, Melbury Abbas.

abbesse (ME) 'abbess'. Abbot's Court.

abbeye (ME) 'abbey'. Abbeycroft, Abbey House.

abbod (OE) 'abbot'. Abbotsbury, Abbott Street.

āc (OE) 'oak-tree'. Broad Oak, Coppleridge, Oakford, Oakley (2), Okeford (2), Waddock.

aecer (OE) 'plot of arable land'. Innsacre.

ǣl (OE) 'eel'. Almer.

aern (OE) 'house or building'. ?Arne, Crockerton, ?Dullar, Minterne (2), Potterne.

aesc (OE) 'ash-tree'. Anderson, Ash (2), Ashcombe, Ashington, Ashley (4), Ashmore, Ashton (2), Nash (2).

aetheling (OE) 'prince'. Agglestone, Allington.

ǣwiell (OE) 'source of a stream'. Alton Pancras.

169

āewielm (OE) 'source of a stream'. Toller Whelme.

alor (OE) 'alder'. Alderholt, Alders Coppice, Aller, Axnoller.

alum (ModE) 'alum'. Alum Chine.

ānstīg (OE) 'narrow track'. Ansty.

ar (Celtic) 'beside'. Orchard.

atten (ME) 'at the'. Nash (2), Nyland.

bāer (OE) 'woodland pasture'. ?Barford, ?Beer Hackett, ?Bere Farm, Bere Marsh, ?Bere Regis, ?Middlebere.

baeth (OE) 'bathing-place'. Moorbath.

bagga (OE) 'bag-like feature or animal'. Bagman's Farm.

baillie (ME) 'bailiff's jurisdiction or district'. Bailey Ridge, Bailie Gate.

balg (OE) 'smooth'. Ballard Down.

bay (ModE) 'embankment to form a dam'. Bay.

bēan (OE) 'bean'. Bainly, Benville, Bincombe, Binnegar.

bearu (OE) 'wood, grove'. Adber, ?Bagber, ?Barford, Beere Farm, ?Beer Hackett, Beerhall, ?Bere Farm, ?Bere Regis, Hazelbury Bryan, ?Middlebere, Plumber, ?Todber.

begeondan (OE) 'beyond'. Yondover.

belle (OE) 'bell-shaped hill'. Belchalwell, Bellows Cross.

bēo (OE) 'bee'. Beaulieu Wood.

beorg (OE) 'hill, mound, tumulus'. ?Bagber, Bulbarrow Hill, Charborough House, Chelborough, Dogbury, Dunbury, Hambury, King Barrow, Limbury, Longbury, Lymburgh's Farm, Seaborough, Stoborough, Symondsbury, ?Todber, Worbarrow.

bere (OE) 'barley'. Barcombe.

bere-aern (OE) 'barn'. Berne.

bere-tūn (OE) 'barley farm'. Barton Hill.

bere-wīc (OE) 'barley farm'. Berwick.

berned (OE) 'burnt'. Barnsfield Heath.

betwēonan (OE) 'between'. Christchurch, Twinwood.

bī (OE) 'by, near'. Bestwall, East Brook, Westport.

bic (OE) 'beak, beak-shaped ridge'. Purbeck.

bile (OE) 'bill, beak'. Portland Bill.

binnan (OE) 'within'. Bindon.

170

biscop (OE) 'bishop'. Bishop's Caundle, Bishop's Down.

blaec (OE) 'black, dark'. Blackdown Hill, Blackmoor, Blackney, Blackrow, Blackven, Black Venn, Blackwater, Blagdon (2), Nutford.

blāecen (OE) 'bleaching'. Blashenwell.

blāege (OE) 'blay, gudgeon'. Blandford (2).

blēat (OE) 'wretched, cold'. ?Bleet.

blinc (OE) 'shining stream'. Blynfield.

bōc (OE) 'beech-tree'. Bockhampton (2).

bōc-land (OE) 'land granted by charter'. Buckland Newton, Buckland Ripers.

boga (OE) 'bow'. ?Boveridge.

bord (OE) 'border'. Chebbard.

bors (OE) 'spiky plant'. Boscombe.

bothen (OE) 'rosemary, darnel, thyme'. Bothenwood.

bothm, botm (OE) 'valley bottom'. Bothenhampton, Coombe Bottom, Empool Bottom, Sleep Bottom.

brād (OE) 'broad'. Bradford (3), Bradle, Bradpole, Broadenham, Broadley, Broadmayne, Broad Oak, Broadwey, Broadwindsor, Sydling St Nicholas.

brāec (OE) 'land broken up'. Breach (2).

brōc (OE) 'brook'. ?Brockham, Brockhampton, Brockington, East Brook, Fern Brook, Holebrook, Honeybrook, Lambrook, Lowbrook, Northbrook, Southbrook, Westbrook.

brocc (OE) 'badger'. ?Brockham.

brocc-hol (OE) 'badger hole'. Brockhill.

brōm (OE) 'broom'. Brimbley, Bronkham, Broom Hill, Broomhill.

brūn (OE) 'brown'. Burngate.

brycg (OE) 'bridge, causeway'. Bridge Lane, Chilbridge, Crawford Bridge, Holmebridge, Kitford Bridge, Stalbridge, Stanbridge (2), Stockbridge, Woodbridge (2), Wool Bridge, Wools Bridge.

bucc (OE) 'buck, male deer'. Bokerly Ditch.

bucca (OE) 'he-goat'. ?Buckham.

bufan (OE) 'above, over'. ?Boveridge, Bowden, Bowood.

bugge (OE) 'hobgoblin'. ?Buckshaw, ?Bugley.

bula (OE) 'bull'. Bowldish Pond, Bowleaze, ?Bulbarrow, Bullhill.

bune (OE) 'reed'. ?Chewton Bunny.

būr (OE) 'cottage'. Bushey.

burh (OE) 'fortified place, pre-English earthwork'. Abbotsbury, Badbury, Berry Hill, Bulbury, Burcombe, Burwood, Buzbury, Chalbury (2), Dudsbury, Ensbury, Flower's Barrow, Henbury, Hengistbury, Maumbury, Melbury (4), Netherbury, Penbury, Poundbury, Rawlsbury, Shaftesbury, Spetisbury, Woodbury.

burh-tūn (OE) 'fortified farm, farm near a fortification'. Bourton, Burton (5).

burna (OE) 'spring, stream'. Bibbern, Bourne, Bournemouth, Cheselbourne, Cranborne, Hoburne, Langbourne, Milborne (2), Oborne, Sherborne, Wimborne (2).

bury (ME) 'manor house'. Eastbury, Westbury.

butere (OE) 'butter'. Butterwick.

butt (OE) 'archery butt'. ?Hillbutts.

butte (OE) 'short strip ploughed at right angles to others'. ?Hillbutts.

byden (OE) 'hollow'. Bibbern.

byxen (OE) 'growing with box'. Bexington.

caerse (OE) 'cress'. Cards Mill, Caswell, Keysworth.

calu (OE) 'bare'. Colway.

canne (OE) 'hollow, deep valley'. Cann.

canonicus (Latin) 'canon'. Whitchurch Canonicorum.

carn (Celtic) 'heap of stones, cairn'. River Cerne, Cerne Abbas, Nether & Up Cerne, Charminster, River Char.

castel (ME) 'castle'. Castle Hill, Castleton, Corfe Castle, Maiden Castle, Sandsfoot Castle.

catt (OE) 'wild-cat'. Catsley.

cauce (ME) 'raised way across marshy ground'. Sherborne Causeway.

ceaf (OE) 'chaff, fallen twigs'. Chaffeymoor.

cealc (OE) 'chalk'. Challow.

ceald (OE) 'cold'. Belchalwell, Cold Harbour, Cole Hill Wood.

cealf (OE) 'calf'. Chaldon Herring.

cearr (OE) 'turn, bend'. ?Charborough House.

ceaster (OE) 'Roman city'. Dorchester.

cēd (Celtic) 'wood'. Chetterwood, Chideock, Lytchett (2), Orchard.

ceole (OE) 'throat, channel, gorge'. ?Chelborough, Chilbridge.

ceorl (OE) 'freeman, peasant'. Chalbury, Charlton (3).

ceotol (OE) 'deep valley surrounded by hills'. Chettle, Chettle Head.

cēping (OE) 'market'. Blandford Forum.

chapele (ME) 'chapel'. Chapel Court, Chapel Marsh.

cierr (OE) 'turn, bend'. Jordon Hill.

cild (OE) 'noble-born son, younger son'. Childhay, Chilfrome, Chilmore, Child Okeford.

cilte (OE or pre-English) 'hill-slope'. Chilcombe.

cinu (OE) 'deep valley, ravine'. Alum Chine, Branksome Chine.

cirice (OE) 'church'. Chescombe, Christchurch, Church Knowle, Frome Vauchurch, Whitchurch Canonicorum, Winterborne Whitechurch.

cisel (OE) 'gravel, shingle'. Cheselbourne, Chesil Beach.

clādo- (Celtic) 'ditch'. Badbury.

clǣg (OE) 'clay'. Claylake, Claywell, Clinger.

clǣne (OE) 'clean, clear of weeds'. Clandon.

clāte (OE) 'burdock, goose-grass'. Clatcombe.

clif (OE) 'cliff, bank'. Catsley, The Cliff, Clifton Maybank, Clyffe, Duncliffe, Eccliffe, Highcliffe, Muscliff, Redcliff, Rockley, Whitecliff.

cnaepp (OE) 'hill-top, hillock'. Crocker's Knap.

cniht (OE) 'thane, retainer, knight'. Knighton (5).

cnoll (OE) 'hill-top, hillock'. Bucknowle, Chartknolle, Chetnole, Church Knowle, Hartland, Hincknoll, Knoll (2), Knowle Hall, Knowlton, Penbury Knoll, Puncknowle.

cobb (OE) 'rounded mass'. Cobb, Cobley.

cocc (OE) 'woodcock or other wild bird', or 'heap, hillock'.

Cockhill, Cocknowle.

col (OE) 'charcoal'. ?Colehill, Cole Street, Cole Wood, ?Great Coll Wood.

cōl (OE) 'cool'. Colmer.

coll (OE) 'hill'. ?Colehill, ?Great Coll Wood.

coninger (ME) 'rabbit warren'. Conegar Hill, Conygar Hill.

conōg (Celtic) meaning doubtful. Combs Ditch.

coppod (OE) 'pollarded'. Coppleridge.

corf (OE) 'cutting, gap, pass'. Corfe Castle, Corfe Hill, Corfe Mullen, Corscombe, Corton, Coryates.

corner (ME) 'corner, nook'. The Corner.

cot (OE) 'cottage'. Cothayes, Woodcutts (2).

court (ME) 'large house'. Abbot's Court, Bere Farm, King's Court Wood, Moor Court Farm, Moorcourt Farm.

crabbe (ME) 'crab-apple'. Crab Orchard.

cran (OE) 'crane, heron'. Cranborne.

crāwe (OE) 'crow'. Crawford Bridge, Tarrant Crawford.

cribb (OE) 'crib'. Cripton.

crōc (OE) 'bend'. Knob's Crook.

crocc (OE) 'crock, pot'. Crockerton Hill.

croccere (OE) 'potter'. Crocker's Knap.

croft (OE) 'enclosure'. Abbeycroft, Crate Wood.

cros (OE) 'cross'. Ivy Cross, Woodhouse Cross.

cross (ModE) 'cross-roads'. Harman's Cross, New Cross Gate, Shave Cross, Three Legged Cross, Trickett's Cross.

crüg (Celtic) 'mound, hill, barrow'. Creech Barrow, Creech Hill, Long & Moor Crichel, Crook Hill.

crundel (OE) 'pit, quarry'. Crendell.

crypel (OE) 'place that can be crept through'. Cripplestyle.

cū (OE) 'cow'. Cowdon Hill, Cowgrove, Culeaze House.

cumb (OE) 'valley'. Ashcombe, Barcombe, Batcombe, Bettiscombe, Bidcombe, Bincombe, Bonscombe, Bookham, Boscombe, Brenscombe, Brimbley Coombe, Bronkham, Burcombe, Chescombe, Chilcombe, Clatcombe, Combe Almer, Compton (5), Coombe (6), Corscombe, Eastcombe, Encombe, Filcombe, Great Coombe, Hillcombe, Holcombe,

Honeycomb, Kingcombe, Lankham, Lewcombe, Longcombe, Loscombe, Luccombe (2), Luscombe, Lyscombe, Mappercombe, Melcombe (2), Morecombelake, Motcombe, Nettlecombe, Purcombe (2), Renscombe, Seacombe, Shatcombe (2), Southcombe, Stancombe, Thorncombe (2), Wakeham, Watercombe, Watcombe, Westcombe, Whatcombe (2), Whitcombe, Woolcombe (2).

cut (ME) 'water-channel'. Cut Mill.

cwēn (OE) 'queen'. Queen Oak.

cȳme (OE) 'convenient'. Kimmeridge.

cymed (OE) 'wall-germander'. Kingcombe.

cyne- (OE) 'royal'. ?The Kendalls, Kington (2).

cyning (OE) 'king'. King Barrow, King Down, King's Court Wood, Kingsettle, Kingsland, King's Mill Bridge, Kingstag, Kingston (5), Kingswood, Winterborne Kingston

cȳta (OE) 'kite'. Kitford Bridge.

dēad (OE) 'dead, disused'. Deadmoor.

dēaw (OE) 'dew'. Dewlands.

decoy (ModE) 'decoy'. Decoy Heath.

denu (OE) 'valley'. Dean (3), Deanland, Tincleton.

deorc (OE) 'dark'. Darknoll.

dīc (OE) 'ditch'. Bokerly Ditch, Combs Ditch, Grim's Ditch, Holditch, Walditch.

dodde (OE) 'rounded hilltop'. ?Dodding's, Duddle.

dogga (OE) 'dog'. Dogbury.

dowere (ME) 'dowry'. Dowerfield.

dulu (OE) 'valley'. ?Dullar.

dūn (OE) 'down, hill'. Bindon, Bishop's Down, Blackdown, Blagdon (2), Bowden, Canon Hill, Chaldon (3), Clandon, Coombe Down Hill, Cowdon, Donedge, Dunbury, Dungrove, Duntish, Eggardon, Farrington, Ferndown, Hambledon, Harley Down, Haydon (3), Jordon, King Down, Langdon, Linton, Littledown, Main Down, Mill Down, Moordown, Morden, Norden, Pilsdon, Pokesdown, South Down, Sutton Holms, Waddon (2).

dunn (OE) 'dark'. Duncliffe.

durno- (Celtic) 'fist'. Dorchester.
duru (OE) 'door'. Durdle Door.
ēa (OE) 'stream'. Christchurch.
eald (OE) 'old'. Old Lawn.
ears (OE) 'buttock'. Arish Mell.
ēast (OE) 'east'. Eastbury, Eastcombe, Easthay, Eastington, East Moors, Easton, East Parley, East Stoke, East Stour, Eype.
ēastan (OE) 'east of'. Bestwall, East Brook.
ēasterra (OE) 'more easterly'. Eype.
ebba (OE) 'ebb, shore visible at low tide'. Great Ebb.
ecg (OE) 'edge'. Donedge.
edisc (OE) 'pasture'. Bowldish.
ēg or *īeg* (OE) 'island, well-watered land, dry ground in marsh'. Brownsea, Chaffeymoor, ?Chewton Bunny, Eye Mead, Furzey Island, Pipsford.
ellen (OE) 'elder-tree'. ?Elwell Lodge.
elm (OE) 'elm-tree'. Walton Elm.
emn (OE) 'even, smooth'. Empool.
ened (OE) 'duck'. Enmore.
ende (OE) 'end'. Townsend.
eofor (OE) 'wild boar'. ?Evershot.
eorl (OE) 'nobleman'. Earl's Hill.
epistle (ModE) 'epistle'. Pistle Down.
etisc (OE) 'pasture'. Duntish.
faeger (OE) 'fair, beautiful'. Verwood.
faesten (OE) 'stronghold'. Handfast Point.
fāh (OE) 'coloured'. Frome Vauchurch.
fearn (OE) 'fern'. Farnham, Farrington, Fernbrook, Furleigh.
feld (OE) 'tract of open country, field'. Barnsfield, Benville, Blynfield, Field Grove, Hethfelton, Hilfield, Merry Field Hill, Sovell Down, Westfields, Whitfield, Woodville.
fenn (OE) 'fen'. Blackven, Black Venn, Bowerswain, Vale Acre, Venn.
fergen (OE) 'wooded hill'. ?Ferndown, Verne Yeates.
fierne (OE) 'ferny place'. ?Ferndown.

fīf (OE) 'five'. Anderson, Fifehead (3).

filethe (OE) 'hay'. Feltham, Filcombe, Filford.

fitt (OE) 'dispute'. Fitzworth.

flēot (OE) 'estuary, inlet'. Fleet, Longfleet.

flōr (OE) 'floor'. ?Flower's Barrow.

folc (OE) 'folk, people'. Folke.

fonke (ME) 'spark of fire'. ?Merritown.

ford (OE) 'ford'. Ameysford, Barford, Blandford (2), Bradford (3), Canford (2), Crawford, Fiddleford, Filford, Ford Farms, Forde Abbey, Fordington, Hanford, Hayward Bridge, Heniford, Huntingford, Langford, Luckford, Lydford, Muckleford, Mudeford, North Haven, Nutford, Oakford, Okeford (2), Pilford, Pinford, Pipsford, Romford, Sandford (2), Sherford, Somerford, West Stafford, Stake Ford Cross, Stinsford, Stokeford, Tarrant Crawford, Thornford, Tollerford, Twofolds Bridge, Twyford, Walford, Walkford, Westford, Woodsford, Wrackleford.

foreland (ModE) 'cape, headland'. Handfast Point.

forest (ME) 'forest'. Forest Farm & Side.

forst (OE) 'ridge'. ?Fossil.

fortune (ModE) 'fortune'. Fortuneswell.

forum (Latin) 'market'. Blandford Forum.

fōt (OE) 'foot'. Sandsfoot.

frāter (Latin) 'brother (of religious order)'. Toller Fratrum.

frere (ME) 'friar'. Friar Waddon.

frogga (OE) 'frog'. Frogmore (2).

frud (Celtic) 'stream'. Winfrith Newburgh, Wynford Eagle.

funtōn (Celtic) 'stream, spring'. Fontmell Magna & Parva.

fyrhth (OE) 'wood, wooded countryside'. Frith.

fyrs (OE) 'furze'. Furzehill, Furzey Island.

gaers-tūn (OE) 'grass enclosure, paddock'. Garston.

gafol (OE) 'tax, rent'. Galton.

galga (OE) 'gallows'. Gallows Hill.

gāra (OE) 'triangular plot of ground, point of land'. Gore Farm (2), Gore Heath.

gāt (OE) 'goat'. Goathill, Goathorn, Gotham.

gēap (OE) 'steep place'. Eype.

geard (OE) 'yard'. Smetherd.

geat (OE) 'gate, gap, pass'. Bailie Gate, Biddlesgate, Burngate, Corfe Castle, Coryates, Crockerton Hill, Picket, Slaughtergate, Verne Yeates, Woodyates.

geolu (OE) 'yellow'. Yellowham.

gerd (OE) 'rod, spar'. Yardgrove.

gierd (OE) 'measure of land'. Yard Dairy.

glida (OE) 'kite or other bird of prey'. Lydford.

gold-hord (OE) 'gold-hoard, treasure of gold'. Gaulter Gap.

gor (OE) 'dirt'. Gorwell.

gouge (early MODE) 'to hollow or scoop out'. ?Gutch Pool.

grāf (OE) 'grove, copse'. Cowgrove, Dungrove, Field Grove, Graston, Grove, Hargrove, Hartgrove, Thorngrove, Weathergrove, Yardgrove.

grange (ME) 'grange, outlying farm where crops were stored'. Grange (2).

grēne (OE) 'a green'. Enmore Green. Giddy Green.

Grīm (OE) a nickname for Woden. Grim's Ditch.

gydig (OE) 'mad, foolish'. Giddy Green.

gyse (OE) 'gush of water'. Gussage (3).

hǣeddre (OE) 'heather'. ?Hatherly.

haefen (OE) 'haven, harbour'. North & South Haven Point, Tadden.

haeg (OE) 'enclosure'. Bilshay, Blackney, Bluntshay, Bowleaze, Champernhayes, Childhay, Colway, Cothayes, Downshay, Easthay, Gummershay (2), Guppy, Hursey, Kershay, Lenthay, Marshalsea, Meerhay, Netherhay, North Hayes, Silkhay, Winterhays.

haeg-thorn (OE) 'hawthorn'. Haythorn, ?Hatherly.

hǣel (OE) 'good fortune' or *hǣele* (OE) 'healthy' or *hǣelu* (OE) 'health'. Elwell.

hǣeme (OE) 'dwellers'. Ashington, Bockhampton, Brockington, Shilvinghampton, Stubhampton, Witchampton.

hǣer (OE) 'rock, heap of stones, tumulus'. ?Arne.

hǣes (OE) 'brushwood'. Hayes.

haesel (OE) 'hazel'. Hazelbury Bryan.

haet (OE) 'hat-shaped hill'. Hatts Barn.

hāeth (OE) 'heath'. Heath Farm, Hethfelton.

hālga (OE) 'saint'. All Hallows.

hālig (OE) 'holy'. Halstock, Holwell.

hām (OE) 'homestead, village'. ?Edmondsham, ?Farnham, Gillingham, ?Petersham, ?Pulham, Wareham.

hamel (OE) 'scarred, mutilated'. Hambledon Hill.

hamlet (ModE) 'hamlet'. Hamlet.

hamm (OE) 'enclosure, river-meadow, promontory'. Attisham, Bagman's Farm, Brinsham, Broadenham, Brockham, Buckham, Densham, ?Edmondsham, ?Farnham, Feltham, Frankham, Gotham, Ham Common, Hammoon, Hampreston, Hamworthy, Hillamsland, Langham, Longham, Milborne Stileham, Newnham, Parnham, ?Petersham, Portisham, ?Pulham, Rampisham, Swineham, Tyneham, Yellowham.

hām-tūn (OE) 'home farm, homestead'. Bockhampton, Bothenhampton, Brockhampton.

hān (OE) 'rock, stone'. Handfast Point, Hanford.

hangra (OE) 'wooded slope'. Binnegar, Clinger.

hār (OE) 'grey'. ?Hargrove, Harpitts, ?Hartgrove.

hara (OE) 'hare'. ?Hargrove, ?Hartgrove.

hēafod (OE) 'headland, ridge, upper end of a valley'. Ballard Down, Chettle Head, Swyre Head (2).

hēafod-stocc (OE) 'head post'. Yewstock.

hēah (OE) 'high'. Hambury, ?Henbury, High Hall, High Lea, Highwood, Hinton St Mary, Sixpenny Handley.

healf (OE) 'half'. Half Hide Down.

healh (OE) 'nook of land'. ?Cudnell, Wraxall.

heall (OE) 'hall, manor house'. Beerhall, High Hall, Kingston Lacy Hall, West Hall.

heard (OE) 'hard'. Harley Down.

hearpere (OE) 'harper'. Harp Stone, Hurpston.

hēg (OE) 'hay'. Haydon (3), Hayward Bridge.

helde (OE) 'tansy'. ?Hilton.

henn (OE) 'water-hen, wild bird'. Encombe, ?Henbury, Hincknoll, Henley.

heorot (OE) 'hart'. Hartland, Hartley.

here-beorg (OE) 'shelter'. Cold Harbour.

hermitage (ME) 'hermitage'. Hermitage.

hīd (OE) 'hide of land'. Fifehead (3), Half Hide Down, Hyde (3), Piddletrenthide.

hielde (OE) 'slope'. ?Hilton.

hīwan (OE) 'religious community'. Hinton Martell & Parva, Piddlehinton, Tarrant Hinton.

hīwisc (OE) 'measure of land that would support a family'. Belhuish, Hewish, Huish (2).

hlēo (OE) 'shelter' or *hlēow* (OE) 'sheltered'. Lewcombe, Lewell, Luccombe (2).

hlinc (OE) 'ridge, bank'. Lydlinch, Lynch, Sydling (2).

hlith (OE) 'slope'. Lily Farm.

hlōse (OE) 'pig-sty'. Loscombe, Luscombe.

hlȳde (OE) 'torrent, noisy stream'. Litton Cheney.

hnoth (OE) 'knoll, hill'. The Nothe, White Nothe.

hnutu (OE) 'nut-tree'. Nutford.

hōc (OE) 'hook, angle, bend'. Hooke, Hookswood, Withy-hook.

hōd (OE) 'hood, shelter'. Hod Hill.

hogg (OE) 'hog, wild boar', also 'young sheep' in later names. ?Hogchester, Hoglease, ?Hogstock, Ogden Down.

hōh (OE) 'heel of land'. Hoburne.

hol (OE) 'hollow, deep' or 'a hollow'. Holcombe, Holditch, Holebrook, ?Holton, Holway, Holwell (2), Holworth, Tadnoll.

holegn (OE) 'holly'. Holdenhurst, Holm & Ivy Farm, East & West Holme, Holmwood, Holnest, Sutton Holms.

holt (OE) 'wood'. Alderholt, Holt (2), ?Holton.

hōp (OE) 'small bay'. Mupe Bay.

horn (OE) 'horn-shaped hill'. Horn Hill.

horu (OE) 'dirt, mud'. Horton.

hramsa (OE) 'wild garlic'. ?Rampisham, Rempstone.

hremn (OE) 'raven'. ?Renscombe.

hrēod (OE) 'reed'. Radipole, Rockley, Rodmore.

hring (OE) 'ring'. Ringmoor, Ringstead.

hrung (OE) 'pole'. Romford.

hrycg (OE) 'ridge'. Bailey Ridge, Boveridge, Bowridge, Coppleridge, Ridge (5), Ridgeway, Wolfridge.

hund (OE) 'hound'. ?Hound Hill.

hūne (OE) 'hoarhound (a plant)'. ?Hound Hill.

hunig (OE) 'honey'. Honeybrook, Honeycomb.

hunta (OE) 'hunter'. Huntingford.

hūs (OE) 'house'. Pithouse, Shade House, Woodhouse.

hwǣte (OE) 'wheat'. Watcombe, ?Whatcombe (2), Whatley.

hwīt (OE) 'white'. Whitchurch Canonicorum, Whitecliff, Whitefield, White Mead, White Mill, White Nothe, White Sheet Hill, Whiteway (2), Whitey Top, Whitfield (2), Winterborne Whitechurch.

hyll (OE) 'hill'. Broom Hill, Broomhill Bridge, Bullhill, Castlehill, Cockhill, ?Cocknowle, Colehill, Cole Hill, Corfe Hill, Creech Hill, Crichel (2), Crook Hill, ?Cudnell, Darknoll, ?Durdle Door, Fossil, Furzehill, Gallows Hill, Goathill, Hilfield, Hillamsland, ?Hillcombe, Hill Farm, Hound Hill, The Kendalls, Knaps Hill, Manor Hill, Marnhull, Osehill, Pamphill, Pussex, Ryall, Sandhills, Sandley, Stapehill, Sugar Hill, Thornhill, Thorn Hill, Totnell, Wadmill.

hylu (OE) 'hollow'. ?Cocknowle.

hyrne (OE) 'angle or corner of land'. Hurn.

hyrst (OE) 'copse, wooded hill'. Bedchester, Hogchester, Holdenhurst, Holnest, Hurst.

īeg-land (OE) 'island, dry ground in marsh'. Nyland.

īfet (OE) 'clump of ivy, place overgrown with ivy'. St Ives.

īfig (OE) 'ivy'. Ivy Cross.

in (OE) 'in'. Eastington, Uppington.

-ing (OE) 'place characterized by, place belonging to'. Dodding's Farm, Fordington, Snelling, Uddens.

-inga (OE) genitive plural case of *-ingas* 'people, followers'. Gillingham.

-ingtūn (OE) 'farm called after'. Baltington, Bovington, Chalmington, Chedington, Didlington, Ibberton, Ilsington, Leeson, Lillington, Mannington, Nottington, Osmington, Pallington, Povington, Poyntington, Putton, Rollington.

intrinseca (Latin) 'inner'. Ryme Intrinseca.

knob (ME) 'knoll'. Knob's Crook.

kyne (ME) 'cows'. ?The Kendalls.

lacu (OE) 'stream'. Bidlake, Claylake, Ebblake, Lake, Morecombelake, Vale Acre, Woodlake.

lǣcere (OE) 'leech-gatherer'. ?Lazerton.

lǣs (OE) 'pasture'. Culeaze, Deans Leaze, Hogleaze, Mogers Leaze.

lamb (OE) 'lamb'. Lambrook.

land (OE) 'land, estate'. Hillamsland, Kingsland, Newland, Newlands, Old Lawn, Portland, Studland, Swalland, Woodlands, Woolland.

lane (OE) 'lane'. Deanland, Long Lane, Winterborne Stickland.

lang (OE) 'long'. Langbourne, Langdon, Langford, Langham, Langton (3), Lankham, Long Bredy, Long Burton, Longbury, Longcombe, Long Crichel, Longfleet, Longham, Long Lane, Longmoor.

lāwerce (OE) 'lark'. Laverstock.

lēac-tūn (OE) 'herb garden'. ? Letton.

lēah (OE) 'wood, clearing, glade'. Ashley (4), Bainly, Barnsley, Beaulieu, Bellows Cross, Bradle, Brimbley, Broadley, Bugley, Bulbury, Cobley, Coltleigh, Filford, Furleigh, Halstock Leigh, Harley, Hartley, Hatherly, Henley, High Lea, La Lee, Leigh (2), Lily, Loverley, Marley, Matterley, Oakley (2), Parley (2), Sixpenny Handley, Sopley, Stockley, Tiley, Wantsley, Westley, Whatley, Whistley.

lēd (Celtic) 'grey'. Lytchett (2).

lencten (OE) 'Lent, Spring'. Lenthay.

līn (OE) 'flax'. Limbury, Linton Hill, ?Lymburgh's.

lind (OE) 'lime-tree'. ?Lymburgh's.

182

lisc (OE) 'reed'. Lyscombe.

lorte (OE) 'dirt'. Lorton.

lūce (OE) 'enclosure'. Look.

lutā (Celtic) 'mud'. Lodmoor.

lȳtel (OE) 'little'. Frome St Quintin, Little Bredy, Little Canford, Littledown, Little Mayne, Littlemoor, Little Puddle, Littleton, Littlewindsor, Little Wood.

mǣd (OE) 'meadow'. Eye Mead, Frome Mead, White Mead.

maegden (OE) 'maiden'. Maiden Castle, Maiden Newton.

mǣle (OE) 'multicoloured'. Melbury (4), Melplash.

mǣne (OE) 'common'. Main Down, Manor Hill, ?Maumbury,

mǣnnes (OE) 'community'. ?Chapman's Pool.

mǣw (OE) 'seagull'. Mupe Bay.

magna (Latin) 'great'. Broadwindsor, Canford Magna, Fontmell Magna, Kington Magna, Minterne Magna.

mailo- (Celtic) 'bare hill'. Fontmell Magna & Parva.

main (Celtic) 'rock, stone'. Broadmayne, ? Maumbury.

mange (ModE) 'cutaneous disease of animals'. Manswood.

mangere (OE) 'trader'. Mangerton.

mapuldor (OE) 'maple-tree'. Mapperton (2), Mappowder, Matterley.

mealm (OE) 'sandy or chalky soil'. ?Maumbury.

mearn (OE) 'soft stone or marl'. ?Marnhull.

meoluc (OE) 'milk'. Melcombe (2).

mere (OE) 'pool'. Almer, Ashmore, Colmer, Enmore, Meerhay, Ringmoor.

mersc (OE) 'marsh'. Bere Marsh, Blackven, Caundle Marsh, Chapel Marsh, Font le Roi, Guy's Marsh, Margaret Marsh, Marsh (3), Marshwood, Middlemarsh, Peacemarsh.

middel (OE) 'middle'. Middlebere, Middlemarsh, Milton (3).

minte (OE) 'mint'. Minterne (2).

mizmaze (ModE) 'maze, labyrinth'. Miz Maze.

molin (Old French) 'mill'. Corfe Mullen.

mōr (OE) 'moor, marshy ground'. Blackmoor, Chaffeymoor, Deadmoor, Dudmoor, Frogmore (2), Littlemoor, Lodmoor, Longmoor, Moorbath, Moor Court, Moor Crichel, Moorside, Moordown, Morden, Morecombelake, Moreton, Pymore, Rodmore, Rushmore, Smedmore, West Moors.

mōt (OE) 'meeting'. Motcombe.

mudde or *mode* (ME) 'mud'. Mudeford.

munuc (OE) 'monk'. Monkton Up Wimborne, Monkton Wyld, Monkwood (2), Tarrant Monkton, Winterborne Monkton.

mūs (OE) 'mouse'. Muscliff.

mūtha (OE) 'mouth, estuary'. Bournemouth, Charmouth, Small Mouth, Weymouth.

myln (OE) 'mill'. Arish Mell, Cards Mill Farm, Chamberlayne's Farm, Cut Mill, King's Mill Bridge, Milborne (2), Mill Down, New Mills, White Mill.

myncen (OE) 'nun'. Minchington.

mynster (OE) 'church of a monastery, large church'. Beaminster, Charminster, Iwerne Minster, Sturminster (2), Wimborne Minster, Yetminster.

myrge (OE) 'merry, pleasant'. Marley, Merritown, Merry Field.

mȳthe (OE) 'confluence of rivers'. Mythe Hill.

nēat (OE) 'cattle'. Notton.

neotherra (OE) 'lower'. Bingham's Melcombe, Lower Sturthill, Netherbury, Nether Compton, Nether Cerne, Netherhay, Netherstoke.

netel (OE) 'nettle'. Nettlecombe.

nīwe (OE) 'new'. Maiden Newton, New Cross Gate, Newland, Newlands, New Mills, Newnham, Newton (4), Sturminster Newton.

north (OE) 'north'. Norden, Northbourne, North Hayes, Northwood.

northan (OE) 'north of'. Northbrook, Northport.

ofer (OE) 'slope, ridge'. ?Owermoigne.

ōfer (OE) 'bank'. Southover (2), East & West Stour, Westover (2), Yondover.

ōra (OE) 'bank, shore'. Broadwindsor, Fitzworth, Goathorn, Ower.

orceard (OE) 'orchard'. Orchard.

pamp or *pempe* (OE) 'hill'. Pamphill.

park (ME) 'park'. Harbin's Park, Leigh Park, Park Farm, Parkstone.

parva (Latin) 'little'. Blandford St Mary, Fontmell Parva, Hinton Parva, Little Canford, Minterne Parva.

pearroc (OE) 'small enclosure, paddock'. Park Farm.

penn (Celtic) 'hill'. Penbury Knoll, Pen Hill, ?Penn, Pentridge, Pilsdon Pen, Sixpenny Handley.

penn (OE) 'pen, enclosure for animals'. ?Penn.

penthouse (ModE) 'outhouse or shed with sloping roof'. Paynthouse Farm.

peru (OE) 'pear-tree'. East & West Parley, Parnham, Purewell.

pīc (OE) 'point, pointed hill'. Picket Farm.

pidele (OE) 'marsh, fen'. Affpuddle, River Puddle, Piddlehinton, Piddletrenthide, Puddletown, Tolpuddle, Turners Puddle.

pīe (OE) 'gnat or other insect'. Pymore.

pīl (OE) 'stake' or 'peak'. ?Pilford, Pilsdon.

pimp (Celtic) 'five'. ?Pimperne.

pimp (OE) 'hill'. ?Pimperne.

pīn (OE) 'pine-tree'. ?Pinford.

pinn (OE) 'pin or peg'. ?Pinford.

pise (OE) 'peas'. Peacemarsh.

plaesc (OE) 'pool'. Melplash.

plūme (OE) 'plum-tree'. Plumber, ?Puncknowle.

plysc (OE) 'pool'. Plush.

pohha (OE) 'pouch'. Bowridge Hill.

point (ModE) 'promontory'. North & South Haven Point.

pōl (OE) 'pool, creek'. Bradpole, Chapman's Pool, Empool, Gutch Pool, Poole, ?Pulham, Radipole.

porcus (Latin) 'pig'. Toller Porcorum.

port (OE) 'port, harbour' or 'market, market-town'. Bridport, Northport, Portesham, Portland, Westport.

pott (OE) 'pot'. Potterne.

prenn (Celtic) 'tree'. ?Pimperne.

prēost (OE) 'priest'. Hampreston, Preston (3).

prior (OE) 'prior'. Briar's Wood.

pūca (OE) 'puck, goblin'. ?Pokesdown, Puckstone.

pull (OE) 'pool, stream'. ?Pulham.

pūr (OE) 'bittern, snipe'. Purbeck.

pyll (OE) 'pool in a river, small stream'. ?Pilford.

pyrige (OE) 'pear-tree'. Perry Copse & Farm, Purcombe (2).

pytt (OE) 'pit'. Harpitts, Pithouse, Pitt, Sandpit, Stanpit, Winspit.

pyttel (OE) 'hawk, mousehawk'. ?Piddles Wood.

rāew (OE) 'row (of houses or trees)'. Blackrow, Crocker's Knap, Rew, Woodrow.

ramm (OE) 'ram'. ?Rampisham.

rāw (OE) 'row'. Woodrow (2).

rēad (OE) 'red'. Redcliff, Red Hill, Rodden.

regis (Latin) 'of the king'. Bere Regis, Melcombe Regis, Wyke Regis.

ric (OE) 'track'. Kimmeridge.

rid (Celtic) 'ford'. ?Chetterwood.

rima (OE) 'rim, edge, border'. Ryme Intrinseca.

rīth (OE) 'stream'. ?Chetterwood.

ryge (OE) 'rye'. Ryall.

rysc (OE) 'rush'. Rushmore, Rushton, Tarrant Rushton.

sāe (OE) 'sea'. Seacombe, Seatown.

sāete (OE) 'dwellers'. Dorset.

salt-aern (OE) 'building where salt is made or sold'. Salterns.

sand (OE) 'sand'. Sandbanks, Sandford (2), Sandhills, Sandley, Sandpit, Sandsfoot, Sandway.

scēacere (OE) 'robber'. ?Sugar Hill.

sceaft (OE) 'shaft, pole'. ?Shaftesbury.

sceaga (OE) 'small wood, copse'. Buckshaw, Bushey, Shave Cross, Shave Hill.

scēap or *scīep* (OE) 'sheep'. Shapwick, Shatcombe, Shipstal, Shipton Gorge.

sceard (OE) 'cleft, gap'. Shade House.

scēat (OE) 'corner or angle of land'. ?Evershot, Shatcombe.

sceort (OE) 'small'. ?Chapman's Pool.

scēot (OE) 'steep slope'. ?Cowherd Shute.

scīete (OE) 'corner or angle of land'. ?Evershot.

scīr (OE) 'bright, clear'. Sherborne, Sherford.

scīr-rēfa (OE) 'sheriff'. Shroton.

scitere (OE) 'sewer'. Shitterton.

scylf (OE) 'shelf, slope'. Shilvinghampton.

scyte (OE) 'steep slope or hill'. ?Cowherd Shute, White Sheet Hill.

sealh (OE) 'sallow, willow'. Silton.

Seaxe (OE) 'the Saxons'. Pen Hill, Sixpenny Farm, Sixpenny Handley.

seofon (OE) 'seven'. Seaborough.

setl (OE) 'seat'. Kingsettle.

sīc (OE) 'stream'. Gussage (3).

sīd (OE) 'large'. Sydling (2).

sīde (OE) 'side'. Moorside.

slaeget (OE) 'sheep pasture'. ?Bonsley, Slait Barn, Sleight (2).

slǣp (OE) 'slippery, muddy place'. Slape House, Sleep Bottom, Slepe (2).

slege (OE) 'sheep pasture'. ?Bonsley.

smael (OE) 'narrow'. Small Mouth.

smethe (OE) 'smithy'. Smetherd.

smēthe (OE) 'smooth, level'. Smedmore.

speoht or *speht* (OE) 'green woodpecker'. Spetisbury.

staca (OE) 'stake'. Kingstag, Stake Ford.

stān (OE) 'stone, rock'. Agglestone, Durlston, Graston, Harp Stone, High Stoy, Hurpston, Parkstone, Puckstone, West Stafford, Stallen, Stanbridge (2), Stancombe, Stanpit, Stanton St Gabriel, Stoborough, Stone, ?Wytherstone.

stapol (OE) 'post, pile'. Stalbridge.

steall (OE) 'stall, fold'. Shipstal.

stēap (OE) 'steep'. Stapehill.

stede (OE) 'place, site'. Ringstead.

steort (OE) 'tail of land'. Sterte, Woodstreet.

steortel (OE) 'small projecting piece of land'. Sturthill.

sticol (OE) 'steep'. Winterborne Stickland.

stīepel (OE) 'steepplace, steeple'. Iwerne Steepleton, Steeple, Winterbourne Steepleton.

stigel (OE) 'stile, steep ascent'. Cripplestyle, Milborne Stileham.

stint (OE) 'sandpiper, dunlin'. Stinsford.

stoc (OE) 'outlying farm buildings, secondary settlement'. Burstock, Cattistock, Halstock, Hogstock, Laverstock, Mandeville Stoke, Netherstoke, Powerstock, Stock Gaylard, ?Stock Hill, Stockwood, Stoke Abbott, East Stoke, Stoke Wake.

stocc (OE) 'tree-stump'. Stockbridge, ?Stock Hill, Stock Hill, Stockley.

stōd (OE) 'stud, herd of horses'. Studland.

stōl (OE) 'stool, seat'. Bussey Stool.

strǣet (OE) 'street, hamlet, Roman road'. Abbott Street, Cole Street, Hammond Street, Stratton.

strōd (OE) 'marshy land overgrown with brushwood'. Strode, Stroud (2).

stybb (OE) 'tree-stump'. Stubhampton.

sumor (OE) 'summer'. Somerford.

sūth (OE) 'south'. South Down, South Haven, Southover (2), Southwell, Sovell, Sutton (3).

sūthan (OE) 'south of'. Southbrook.

swan (OE) 'swan'. ?Swanage.

swān (OE) 'herdsman, peasant'. Swalland, ?Swanage.

swelle (OE) 'steeply rising ground'. ?Poxwell.

swēora or *swȳra* (OE) 'neck of land, col'. Swyre (3).

swīn (OE) 'swine'. Swineham, Toller Porcorum.

tacca (OE) 'young sheep'. Acton.

tāde (OE) 'toad'. Tadden, ?Tadnoll.

tēafor (OE) 'red lead'. ?Evershot.

thorn (OE) 'thorn-tree'. Mosterton, Thorncombe (2), Thornford, Thorngrove, Thornhill (2), Thorn Hill, Thorton.

thornig (OE) 'growing with thorns'. Thorney Down.

throp (OE) 'outlying farm, secondary settlement'. Droop, Throop (3).

thȳfel (OE) 'thicket'. Holly & Ivy Farm.

thyrel (OE) 'hole'. ?Durdle Door, Durlston.

thyrne (OE) 'thorn-bush'. Thurnwood, Turnworth.

tige (OE) 'goat'. Tyneham.

tigel (OE) 'tile'. Tiley.

tōte (OE) 'look-out'. Hambury Tout, Todber, ?Totnell, Worbarrow Tout.

tōt-hyll (OE) 'look-out hill'. Tout Hill, Tut Hill.

trente (Old French) 'thirty'. Piddletrenthide.

trēow (OE) 'tree'. Loxtree.

trigon (ModE) 'triangle'. ?Trigon Farm.

trog (OE) 'hollow, valley'. Dunster.

troy town (ModE) 'maze'. Troy Town.

tūn (OE) 'farm, estate, village'. Abbott's Wootton, Acton, Afflington, Allington, Allweston, Alton Pancras, Anderson, Ashington, Ashton (2), Athelhampton, Basan, Barnston, Bexington, Bhompston, Blackmanston, Bockhampton, Brockington, Bryanston, Buckhorn Weston, Burleston, Burton Bradstock, Castleton, Catherston Leweston, Charlton (3), Chewton Bunny, Clifton Maybank, Compton (5), Corton, Cripton, Cruxton, Drimpton, Durweston, Eastington, Easton, Egliston, Ellston, Fordington, Forston, Frampton, Galton, Gatemerston, Glanvilles Wootton, Godlingston, Godmanston, Hampreston, Herrison, Herston, Hethfelton, Hilton, Hinton (3), Holton, Horton, Iwerne Steepleton, Kingston (5), Kinson, Knighton (5), Knitson, Knowlton, Langton (3), Lazerton, Leweston, Littleton, Litton Cheney, Lorton, Luton, Lutton, Madjeston, Magiston, Maiden Newton, Mangerton, Manston, Mapperton (2), Milton (3), Minchington, Monkton Up Wimborne, Moreton, Muston, Newton (4), Notton, Piddlehinton, Poorton, Preston (3), Puddletown, Pulston, Quarleston, Ranston, Rempstone, Rushton, Seatown, Shroton, Shillingstone, Shilvinghampton, Shipton Gorge, Shitterton, Silton, Stalbridge Weston, Stanton St Gabriel, Stratton, Stubhampton, Sturminster Newton, Sutton (2), Tarrant Hinton,

-Keynston, -Launceston, -Monkton, -Rawston, -Rushton, Tatton, Thorton, Townsend, Tuckton, Uppington, Upton (2), Walton, Waterston, Watton, Weston, Winkton, Winterborne Clenston, -Herringston, -Houghton, -Kingston, -Monkton, -Muston, -Tomson, -Zelstone, Winterbourne Steepleton, Witchampton, Wolfeton, Wonston, Woolgarston, Wootton (3).

twī- (OE) 'double'. Twofords Bridge, Twyford.

tȳnincel (OE) 'small farm'. Tincleton.

tyrch (Celtic) 'boar'. Pentridge.

tyrl (OE) 'the rolling or turning one'. Trill (2).

uferra (OE) 'higher'. Over Compton, Overcombe.

uindo- (Celtic) 'white'. Badbury Rings.

ūle (OE) 'owl'. Ulwell.

upp (OE) 'up, higher up'. Piddletrenthide, Higher Sturthill, Up Cerne, Uploders, Uppington, Up Sydling, Upton (2), Upwey, Wimborne St Giles.

vale (ME) 'wide valley'. Marshwood Vale.

varia (Celtic) meaning unknown. Dorchester.

wacu (OE) 'watch, wake'. Wakeham.

wād (OE) 'woad'. Waddon (2).

waed (OE) 'ford'. Waddock.

wāet (OE) 'wet'. ?Whatcombe (2).

waeter (OE) 'water'. Blackwater, Watercombe.

walu (OE) 'ridge, bank'. Holwell, ?Walditch.

wareine (ME) 'warren, game preserve'. Warren (2).

weald. (OE) 'woodland'. ?Walton.

weall (OE) 'wall'. Bestwall, ?Walditch, Wall Farm, ?Walton.

wealt (OE) 'shaky, unsteady'. Walford.

weard (OE) 'watch'. Worbarrow.

wearg-rōd (OE) 'gallows for criminals'. Worgret.

wearm (OE) 'warm'. Warmwell.

weg (OE) 'way, road'. Challow, Corscombe, Crockerton, High Stoy, Holway, Ridgeway, Sandway, Waytown, Whiteway (2), Whitey.

wella (OE) 'spring, stream'. Armswell, Askerswell, Belchal-